MAKING BETTER READERS

MAKING

BETTER READERS

by

RUTH STRANG

Professor of Education
Teachers College, Columbia University

AND

DOROTHY KENDALL BRACKEN

Director, The Reading Clinic
Southern Methodist University

D. C. HEATH AND COMPANY

BOSTON

Library of Congress Catalog Card Number

57–8434

PREFACE

THIS BOOK was designed to help prospective teachers and teachers-in-service to understand reading development and ways of furthering it, and to help every member of the school staff to see more clearly his responsibility as part of the total reading program. The book should be useful not only in introducing the field of reading to teachers, administrators, and guidance workers, but also in giving them concrete, practical suggestions to apply in their own classrooms and schools. It will also serve as an orientation, introduction, and supplement to the more comprehensive and technical books on reading already available.

To meet these needs, the book has been planned as follows: First, to describe the development of reading and major methods of teaching reading in the elementary school. This is valuable to persons in junior and senior high school, not only in giving a genetic approach to the reading development and problems during adolescent years, but also to acquaint them with procedures that may be used in modified form with high school students having difficulty with reading.

Since, under present school conditions, there is a wide range of reading ability represented in our junior and senior high schools, a description of this diversity of reading interest and ability and how to deal with it is given in Chapter 2. Here the special reading problems of the gifted, the student who can read better, and the slow learner are considered.

Despite the diversity of reading ability, there are certain common reading abilities which should be taught. How to provide for reading development and personal development through reading during high school years is treated in Chapter 3. In this chapter basic reading skills and methods of teaching them are described.

Since reading is everybody's business, it is necessary to describe some of the common opportunities and responsibilities of the whole school staff. These responsibilities have been translated in Chapter 4 into concrete procedures for understanding the individual student, giving instruction in reading while teaching any subject, and providing other language arts experiences.

There are, however, special approaches, a special vocabulary, and special procedures for teaching reading in each subject. Although the English teacher has usually assumed major responsibility for the language arts, there is much that the teacher of every subject can do. In Chapter 5 this is described with many illustrations of classroom procedure.

Even though every teacher has become a teacher of reading of his subject, there are still some individual students who cannot read well enough to profit by regular classroom instruction. For these individuals, special reading groups and clinical facilities should be made available. These are described in Chapter 6, which emphasizes the training value of teachers to clinic work with small groups and individuals, as well as the benefit to the limited number of clients served in the clinic.

To supplement the references to methods and instructional materials, given in each chapter, additional lists of books for teachers and students, audio-visual aids, and standardized tests are given in the Appendix.

A special feature of this book is the illustrations, each selected to emphasize a point of major importance. The busy teacher will be likely to read the book selectively, getting a general impression from thoughtful skimming and coming back again and again to parts that meet his immediate needs.

The authors wish to thank the teachers who so kindly described their procedures of improving reading and permitted our use of them. They also wish to thank Miss Hettie Dougherty, Reading Clinic Teacher, Dallas Independent School District, Dallas, Texas, for checking references and expertly handling some other routine matters connected with preparation of the manuscript.

Acknowledgment is gratefully made to the staff of the High School and College Reading Center, Teachers College, Columbia University — Dr. Helen Carey, Dr. Beulah Ephron, Miss Amelia Melnik, Mr. Frank Perry, Mrs. Meriam Schliech, Mr. Russell Wray, Dr. Dorothy Withrow, and Dr. Nancy Young — for their insight and supervising skill in working with Reading Center cases; to the graduate students working in the High School and College Reading Center, especially Mrs. Frank Cyr, Miss Jean Rennolds, and Mr. John McInness, whose cases are reported in some detail in Chapter 6; and to the graduate students taking the basic course, "The Improvement of Reading in High School and College," who contributed concrete descriptions of procedures and suggestions for games and other materials of instruction.

CONTENTS

1

Overview of Reading Development   3

vii

2

Diversity of Reading Ability and Interest 59

3

Essential Reading Abilities   105

4

Responsibilities of the Whole School Staff   157

5

How to Teach Reading in the Content Fields 203

⑥

Special Reading Groups and Reading Clinics 289

Appendix 345

Index 361

ACKNOWLEDGMENTS

The authors are indebted for help with photographs:

To Dr. Frank Williams, Assistant Superintendent of Schools in Charge of Instruction, and to Don Mathews, Assistant Superintendent in Charge of Special Services, Dallas Independent School District, Dallas, Texas, for the pictures on pages 23 (top), 37, 45 (bottom), 66 (top), 79 (top), 83 (bottom), 119 (bottom), 147, 249, 268 (bottom), 275 (bottom), and 316 (center).

To Dr. J. Ernest Kuehner, Director of Education, and to Dr. William Kottmeyer, Assistant Superintendent, The Board of Education of the City of St. Louis, for the pictures on pages 134 (top), 207, 289 (bottom), 297 (bottom), 303, 317 (top and bottom), 321, 325 (center and bottom), and 339.

To Z. T. Fortescue, Superintendent, to Paul Hensarling, formerly Director of School-Community Relations, and to E. S. Spradley, Director of Administrative Research, Port Arthur Independent School District, Port Arthur, Texas, for the pictures on pages 31, 108 (center) 161 (bottom), 167 (bottom), 184, 196, and 215

To Harry A. Becker, Superintendent, and to Benjamin Isenberg, Director of Audio Visual Workshop, Norwalk High School, Norwalk, Connecticut, for the pictures on pages 108 (top), 119 (top), 161 (top), and 167 (top).

To Martin Innett, Student Photographer, to David Shepherd, Consultant in Reading, and to John Mack, Sponsor of Photography Club, Dobbs Ferry Junior-Senior High School, Irvington, N.Y., for the pictures on pages 83 (top). 89 (bottom), 108 (bottom), 254 (top), and 275 (top).

The authors are especially indebted to George Patton, Photographer, to the staff of the Southern Methodist University Reading Clinic, to the children enrolled in the Clinic, and to the children's parents — all of whom gave up a holiday in order that the activities of the Clinic might be photographed — for the pictures on pages 66 (bottom), 289 (top), 297 (top), 316 (top and bottom), 317 (center), 325 (top), 330, 331 (top and bottom), and 340.

Acknowledgment is also made to the following sources for their kind permission to reproduce photographs:

PAGE

11 (*top*) Louise Van Der Meid
(*center*) Eva Luoma Photo
(*bottom*) Three Lions

23 (*bottom*) Eastern Washington College of Education

41 (*top*) Courtesy of *Illinois Education;* Belleville News-Democrat Photo
(*center*) Denver Public Schools; J. G. Bruce Photo
(*bottom*) Chicago Public Schools

45 (*top*) Audio-Visual Aid Department, Milwaukee Board of School Directors
(*center*) The Los Angeles Public Schools

53 Associated Press Photo

54 Louise Van Der Meid

PAGE

79 (*center*) Plandome Road School Library, Manhasset, N.Y.
(*bottom*) Chicago Public Schools

89 (*top*) Royal C. Crooks Photo
(*center*) *Chicago Tribune* Photo

97 (*top*) Ewing Galloway
(*bottom*) A. Devaney; David W. Corson Photo

101 Marie Fraser, *The Indiana Teacher*

102 Frederick Lewis

131 (*top*) Courtesy of Stephen F. Austin State College, Nacogdoches, Texas
(*bottom*) Monkmeyer; Max Tharpe Photo

134 (*bottom*) Ewing Galloway

153 Don Knight

175 Monkmeyer; Merrim Photo

xiv

MAKING BETTER READERS

r information and understanding, for entertainment, for sheer enjoyment, nd for personal growth.

Learning to read, like learning to live, is a lifelong process; it begins t birth and continues into old age. Preschool experiences are a prelude o school success. Early school experiences may contribute to later ailure in reading and dislike of school. There is a certain psychological redestination — which may be favorable as well as detrimental. It is aerefore desirable for high school teachers to have some insight into ae development of reading during preschool and elementary school ears. They often have opportunities to help parents provide favorable onditions for their younger children.

reschool Prelude to Success in Reading

The foundation for reading is laid in the early preschool years. It is aen that the child begins to build attitudes and habits of meeting life ituations — to be independent or dependent, self-confident or fearful. Dorothy Barclay's slogan for parents, "Live the good life and love that aby," is supported by sound research. Other ways in which parents aay pave the way for future school success are to let the young child do s many things for himself as possible — to let him solve his own daily roblems and be free to explore and discover things for himself. Such xperiences help to develop self-esteem, self-confidence, initiative, and re-ponsibility — all very important conditions for effective reading.

rereading Development of the Language Arts

During the preschool years the child also learns to look and listen and alk. Reading is the fourth language art to be acquired; learning to ook and listen comes first. Among the many sounds a baby hears he oon learns to recognize and respond to certain ones in the "buzzing onfusion" of the world about him. He learns some of these sounds as ae repeats them over and over with pleasure. Soon he begins to expect hese sounds and to listen for them; thus his listening skill develops. Ability to hear sounds accurately and to distinguish between them is one mportant element in reading readiness.

Another language skill is the ability to see similarities and differences n the things around one. The baby develops this ability; he learns to ook. At an early age he begins to identify and choose objects with which o play. During later preschool years he will point out details in pictures and recognize certain words that he sees in the story book his mother eads to him. All his school subjects — reading, writing, and spelling — vill require this ability to perceive accurately.

OVERVIEW OF READING
DEVELOPMENT

WE NEED TO HAVE a clear idea of the reading pro
view of reading determines how we will teach it. If we thi
as "word calling," then the phonic method will serve our pu
think of reading as "getting meaning from the printed pag
meaning into the printed page" (6, p. 2), then we will pr
with reading material that is meaningful, interesting, and
student.

Reading is a means to an end — finding out something
know, learning to do something we want to do, or getting
sense of adventure from the reading. To do this, it is necessa
the mechanics of reading and to learn the approaches, voc
special skills needed in different fields. Then we shall be

The third language art developed and practiced before school age is the speaking, or talking, skill. Having heard and identified certain spoken sounds in his environment, he says them over and over. As he observes that certain sounds produce certain effects — saying *Mama* brings mother to him; saying *milk* causes his hunger to be satisfied — he learns these words. The speaking skill, beginning haltingly with a few words, is built rapidly after the second year. By the time the child enters school he has, on the average, approximately 2,500 words in his speaking vocabulary. Vocabularies vary enormously for children of different ages, for individual children of a given age, and with the method used to study the words they know. Their oral vocabulary serves as a basis for building the sight, or reading, vocabulary they will begin to acquire during their first years at school.

Like the reading process itself, the language arts show much overlapping in their development. While the young child is listening, he is also looking. While he is looking, he is also beginning initial attempts at speaking. In other words, while his chief concern at the moment may be to get what he wants through speech, he is also expanding and improving his listening and looking skills.

Learning to read is a difficult and discouraging experience for a child who has defects of sight, hearing, or speech, and who lacks adequate language readiness. Children who cannot distinguish likenesses and differences in the sounds of words and in their forms become confused in learning to read. They are helped by systematic practice in visual and auditory perception. If the child is a slow learner, or is generally immature, he is sure to find learning to read difficult. If, in addition, he does not like the teacher, is disturbed about his home relations, wants to remain dependent — and babies do not read — or is otherwise emotionally disturbed, he cannot put forth the effort that reading requires. In fact, these same conditions may prevent high school students from getting anything out of the books they are expected to read.

Five Periods of Reading Development

After the preschool years, five periods of development in reading may be identified. According to *The Twenty-Fourth Yearbook* of the National Society for the Study of Education (24, p. 24), they are:

1. The period of preparation for reading.
2. The initial period of reading instruction.
3. The period of rapid progress in fundamental attitudes, habits, and skills.
4. The period of wide reading to extend and enrich experience and to cultivate important reading attitudes, habits, and tastes.

5. The period of refinement of specific reading attitudes, habits, and tastes.

These periods of growth correspond roughly to the reading experiences offered in the primary grades, the intermediate grades, and the junior-senior high school. For example, in the primary grades some of the children are given prereading, or reading readiness experiences, to prepare them for the initial steps in learning to read. As soon as they are ready, they acquire a basic sight vocabulary of fifty to a hundred words. Chart-reading experiences tie in the meaning of reading with the children's everyday activities, and prepare them to read beginner's books. In the intermediate grades, pupils become increasingly independent in their reading. They use a variety of word recognition skills to get the meaning of words. In addition, they learn to use reading in different subject fields for many and varied purposes. Finally, in the junior-senior high school, students continue to apply the skills, techniques, and abilities learned in the elementary grades, to extend and refine these, and to make wider use of reading in their search for information and as a source of recreation and personal development.

While this growth in reading has been related to certain school grades, actually almost all reading abilities develop early and are reinforced, modified, and expanded as the pupil progresses through school. One period or stage merges imperceptibly into the next.

Readiness for Reading

Much attention has been given to the problem of reading readiness. It boils down to this: Children grow at different rates. A few are ready to read at five; many at six; others are not ready until seven or later. From the beginning of their reading instruction they need sufficient maturity to get meaning from printed words. A child is not ready to read just because he has reached the chronological age of six years.

Nature of readiness

Many factors are involved in readiness to read: physical, emotional, social, intellectual, and environmental. Preschool experiences with things, places, and people; a desire to learn; interest in books; security in his relationship with parents; ability to talk about his experiences and understand what others say; all these play an important part in readiness for reading. A child is not ready to read if he has visual defects that cause strain or discomfort when he tries to see likenesses and differences in words. He is not ready to read if he cannot distinguish similar sounds and note their differences. He is not ready to read if he cannot speak plainly but uses "baby talk." He is not ready to read if he has not learned to pay attention, to relate events in sequence, and to remember simple directions; he needs to grow mentally. He is not ready to read if he has no desire to hear and tell stories or find out what those black marks on paper say. He is not ready to read if he comes to school rebellious, fearful, and uncooperative.

Time, too, is a factor. Six months may make the difference between success and failure in the initial attempt to read. Some children need much more time than others to build this foundation for initial reading instruction. Some children are ready to read at five years of age or earlier; others are not ready to read until later. Readiness is not synonymous with a fleeting interest. It is more fundamental than that, important as interest is. Nothing is gained by giving instruction in reading before the child is physically, mentally, socially, and linguistically ready to read. In fact, such premature teaching of reading may be definitely detrimental. The experience of failure in beginning reading often creates a fear of reading and lack of confidence on the part of the child, which may persist into high school years. It is much more difficult to teach a "burnt child" to read than one who has not previously experienced failure.

Another kind of readiness stems from motivation or desire to engage in a particular reading activity. In general, readiness for reading blossoms in response to a need. For example, Mary Jane receives a valentine with a message on it just for her. As she looks at the letters, she suddenly realizes that they form printed words and that printed words have personal meaning for her. Throughout elementary and high school years, skillful teachers introduce new reading experiences in such a way as to relate them to the pupil's interests and needs.

How parents can help

Parents can help children become ready to read by:

1. Reading stories to them.
2. Giving them interesting experiences to talk about.
3. Playing listening games such as imitating and guessing animal sounds; finding descriptive words for sounds like *bang, crash, whisper;* recognizing the sounds made by different objects such as a saw, hammer, egg beater.
4. Providing picture books for them to look at and, through their own interest in reading, giving them the idea that reading is important.
5. Pronouncing and telling them the meaning of words in their environment which the children want to know — words like *hot, cold, off, on, go, stop;* the labels on cans and jars, the slogans on billboards, the captions on television. For example, a four-year-old points to a slogan on a

billboard and shouts, "Daddy, I can read the sign." A six-year-old, riding in an auto, asks the meaning of and later points out signs, such as "Slow — School Crossing." Another preschool child brings her mother the salt box and says, "This says *salt*, doesn't it, Mother?" Such experiences increase the child's speaking vocabulary, help him to recognize similarities and differences, and reinforce his interest in books and meaningful printed words. All this should be done in a natural, casual, relaxed way, without creating anxiety over learning to read.

How teachers can help

Teachers are guided in helping children build readiness for reading by finding out through observation (13) or a reading readiness test (see Appendix, page 345) where individual children need help. Better still, informal observations may be combined with reading readiness test scores. The results of reading readiness scores when coupled with a teacher's day-by-day observation can predict a child's success in reading quite reliably.

After studying individual pupils the teacher will try to do what that study shows to be desirable and necessary. She will obtain the cooperation of the school doctor, nurse, or parent in the correction of physical defects. She will give practice as needed in auditory discrimination. Boys seem to have more trouble with auditory discrimination than girls. Giving boys practice in distinguishing sounds in words has helped to reduce failures in learning to read. Monroe (22) has suggested ways of developing sensitivity to the qualities of vocal and of non-vocal sounds and to sounds in words. For example, the teacher may select pairs of words somewhat similar in sound but different in meaning and ask, "Which can you ride on — a penny or a pony?" "Can you climb a letter or a ladder?" "Do we have turtle for Thanksgiving?" "No, turkey." Detecting and supplying words that rhyme and words that begin with the same sound and identifying sounds in the beginning, middle, and end of words are other exercises that build auditory skills.

It is also important for the teacher to help children form the habit of reading from left to right. Series of pictures used for visual and auditory discrimination should be arranged in a left-to-right order. When reading picture stories, the children should begin with the upper left-hand picture and continue toward the right.

In addition to special exercises and games, the teacher provides many stimulating natural opportunities for speaking and listening. Thus the children build oral vocabularies which are basic to beginning reading.

The desire to read is of central importance. Without the desire to read, the child will not put forth the effort that learning to read requires.

Listening to stories, looking at picture books, and talking about them interest children in reading, as well as improving their auditory and visual perception. As they listen, they follow the thread of the story. This helps them to anticipate words and meanings when they begin to read. In addition to providing for all these experiences, the teacher will in many ways contribute to his pupils' personal and social development, for reading is part of the total development of the child.

Teachers do not need to *wait* for reading readiness; it can be developed through experiences of listening, looking, talking, and giving whole-hearted attention. Skillful teachers take advantage of readiness to read whenever it appears. They will neither hold back a child who is ready to read nor plunge him into reading instruction prematurely.

To wait until the child can succeed in his initial attempt at reading is not to waste time. It may save time in the end by preventing confusion and discouragement. There is good evidence of this from an extensive experiment in England. During World War II children who usually started school at five years of age and began to learn to read then, could not attend school. But when they did begin their regular schooling one or two years later they made up for lost time. As a result, in the higher grades children who had not gone to school at the usual age of five were reading as well or better than a comparable group of children who had gone to school at the regular time.

First Reading Experiences

The child first learns words as wholes. Then he begins to note details. At this second stage he is using phonics and other word recognition skills. In the third stage he makes whatever analysis is necessary instantaneously; he no longer needs to puzzle out each word.

In the early school years the teacher should be very much concerned with the kinds and qualities of experiences provided for children. She should help them to relate ideas and to generalize, as well as to use each new word or concept in a variety of situations.

Reading begins with the child's own immediate vivid experiences. Boys and girls suggest many things in their environment that they need or want to read — their names on drawings or lockers, signs, labels, luncheon menus in the cafeteria, advertisements, road maps, calendars, greeting cards, invitations to a party, or directions for field trips. They dictate their most interesting experiences to the teacher, who prints the stories they tell on a chart or on the blackboard. Then the children read the stories they have told. The following story was dictated when the children came in to a class enthusiastic about going on a trip to the aquarium:

We are going to go to the aquarium and see one of the biggest turtles in the world. The turtle can eat a big fish whole. He is about a thousand years old.

We will see the crocodiles and fish with whiskers. We are going to see a seal and a porpoise, too.

As children's interests expand, audio-visual aids can be used to supplement their firsthand experiences. Pictures, filmstrips, motion pictures, and recordings help children develop understandings of people, places, and events that enrich their reading.

Children like to read about themselves. One teacher wrote short, simple paragraphs about individual children's activities; these were then mimeographed for each child to read. Some of these paragraphs contained conversation which two children read in front of the class, each taking a part. Another teacher typed simple directions for individual pupils to follow, such as, "Ted will put a book on his head and walk across the room." She held up the sentence and the child whose name appeared in it carried out the directions. His performance was checked by the other children and, if correct, applauded.

Soon the teacher may point out certain words on the experience chart or directions and ask, "What does this word say?" In this way children build up a meaningful vocabulary which they can recognize readily on sight. Learning a sight vocabulary of from fifty to sixty words is not easy. That is why the teacher presents these first words in many interesting ways until the children have mastered them. Experience in reading directions and in identifying words in their dictated stories are some of the best initial reading experiences of children.

In this approach to reading children are motivated in various ways. They want to read about interesting things. They want to succeed in this game of learning new words. They may want to please a teacher whom they like. The important thing is that while learning to read, they learn to like reading. In the long run nothing is gained, much is lost, by meaningless drill on letters and sounds that makes them dislike reading or think of it merely as mechanical pronunciation of words. The modern method is to build a basic sight vocabulary of fifty to one hundred words before teaching the use of phonics in word recognition.

Teaching reading is a highly complex procedure. Therefore, it is essential that teachers have clearly in mind the various methods which have been used in the past and those methods which have proven effective in modern practice. Both elementary and high school teachers should have a repertory of reading methods which they can adapt and use as needed by an individual child or a group.

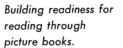

Building readiness for
reading through
picture books.

Reading traffic signs in the
beginning stages of reading.

Reading can be based on
first-hand experience.

Methods of Teaching Beginning Reading

Historically, the alphabet method, the phonic method, the word-phrase method, and the sentence-story method have been introduced as *the* methods of teaching groups of children to read. Children show individual differences in the methods by which they learn most easily and quickly. (For methods of determining how *individual* children learn to read most easily see the section, "The right methods for the right child," on page 18.) Today a *combination* of methods seems best since each method, while having advantages, usually has limitations also. If all methods are used *at appropriate times* in the learning process they each reinforce the other.

Alphabet method

The alphabet method (*naming* the letters in the alphabet and *sounding* the letters in the alphabet) proceeds from smallest unit, the letter, and builds up to the word. This method was used widely during the nineteenth century and early twentieth century and, generally speaking, produced slow readers and good spellers. Published in 1836 in *Mr. Midshipman Easy* by the English sailor-novelist Frederick Marryat, the description of the application of this method suggests the difficulty in arousing intrinsic interest in the alphabet method!

"Look now here," continued Mr. Bonnycastle, opening a book with large type. "Do you see that letter?"

"Yes," replied Johnny, turning his eyes away, and picking his fingers.

"Well, that is the letter B. Do you see it? Look at it, so you may know it again. That's the letter B. Now tell me what letter that is."

Jack now determined to resist, so he made no answer.

"So you cannot tell; then we will try what one of these little fellows will do," said Mr. Bonnycastle, taking down a cane. "Observe, Johnny, that's the letter B. Now, what letter is that? Answer me directly."

"I won't learn to read and write."

Whack came the cane on Johnny's shoulders, who burst out into a roar as he writhed with pain.

Mr. Bonnycastle waited a few seconds.

"That's the letter B. Now tell me, sir, directly what that letter is."

Thus Johnny learned to read by the alphabet method only through a powerful, painful supplementary appeal.

Phonic method

Phonetics is the scientific study of speech sounds. *Phonics* is an application of phonetics to reading and spelling; it is a method of sounding letters or groups of letters so as to get clews to the meaning of printed words that the child cannot recognize at first sight. By sounding *t* he gets a clew to the word *tell.* By sounding *thi,* which is familiar to him in the word *thin,* he has a good start on the pronunciation of *thing, think,* and *thick.* Once having correctly pronounced the unfamiliar printed word, he can read it — if he already knows the meaning of the spoken word.

Frequently we hear the question, "Do we teach phonics in the primary grades?" Yes, we do teach phonics; only 2 per cent of the teachers in one study said they did not teach phonics in some way. It is best taught as *one* way for a child to recognize an unfamiliar word in a story he partly understands. Phonics is *one* method of word recognition; it sharpens visual and auditory perception. It is the seeing-sounding path to recognition, hence to the word's meaning. Used after the child has begun to look for meaning in words as wholes — words that have something to say to him — phonics is "a technique which is very helpful to *some* children under *some* circumstances" (16, p. 159).

Most schools today teach children the initial consonants, consonant blends, simple endings, and vowel sounds. They help children to discover certain rules, like observing that adding an *e* to certain words like *rip, can,* and *rat* changes the vowel sounds, making *ripe, cane,* and *rate.*

We give instruction in phonics only after the child has learned some words and with material he wants to read and partially understands. Then he has a motive for trying to recognize and to blend the sounds in an unfamiliar word he needs to know. Bright children seem to be helped more by phonics than slow-learning children.

We do *not* teach phonics as it was taught in the nineteenth century or at the beginning of this century, as a *separate drill* or as the *first step* in reading. If phonics is taught as a system of sounds there is grave danger of focusing the reader's attention on the sounding out of words rather than on the meaning of the passage. One exponent of a system of phonics boasted that she could teach any first-grader to "read" the Bible! She had no concern for using appropriate reading material that a six-year-old could read and comprehend.

To be sure, little children often get a good deal of satisfaction from learning the letters and from phonic drills if the teacher is enthusiastic. They beam when she praises them for saying the sounds correctly just as they do in other situations when they are successful. But many children, taught exclusively by the phonic method, do not learn to read for meaning. They learn reading as a word-calling game. *Reading for meaning* is quite a different process. Reading clinics and upper elementary and high school classes are filled with youngsters who have not learned to read *for meaning.* Some pupils are able to pronounce all the words correctly but they do not know or care what the author is saying. Others are hopelessly confused and pronounce words in weird ways. According to Samuel and Winifred Kirk (16), hundreds of children, drilled in phonics, have become antagonistic to reading and hopelessly discouraged and befuddled because they did not have the ability or because no one ever taught them to blend a series of sounds into a word. "Without this sound-blending ability phonics is more confusing than other methods" (16, p. 160).

In the first three grades a large amount of phonic instruction has been found to be a deterrent to silent reading comprehension but it does improve the oral reading skills of word recognition and pronunciation. Much phonetic instruction tends to take the fun out of reading, but develops word analysis skills. However, "saying words is not reading thoughts" (3).

Most children learn to recognize details in words without the aid of special drills. They group letters by syllables as an aid to pronouncing words. They may also use prefixes and suffixes and roots in pronouncing certain words. If the reader knows these larger groupings of letters, he does not need to use single speech sounds or blended letter sounds; he can get the meaning by pronouncing the larger sound units. That is why with older students teachers may begin with familiar syllables and structural parts of printed words as clews to their meaning.

Teaching speech sounds is a complicated business; it may create almost as many problems as it solves. Phonics should be taught by a person well trained in this field; otherwise reading will become for the child "a great big bloomin' buzzing confusion." He will have to unlearn the sound of *oo* which he has learned to use in *good* when he meets the same letters in *noon* or *soon*. He will be confused when the sound he has learned as a long *i* may be heard in words spelled quite differently, such as *eye*, *high*, *buy*, *cried*, *aisle*. He should be frankly told that at least 13 per cent of the words in the English language are not sounded according to a consistent rule. These words will have to be learned as wholes. Even linguists are embarrassed by the erratic pronunciation of the English language, for many letters make the same sound.

The best way to avoid this confusion is to teach the child how to recognize unfamiliar words as they occur in his reading. This approach gives the child an immediate motive for learning word recognition skills and enables him to check his method against the sensible meaning of the word in its context. In fact, some words like *live* and *read* can be pronounced correctly only if he knows how they are used in a sentence. The exact meaning of almost any word in context depends upon the rest of the sentence or paragraph.

The relation of spelling to phonic instruction is not clear. Certainly instruction in phonics does not insure correct spelling. This is partly because if we spelled words the way they sound, our language would look very funny to us. When we see our pupils spelling words the way they sound to them we realize how unphonetic English really is. Betts stated that "a writer does not have a 50–50 chance of spelling correctly if he spells the word the way it sounds. . . . One of the major causes of poor spelling is an overemphasis on the way a word sounds" (2, p. 554).

Word-phrase method

The word-phrase method was introduced after Cattell demonstrated with the tachistoscope that much more than a single letter can be recognized at one quick glance. Since "the experiment definitely proved that we do not ordinarily read by letters but by whole-word units" (1, p. 212), why not begin with this unit? Although an important method of building a sight vocabulary quickly, the word method should not be carried too far or used exclusively. The word method, and the phrase method, are often spoken of as the "look-say" methods since the procedure is simply one of looking at a word or phrase and saying it. This method is used in the first and second stages of learning to read.

Sentence-story method

The last method to be introduced, chronologically speaking, was the sentence-story method. In this case the object is not to present the child with an "eyeful" but with a *thought* unit (1, p. 240). This method also leans heavily on the theory that it is best to begin with the large, meaningful whole and proceed from there to the smaller parts which make up the whole. The chief advantage of this method is that of making first experiences in reading meaningful and interesting to the child. But like the word-phrase method, the sentence-story method, if used singly and persistently, may produce readers who are inaccurate in word perception, insensitive to detail, and lacking in word recognition skills.

Kinesthetic method

No discussion of reading methods would be complete without mention of one other famous method. The kinesthetic method, carried to perfection by Grace Fernald (8), is a tactile method and one not ordinarily used by developmental reading teachers. Although not primarily a "desperation" method, it is used most often by remedial reading teachers or clinicians after other and quicker methods have failed. Because it employs a tracing-with-fingers approach, it is slow and laborious. For some readers, especially those who are severely retarded or immature, it appears to be the best method. In most reading clinics sand trays are available for tracing words and phrases. Pupils using the sand tray may be seen observing, sounding, and tracing — employing a multiple approach through eyes, voice, ears, and muscles.

Combination of methods

Strangely enough, primary reading practices today reverse the order of methods in which they were introduced during the past one hundred years. At present, children are taught first by the sentence-story method, then by the word-phrase method. Along with the introduction of writing and spelling, the alphabet and phonic methods serve to reinforce the two beginning reading methods.

Two important conclusions concerning the use of appropriate reading methods are:

1. A *combination* of methods is best.
2. No *one* method should be used exclusively.

A good order to use is as follows:

First, use the sentence-story method. Start with the reading of experiences dictated by the children in sentences. When the children in one first-grade class came in out of the first snowstorm of the season, the teacher wrote on the blackboard their eager comments about it:

> Snow, snow, everywhere.
> White snow.
> Soft snow.
> Snow to play in.
> We made snowballs.
> We made a snow man.
> We played in the soft, white snow.

This method of reading about their experiences gives the children the "feel" of reading to get the thought. It makes reading meaningful and enjoyable; it is interesting to them. However, some children memorize rather than read the sentences and paragraphs and fail to learn the individual words, unless other methods are used.

Second, use the word-phrase method. Help the children to distinguish one word from another by its size, shape, and unique features. See if they can identify separate words and phrases in their experience stories. Use the preprimers, which associate words and pictures. The quickest method of building a basic sight vocabulary is to associate the printed word with its meaning, either by tying it up with the familiar spoken word or with a picture, object, or action. One successful first-grade teacher began by writing words on the board. First she used the names of the children gathered around the board in a small group while the others were working at their seats. As she wrote, she said, "This word says *Mary*." Then, when she thought that each child had learned to identify his name, she armed each with an eraser and let them erase their own names as fast as she could write them on the board. Next she scattered on the floor many cards with the children's names printed on them, and there was a merry scramble to find all the cards with their names on them. After they had thoroughly mastered their names, she introduced other words in the same way: "This word says *jump*. Let's see you do what it says." In this way, by associating words as a whole with their meaning, this teacher helped the children to build a basic sight vocabulary. This paved the way for the introduction of other methods.

Third, introduce the alphabet and phonic method to help children analyze words difficult for them and to gain independence in identifying unfamiliar words. Gradually acquaint children with consonants. A child who has learned the letter *m* will not say *brother* when he comes to the word *mother*. The modern methods, however, differ from the historical alphabet and phonic methods. Reading authorities now place emphasis on *patterns* of letters and on *understandings* and generalizations derived by the child from experience with words viewed as meaningful wholes (11). Modern children are taught to group letters in patterns which are frequently found in our language. They are taught phonograms, consonant and vowel blends, structural elements of words; they learn to divide words into syllables, roots, and endings. In short, it is widely conceded today that sounding separately the letters in the word *cat*, as *kuh-a-tuh*, was never an aid to word recognition or memory. Any reader who continues to depend upon phonics to comprehend each word is using a slow, laborious process. Now phonics is used to help readers over difficult places, not to lean on at every step they take. Writing, spelling, and sounding can be definite aids to boys and girls in their struggle to learn to read.

Children learn to read by all sorts of methods. There have been systems of reading that used only phonics. Children were drilled on word sounds, with no relation to meaningful reading. This system has been called "the 'hiss and groan' method of teaching reading" (2, p. 549). Some children learned by this method; others became word callers who could pronounce a passage but had no idea of its meaning. Still others became word-by-word readers. A few, such as we see in our high school reading clinics, became hopelessly confused about reading.

In a developmental reading program an overemphasis on phonics may decrease a child's interest in reading. If the child is bright the unnecessary drill becomes boring. If the child is mentally retarded, he may become confused because he does not have the analytical and sound-blending ability that the study of phonics demands. Children with mental ages lower than seven years, according to one reliable piece of research, may not be successful in applying phonic principles. Some of the difficulties in learning by phonic methods may be due to beginning such training at too early a mental age. In practice there has been a trend toward having children begin learning the consonants after they have acquired a sight vocabulary of fifty to one hundred words. They go on to the vowels in the second grade and other word sounds later. Phonic instruction, as needed, may be given beyond the primary grades and to retarded readers at any age who seem to learn readily to recognize words by this method.

Teachers should be alert to detect signs of readiness for phonic instruction on the part of individual children, such as:

1. Distinguishing between words that sound somewhat alike.
2. Recognizing words that rhyme.
3. Identifying words that begin with the same sound or that have the same endings and the same middle vowel.
4. Having acquired a basic sight vocabulary with which to identify sounds of unfamiliar words.

It is also true that sounding out words is of little or no use to the pupil unless the word is in his oral vocabulary. The purpose of word recognition skills is to associate the printed word with meaning already known by the individual.

When teachers do not succeed with one method, they tend to swing to another way of teaching reading which "gets results." When the "look and say" or word method was in its heyday, a few teachers may have used it exclusively. But before long the pendulum swung back to the sensible position of using an orderly sequence of different methods modified as needed for individual children.

Today the best teachers of reading lay stress on the use of *several methods* and authorities agree that no *one* method should be used exclusively. The effective reader uses various methods ranging from identification of the general form or distinguishing characteristics of a word (configuration), through comparison with other words, context, picture clews, and on to phonic and structural analysis.

The right methods for
the right child

The teacher's reading approach and method must fit the individual. Some approaches are more effective with some individuals than with others. The same method will not bring the same results with different

. Her teaching is personalized; she uses the children's names in
1es and in simple directions that they can carry out. In her class
ding is fun, even though it requires the children's best efforts. Some-
es they play teacher, have puppet shows, make up rhymes to say and
ɡ, play games that require acting out some of the words they are learn-
, and draw pictures to illustrate the story they have read.

The effective teacher takes an attitude of positive expectancy toward
h pupil and an objective attitude toward herself. She finds satisfaction
the personal growth possible in her work. Because she is skillful in
ching she helps the children to learn to read without unnecessary failure.
a child fails occasionally, as everyone does, she helps him to accept
limitations and to view failure as an opportunity to learn not to fail
.t way again. By her own attitude of respect for each individual, she
ates a similar feeling on the part of children for one another.

Word to the Wise — Parent

Parents need to build up a resistance to the plausible advocates of
onics as the cure-all of reading difficulty. They need to be convinced
.t:
1. There is no one cause of reading difficulty.
2. Inability to identify words may not be the cause of their child's
ding difficulty; it may be only a symptom.
3. Drill on phonics alone will not make their child an independent,
ective reader.
4. There are other ways than phonics of identifying unfamiliar words,
d the good reader uses a variety of methods instead of giving up after
ing a single method.
5. Reading for meaning requires many more skills than merely identi-
ing words.
6. Overattention to sounding out words will make a child a slow reader.
7. Overattention to sounding out words takes the joy and adventure
.t of reading.
Instead of beginning with phonic drill, parents should reinforce chil-
en's natural interest in reading as a means of finding out something
at they want to know, such as the label on a can in a store or the name
a gift package. Both parents and teachers should avoid giving children
oks that are too difficult. Often a child will decide which is the best
ok for him to read — one that makes sense to him and is interesting.

Beginning Reading Practices Today

A visitor to primary classes in any good school will see lessons like the
llowing in first-grade classes.

children and young people. The question then arises,
various methods are appropriate for individual pupils?'
concerns not only primary teachers, but others who have
in their classes. If a pupil does not respond well to one
not learned to read by using it, the teacher, on the basis
about the individual, may select another combination
may be more effective. There is also a *Learning Method.*
consists of four standardized reading lessons, each of which
teaching procedure. The purpose of the test is to ascertai
of teaching word recognition is most effective for a
Having learned this, the teacher may select the materials
that will enable the child to learn in the shortest time a
effort.

From a more detailed analysis than is usually made
Merrill Revision of the Binet Intelligence Test or the
gence Scale for children, a teacher may get clews as to
learning — auditory, visual, kinesthetic — by which i
best. Some of the tests, such as those of identifying (
picture vocabulary, word definition and combination,
comprehension. Some, such as stringing beads, copyii
figure, require manipulative ability. Others, such as
obeying simple commands, remembering words, sente
similarities and opposites, involve auditory impressio
such as picture memories, memory for design, discrimi
picture absurdities, demand accurate visual impressions.
on certain of these groups of tests, one may infer that he le
that particular medium. The teacher may then give i
periences along that line.

Conditions Conducive to Learning

The way in which a teacher uses any method, and
relation are of utmost importance in children's learnii
sirable behavior should be rewarded as soon as possibl
is really rewarding to the individual child. The better t
teacher, the more effective will be her approval. The
of optimism, patience, understanding of the way chilc
and feeling, and recognition of individual differences un
of any specific method. The understanding teacher bt
self-esteem. She gives the child recognition and appro
is good in his response. She does not hurry the slow (
gifted child feel that he is wasting his time. When a
the teacher gives him just enough so that he can solve t

A visit to two
first-grade classes *

Teacher: What did we read about yesterday?

Pupil: Mr. Pig.

Teacher: What did he do?

Pupil: He always wanted to eat.

Teacher: When we met a new word, how did we tell what it meant?

Pupil: Sound it out. Skip it and see if the sentence tells what the word
means.

Teacher: Let's read today's story out loud. When reading out loud, what
are two important things to do?

Pupil: Read with expression.

Teacher: What does that mean?

Pupil: Like someone talking.

Teacher: And what was the other thing to do?

Pupil: Read loud enough so everyone can hear us.

(They begin reading a new story.)

Teacher: Read to find out how many letters he thought he was going to get.

Pupil: Very many.

Teacher: Did he get a letter for Mrs. Cow? Show me the sentence that tells
us.

(Pupil does this correctly.)

Teacher: What new word did you find?

Pupil: *Stopped.*

Teacher: What part of this word did you already know?

Pupil: *Stop.*

Teacher: What did we have to add to make it say *stopped?*

Pupil: Added *ed.*

(Pupil had trouble with the word "by.")

Teacher: What does this word *by* mean?

Pupil: *Good-bye.*

Pupil: To *buy* things.

Teacher: Those are meanings of two words that sound the same as *by,* but
this word *by* means near— as Billy is standing by the blackboard.
Why was Mrs. Cat sitting by the road?

Pupil: She wanted to get a letter.

Teacher: Read to find out whether she got a letter.

Pupil: She didn't get a letter.

Teacher: Yes. Read the two sentences that tell us Mrs. Cat didn't get a
letter.

* Observations made in the elementary schools of Euclid, Ohio, Lillian Hinds,
Director of Reading.

In this class the group of seven children gathered around the teacher were reading a story that interested them and were reading for meaning. The teacher used a combination of oral and silent reading. She used oral reading as motivation for effective reading, to diagnose difficulties, and as a springboard in word recognition skills. She used silent reading to give the children practice in reading for meaning. The children were learning methods of word recognition as they needed them and immediately applied what they had learned. One pupil from Sweden, who could not even speak English at the beginning of the school year, was now in May reading as well as the other children as a result of this approach: Reading for meaning and learning word recognition and other reading skills as the need for them arose.

Another first grade was reading an experience chart:

Teacher: Linda has just come into our room and would like to know what we've been doing.

(*Children read the experience chart telling what they have been doing.*)

Teacher: We have a new word, *clay*, on this chart (*points to it*). As you look at it, what do you notice?

Pupil: It looks like *play*.

Teacher: What other words do you know that look like *clay* in some way?

Pupil: *Day*.

Teacher: With what letter does *day* begin?

Pupil: *D*.

(*Other pupils give similar words which teacher writes in a column on the board:*

> clay
> play
> day
> away
> May)

Teacher: Will someone show me why these words are alike? Draw a line under the part that is alike in each word. Why did I write *May* with a capital letter?

Pupil: It's the name of this month.

(*Teacher asks children to pick out certain words and sentences and helps each child to succeed, if he hesitates, instead of calling on someone else.*)

Teacher: We wrote another story about animals in the circus. What was one of the most interesting things we learned about the giraffe? It was something he *couldn't* do.

Pupil: He couldn't make a sound.

Teacher: Can you find the sentence that tells us that?

(*Pupil indicated only one line of the sentence.*)

In the image: "This is the farmer's wife."

Now We Spell
can   Can
run   Run
you   You
me   Me

"The farmer lives here."

"Here is the..."

"See the big barn."

Books We Have Read

Children learn by matching sentences with pictures
that illustrate them.

Guidance and instruction in reading
in a small group.

Teacher: There's no "stop" sign at the end of that line so you must swing back to the beginning of the next line. In what way is the giraffe somewhat like a camel?

Pupil: He can go without water for a long time. (*Shows the line that says that.*)

Teacher: We have a new word on the chart that begins with the letter *w*. What is it?

Pupil: *Without.*

Teacher: *Without* is really made of two words you know — *with* and *out.* How do you make your mouth go when you begin the word *without?*

(*Children look at one another as they say the word.*)

Teacher: What other words that we know begin like *without?*

Pupils: will

                       we

                       wow as in *bow-wow*

                       water

(*Pupil underlines the "w" in each of these words.*)

This teacher started with familiar experiences of interest to the children. All the words were in their oral vocabulary. She asked questions that were answered in the stories and made sure they had learned to recognize individual words. Since they seemed ready to learn some word analysis skills, she went further and gave practice in ways of recognizing new words.

Children need phonics and other word recognition skills so that they can tell one word from another. This teacher was wise to teach phonics *only* after children had learned a basic sight vocabulary of about fifty words. As William S. Gray said, it is too much to confront a child with three unknowns at the same time — the unknown printed word, the unknown pronunciation of the word, and the unknown meaning (11).

**Teaching auditory
and visual discrimination**

Recent research has shown that visual and auditory perception are clearly related to reading success, perhaps even more so than mental age. Auditory perception and discrimination are therefore important parts of a comprehensive word analysis program. Children first need help in hearing the sounds of words they have been using. This ability should be acquired before they are introduced to the letter or letters representing these sounds. In teaching consonant sounds the teacher may say, "Who can think of a person in this room whose name begins like Mary's?" Perhaps Mildred or Milton will speak up. Then the teacher may ask them to mention other words that begin with the same sound. After they have mentioned a number of familiar words that begin with *m*, they can point out one of three words that begins with a different letter — *Mary, moon, Bobby.*

An illustration of informal instruction in auditory discrimination was reported by Mrs. Ann Kerr Carlyon, Instructor in the Reading Clinic, Southern Methodist University, in the following incident:

> During one of our phonics games, it was necessary for Tom to give correctly the sound made by the letters *ou.*
>
> "*ōō*," said Tom.
>
> "Look at our chart, Tom," I said, pointing to the illustrating picture of a mouse. "If the letters *ou* made the *ōō* sound, then we would say, 'The moose is eating the cheese.' Is that correct?"
>
> Tom laughed. "No. The sound is *ou.* I hear the difference now."
>
> Thus by hearing his mistake, Tom was able to get the correct sound and to remember the correct sound by recalling the humorous side of the "moose eating the cheese."

The following exercises to give practice in associating consonant letters and their sounds were suggested by Dr. Nancy Young:

> Begin by writing certain consonant symbols on the board or chart.
>
> 1. Say, "These letters stand for sounds. Can you think of words that *begin* with the *r* sound?" (Point to the letter *r*.)
>
> Encourage pupils to give not only such familiar words as *run, ride, rabbit* but also more unusual words: *refrigerator, radio, radar.*
>
> 2. Next ask pupils to think of words that *end* with the *r* sound; e.g., *far, feather, engineer.*
>
> 3. Last, ask for words in which the *r* sound is heard in the middle of the word: *squirrel, furnace.*
>
> If pupils have difficulty in thinking of words, you may suggest some, asking pupils to listen carefully to the beginning, middle, and final sounds. Pronounce, e.g.:
>
> | *tar* | *parrot* | *radio* |
>
> and ask pupils to tell where they heard the *r* sound. Follow the same procedure with each of the other consonant symbols on the board.
>
> This exercise should be repeated as often as needed until pupils can "connect" the correct sound with each consonant letter, and can think of words containing the sounds in
>
> *initial, medial,* and *final* positions
>
> and can use the initial and final consonants of a word as a clue to the total word in the light of its meaning.

Maney (19, p. 43) suggested the following teaching techniques for the development of auditory perception:

Stage I. Identifying Sounds

Primary: "We are going to play a game. Close your eyes. Who can tell what is making this sound?" (Example: bell ringing, pencil sharpener.)

Upper grades: "Let's find out how keen your ears are. Close your eyes." (Make a sound.) "Now tell or write what you think made that sound." . . . (Easy: Ringing a bell, closing a book, snapping the fingers, tearing paper, bouncing a ball. Harder: Closing a purse, striking a match, running a pencil over a comb, opening and closing a zipper.)

Stage II. Identifying Rhyme

A. Identifying Rhyme in Context

Primary: "I am going to repeat a jingle. Two of the words will sound alike or rhyme. Listen and tell me which two words rhyme: 'Little Jack Horner sat in the corner.' "

Upper grades: "Listen while I say two lines of a poem. Then tell me which words rhyme: 'There was a young lady of Ryde who ate a green apple and died.' "

B. Identifying Rhyme in Controlled Isolation

All levels: "I am going to tell you a word (*rain*). Now I shall tell you three more words. One will rhyme with *rain*. Listen and tell me which one rhymes with *rain*." (Example: *rain — them, can, pain*.) Gradually increase the difficulty of the exercises by including words which are almost rhyming words. (Example: *dine — heard, hard, dime, fine*.)

C. Identifying Rhyme in Complete Isolation

All levels: "I am going to repeat some words. Listen and then tell me which words rhyme: *level, broke, shell, soak*." Variation: "I am going to repeat some words. All rhyme except one. Which word does not rhyme: *check, pick, wreck?*"

Stage III. Supplying Rhyme

A. Supplying Rhyme in Context

All levels: "I am going to repeat a jingle and ask you to supply the last word." Examples: Primary — "Jack and Jill went up the ——." Upper grades — "I think that I shall never see a poem lovely as a ——."

B. Supplying Rhyme in Riddles

Primary: "Who can guess this word? It rhymes with *sled*. You sleep in it. What is it?" (*bed*)

Upper grades: "Can you guess this word? It rhymes with *flower*. It means light rainfall." (*shower*)

C. Supplying Rhyme in Isolation

All levels: "Who can think of a word that rhymes with —— (*dirt*, for example)?" Accept any rhyming word such as *skirt, hurt, shirt*, etc.

D. Check Point

Section C above may be used to appraise the child's rhyming ability. If he is able to rhyme readily, it is unlikely that he will need help on the preceding stages. Next check point is with initial consonants.

Stage IV. Identifying Sounds of Spoken Words

A. Identifying the Initial Sounds of Objects Shown in Pictures

All levels: Choose a picture that has objects familiar to the child. Begin with initial consonants most frequently met in beginning reading, for example, the letter *M*: "What do you see in this picture? Some of the things you mentioned have names that begin like *Mother*. Which ones begin like *Mother?*"

B. Identifying the Initial Sounds in Oral Context

"Listen to this sentence. Some of the words begin like *Mother*. Tell me which words you hear that begin like *Mother*." Example: The *moon* shines at *midnight*. Variation: Identify words that do not begin like a given word.

C. Identifying the Initial Sounds of Words in Isolation

"Listen to these words and then tell which ones begin with the same sound — or which one does not begin like the others."

D. Identifying the Name of the Letter with the Sound (Follows the Association of the Name with the Printed Symbol)

"We know that the first letter of *Mother* is *M*. Other words which have a beginning sound like *Mother* begin with *M*, too. Which of these begin with *M?*" Example: (easy) *hand, coal, market;* (hard) *fork, moth, pine.*

Stage V. Supplying the Initial Sounds of Words

A. Matching the Initial Sound

Primary: "Mary went to the circus. She saw something that begins like her name. What might she have seen?" Variation: "I packed my trunk and in it I put something that begins like *ball*. What might it have been?"

Upper Grades: "Let us try to think of some catchy advertising ideas for these articles on the table. The idea might be a name for the product or a slogan that would promote its sale. There is one rule — most of the words you choose must begin with the same sound." (Examples: *Pin-sharp pencils* and *Sudsy soap.*)

B. Associating the Name of the Letter with the Oral Symbol

All levels: "With what letter do you think this word begins? *Bench, pitcher, midnight*, etc."

C. Check Point

If the reader shows competency in a test based upon B above . . ., it is unlikely that he would need help on the previous jobs pertaining to the development of auditory perception of initial consonant sounds.

> The next check would determine the individual's ability to apply the previous skills to the pronunciation of a new word. . . .

Similar practice in visual discrimination should be given after the children have learned by sight several words beginning with the sound to be taught. Children should not be confused by practice in recognizing the sounds or the form of words they do not know. To avoid doing this, any auditory or visual discrimination exercises needed should be given in small groups with children who have acquired a common sight vocabulary.

From basic words to books

In reading instruction the aim always is *independent, interested readers.* Through reading about their experiences and identifying their names, simple directions, and some other words in their environment, children have learned most of the words in the preprimer and are ready to begin to read their first books. There is probably no greater educational thrill than the one which comes to a first grader who ventures into a bit of reading on his own. If he can be completely absorbed and successful he will announce triumphantly, as one youngster did, "Look! I've read a *book!*"

Other equally simple books using about the same vocabulary are available. Children should read as much as possible of this easy material before going on to the next level book in the basic reading series. Reading a great deal of easy material is fun, develops fluency, and builds confidence. In a way, it clinches the initial stage of reading development and allows for reading maturation before more complicated skills are undertaken at higher levels.

There comes a time when pupils meet unfamiliar words in books where they know most of the other words. They want to learn these new words; they *need* to know them. Then they notice that some words are much alike and some are very different. When they begin an intensive study of writing and spelling, then is the time to help them with word recognition skills.

Teaching Word Recognition Skills

When a child meets a word difficulty, that is the best time to teach him to recognize initial sounds and to blend the consonants with that particular combination of letters. It is better to have the child proceed in this way than learn lists of "family names," such as *tall, ball, call, fall,* in isolation. Such parts of words are not of much help in pronouncing polysyllabic words, though they do help him in working out words of one syllable.

The problem of reading was dismissed very quickly by an optimistic schoolman: "It is all very simple," he said. "You just know the little words, you sound out the big ones, and you know what it says. No one can stop you." Dolch, who has contributed so much to children's learning of the little words through his basic sight vocabulary (see Appendix, page 348), gives the following suggestions for attacking the long words (7):

1. Take off the prefixes and suffixes to see how they alter the meaning of the root word. This should be done slowly, with the children taking the lead in discovering the effect certain prefixes and suffixes have on words.

2. Identify the root word, as *look* in *looking*. This is not the same as finding small words in large words, which may lead to error 60 per cent of the time.

3. Divide words into syllables. (See section on syllabication of this chapter.)

By the time the children have completed three years in school and have read many easy books in addition to their basal readers, they are ready, in the upper elementary grades, to encounter many books, on many subjects, by many authors. The pupils will need a great deal of versatility as they move from books which contain primarily story material presented through a controlled vocabulary to material that is written to answer questions, solve problems, and give information or just pleasure.

At this stage they need reading instruction and practice in word recognition and word meaning skills and reading in different subject fields and for various purposes. They also need encouragement and guidance in reading more widely for pleasure and for personal development.

Boys and girls in the upper elementary school can learn to be quite independent in their use of word recognition skills, that is, in solving new words on their own. Skillful teachers study the methods pupils use when they come to unfamiliar words and teach them all the known techniques of "unlocking" new words. The same procedure would be appropriate for students in high school who have never acquired the word recognition and word meaning skills which would make them independent readers.

One teacher begins by asking, "What do you do when you come to a word you do not know or cannot recognize at once? How do you go about getting the meaning of new words?" Some say, "I guess what the word might mean in that sentence." Others say they try to sound out the word. Some try to get the meaning by dividing it into syllables. Others say, "I see whether it looks like some other words I know." A few get the meaning from known prefixes, suffixes, and roots. Then the teacher proceeds to highlight the good methods her students have described and to instruct the class in other word recognition or word attack skills.

**Five ways to recognize
unfamiliar words**

There are five things readers of all ages can do to recognize unfamiliar words. They are:

1. Use context clews — this means to look at the context, or surroundings, of the word to see if another part of the sentence, or other sentences, will help you "guess" what the word might be. For instance:

In the sentence, "We see with our eyes," if the unknown word is *eyes*, the words *see* and *with* would be contextual clews. The contextual clew in this sentence came *before* the word.

Here is another example: "*Cartoons* are drawings that interest and amuse people." Suppose you did not know the first word, *cartoons*. If you looked at the context, the words *drawings, interest,* and *amuse* would give you clews as to the meaning of *cartoons*. In this sentence the contextual clews came after the unknown word.

Sometimes the clew may be both *before* and *after*. For example, "It was the prairie loneliness that *depressed* his spirits with homesickness." The contextual clews are *loneliness* and *homesickness*.

The contextual clew may be a phrase as in this sentence: "The money was deposited in a bank." The phrase *in a bank* helps to explain the unknown word *deposited*. The clew may also be a sentence or a group of sentences.

It may be another word explaining the unknown word — a word in apposition, as "The *musket*, an early type of rifle, was used by soldiers in the Revolutionary War."

It may be a definition, as "A *turban* is an Arabian head covering."

It may be an example, as "Some grasses look like trees; for example, *bamboo* is a grass" (26, p. 146).

2. Get help from the word form — this means use the form, or shape, of a word that you know to help you recognize the unknown word. For instance, suppose you met this sentence, "Quickly he swam across the *moat*," and you did not know the last word, *moat*.

"Can you think of a word that looks like *moat* but begins differently? Yes, *boat* looks like it, or has the same word form, except for the initial consonant. So, having thought of *boat*, we can now say *moat*. If you have heard the word *moat* before, you will now know the meaning of the sentence."

3. Use structural analysis — this means use the structure of the word to help you recognize it.

If a long word is built of two or more words, it may not be difficult to recognize if you break it into the two smaller words which you may know. You can use this method on words such as these: *outline, newspaper, handbook*.

Phonics is taught as needed in connection with familiar words and sentences.

Children should read many easy books of their own choice.

If the word is not made up, or constructed, of two small words, look for the main part of the word or the root of the word. For example, in the word *misspelled*, the main part, or root, *spell* will help you, since adding the prefix *mis* and the suffix *ed* will lead you to the whole word.

Sometimes removing the prefix and suffix and then placing them back again will be all the help you will need. In the word *ineffectively*, you can remove the *in* and the *ly*, discovering *effective*. When you replace them you can recognize this polysyllabic word.

4. Use phonetic analysis — this means sounding out the word. But this does not mean you have to sound out each letter separately! Certain letters are still taught but combinations of letters, when grouped together, aid recognition of the word more effectively. Children are encouraged to use phonics as the need arises *in the reading situation*. The order in which phonics is learned is somewhat as follows:

Phonetic instruction in our schools today usually begins with initial consonant sounds, for example, *b, c, d, f, g, h*, etc.

The consonant blends come next: *dr, gr, tr, cl, sl, fl, sp, sw*, etc. There are four consonant combinations, however, which must be learned apart. They are *sh, ch, th, wh*, which have an entirely different sound from that of any of the letters alone and are not blends, either.

A little later, instruction is given in simple endings, such as *s, ed*, and *ing*, as in *plays, played, playing*.

About this time also children are often taught the short and long sounds of the vowels. Many three-letter words have short vowels in the middle. But since the middle sound is difficult to hear, the easiest way to teach the short vowel sounds is to identify them with words which *begin* with the vowel sounds, such as:

> "a as in apple
> e as in elephant
> i as in ink
> o as in ostrich
> u as in umbrella" (17, p. 80).

Some *understandings* of the operation of phonics in the English language are gained by pupils as they have further experiences with words. They discover, for instance, that there are some word patterns that they may expect. One teacher presented this idea to primary-grade children by leading out from a discussion of the children's pets:

Teacher: And what sound does your dog make?
Child: Bow-wow.
Teacher: And what sound does your cat make?

Child: Meow.

Teacher: Now suppose I was visiting my uncle and went to the barn to see the cow. And I stroked the cow and it said "Meow." (Children laugh.)

Teacher: You all know that I said the wrong sound for a cow. You knew right away I had made a mistake. Now I want you to know the sounds in words so well that you could tell right away if it was the wrong sound.

(1) The short vowels in three-letter words are often converted into long vowel sounds by the addition of a final silent *e* which "makes the vowel say its name," as

hop — hope

cut — cute

Tim — time

A game that has an element of magic in it consists of a long strip of light-weight oaktag with two slits cut after each three-letter word. Through the slits another piece of oaktag with *e*'s printed on it is drawn. As the *e* appears after each word, the children pronounce the words showing how the *e* has changed the pronunciation and meaning of the first word; for example, from *fat* to *fate*.

(2) Another generalization children with a beginning sight vocabulary may make is that often the first vowel is long in two-vowel combinations, such as "ai" in *wait*, "ea" in *each*, etc. The first vowel does not always give a long sound and the second remain silent, but this is a pattern which occurs frequently enough in the words used in beginning reading vocabularies to warrant paying some attention to it. Some teachers use the rhyme to help children remember this rule: "When two vowels go walking, the first one does the talking."

(3) Then there are some letter combinations which often have unique sounds. Third and fourth graders should be able to pronounce these at sight:

"ou" as in *house* and "ow" as in *owl*

"au" as in *daughter* and "aw" as in *strawberry*

"oo" as in *boot*

"oi" as in *oil* and "oy" as in *boy*

"ew" as in *blew*

"ir" as in *bird*

"ur" as in *fur*

"er" as in *term*

"or" as in *north*

"ar" as in *star*

"ay" as in *day*

In a demonstration lesson Mrs. Lillian Hinds introduced the idea of "two letters that are pronounced as one sound" in this way:

Teacher: What kinds of things do you like to do on a nice, clear day?

Kenny: Sometimes when it's sunny we get out our wagon, and we go on the hill.

David: Me and my brother and some kids on our street, we got a big box and someone pulls it and we pretend it is a covered wagon. . . .

Teacher: Somebody said *train* and *truck;* let me write that on the board. *Train* — now listen carefully — *train, train.* And *truck, truck.* What is there alike about these two words?

Charlie: They start with the same letter.

Cindy: They start with the same two letters.

Teacher: What are they?

Cindy: *Tr.*

Teacher: These two letters have one sound. Now suppose I cover up the first two letters with the sound *tr,* what do I have left?

Jerry: *ain.*

Teacher: Can you think of a word that would end with *ain* and rhyme with *train?*

Jerry: *Pain.*

Teacher: You make *pain* by adding the *p* to *ain.* Now it's not going to snow today; it's going to ——.

Garry: *Rain.*

(*Another child adds "plain" to the list.*)

5. Use the dictionary — this means that if you cannot recognize a key word by its context, by word form, by structural or phonetic analysis, the next thing to do is to look it up in a dictionary and learn how to pronounce the unfamiliar word. Independent use of the dictionary, of course, requires skill in:

> use of the alphabet
> use of guide words
> use of pronunciation key (with emphasis on this skill)
> use of the several definitions given for aid in recognition

When these five techniques of word recognition are taught to children in the elementary grades, or to readers at any level, they usually become more independent and more confident in helping themselves with new words. Once the ways of helping themselves are discovered they seem to gain confidence for more difficult reading tasks. Likewise, success in applying word recognition techniques gives them confidence; and confidence gives them renewed interest and ambition. As one mother said to Mrs. Hazel Horn Carroll, "It was what you did the fourth time Joe came to the Reading Clinic [word recognition skills were introduced to Joe at that session] that first gave him a new lease on reading!" A fifth-grade boy likewise gained confidence through learning word attack skills. The following incident was reported by Mrs. Ann Kerr Carlyon:

"Mrs. Carlyon," Fred said to me as we worked at dividing a word into syllables. "I had a contest with a boy at school on figuring out hard words. He's one of the best readers in our class, and he said I couldn't read. I told him I could read just as many hard words as he could."

At this point I thought, "Oh, no, Fred! Not another defeat for you!" But my despair changed to joy as Fred continued.

"And you know what? I beat him! I divided the words just like we do here at the Clinic. I may be slow, but give me a little time and I can get just about any word. He may be a better reader than I am, but he didn't know how to figure out the hard ones."

Of course, I hadn't been teaching Fred how to attack words so that he could qualify in a word-reading contest; but his expression told me just how much this triumph had meant to him in the struggle to overcome the feeling that he would never read as well as other people.

Syllabication

A knowledge of some rules of syllabication will often aid pupils to become independent readers. Dividing some words into syllables or other discernible parts will be quite complicated. No rules will work every time. But they do function often enough to warrant teaching them.

1. A word has as many syllables as there are vowels, or vowel combinations. In the word *complicated* there are four vowels and hence four syllables. In the word *vacation* there are two vowels and one vowel combination, so we have three syllables. But note this exception: Do not count the silent *e* that you find on the end of many words. For instance, the word *valentine* has four vowels, but since we do not count the final *e* in determining the number of syllables, we have only three syllables.

2. When the word is built on the vowel-consonant-consonant-vowel pattern the division is between the consonants, like this:

$$v\,c\,/\,c\,v$$
$$l\,i\,t\,/\,t\,l\,e$$
$$p\,i\,c\,/\,n\,i\,c$$

3. When the pattern is vowel-consonant-vowel, the consonant generally goes with the vowel that follows it, like this:

$$v\,/\,c\,v$$
$$b\,a\,/\,b\,y$$
$$s\,e\,n\,s\,a\,/\,t\,i\,o\,n$$

4. When there is a closed syllable (a syllable ending in a consonant) the vowel is usually short. For example, in the word used above, *sensation*, the first syllable is a closed syllable because it ends in a consonant. Therefore, the *e* is short. When there is an open syllable (a syllable ending in a vowel) the vowel in that syllable is generally long. Using *sensation* again as an illustration, the second syllable is an open syllable because it ends in a vowel. Therefore, the vowel *a* is long.

These rules enable the reader to divide words correctly into syllables and so recognize long words in silent reading. They give him a method, or a way of attack. For correct pronunciation, he will have to check the sounds and accents with the dictionary. As children grow older they become more interested in knowing and studying the exceptions to these general rules.

Teaching Word Meaning Skills

The use of the word recognition techniques presupposes the unknown word to be in the listening or speaking vocabulary of the reader. If the pupil knows the meaning of the spoken word, he knows the meaning of the printed word, once he has pronounced it. Then he may proceed with his reading. But, if by use of these techniques he calls the word and does not know what it means, then he must move over to other methods for "unlocking" the *meaning* of the word.

Much attention is given to word meaning or vocabulary skills in the upper elementary grades. In general, pupils are taught that there are four things to do when they meet a word, recognize it, but cannot define it. The first and last techniques are similar to the word recognition skills. These four word meaning techniques are:

1. Use context — this means to guess at the meaning of the word by looking for other words, phrases, and sentences that will tell you what the word means. For example, suppose you came to the word *impenetrable* in this sentence, "The language in which some scientists speak is impenetrable." You might not know what sort of language most scientists speak. But if this sentence, "Even other scientists often are puzzled by it," were added, you might "guess" that *impenetrable* means hard to understand.

2. Use the known meaning of related words — this means using knowledge of words very nearly like the one in question. For instance, suppose the word in question is *micrometer* and you know what a *speedometer* is — an instrument for indicating speed or velocity. By using this information you may conclude that a micrometer is an instrument for measuring microscopic or minute distances.

3. Use roots and affix meanings — in other words, find the root of the

Using structural analysis in recognizing words.

Many examples help children learn the different ways of making words plural.

word and use its meaning plus the meaning of the prefix and suffix. For example, in the sentence, "An equitable settlement was made," if you know that the Latin word *aequus* means "equal" then you would conclude that the settlement made was an equal, just, or impartial one.*

A knowledge of the meaning of the common affixes is an aid to vocabulary improvement. Many times students will know the meaning of the root, or small word, and are able to ascertain the whole word by the addition of the prefix meaning. For instance, if the word in question is *abnormal*, the meaning of *normal* is changed by the prefix *ab*, which means "away from." Thus *abnormal* means literally "away from the normal." Likewise, if the root is known, the suffix may be used to determine the specific meaning. In the word *aqueduct* the *aque* means water and *duct* means to lead or carry. Literally, then, an aqueduct is a structure for conveying a large quantity of flowing water. Similarly, a *viaduct* would be a structure for carrying a road or railroad, as over a valley.

4. Use the dictionary, which is the best guide for word meaning. The fundamental dictionary skills are an essential part of the program of improving vocabulary in the elementary grades. To use the dictionary effectively, it is necessary to know how to locate the word, to use the dictionary markings to pronounce it, and to select from the range of meanings given in the dictionary the one that makes the best sense in the sentence being read.

Abstract words are more difficult to learn than words that stand for objects or actions. That is why some pupils have trouble with "little words" like *that, than, these, every, very*. Knowing this, teachers will not become impatient with children's failure to recognize these little words.

The Language Arts Core Class

Toward the end of the primary period is a good time for teachers to review the word attack skills children have been learning during their first three years of school. The course of reading development does not always run smoothly; some children do not acquire the vocabulary, the word recognition, and other reading skills expected of them on a certain grade level. Consequently, they need special instruction. In St. Louis and in Euclid, Ohio, an important part of a "total school" developmental program is the Language Arts Core Class for children who would benefit from more intensive reading instruction at the end of the third year. Up to that time each child has progressed in reading as fast and as far as he was able without the experience of failure from being "left back" if he was slower than other children of his age in learning to read. If, after

* For a list of roots, prefixes, and suffixes, see reference 30, pp. 407–410.

three years in school, he is still not ready to cope with the reading required in the fourth grade, he is put into a special section of the fourth grade. In this special section the pupil learns fourth-grade content but is also given intensive instruction in the aspects of reading in which he is weak. If he has gained sufficient reading skill at the end of the fourth grade, he is promoted to the fifth grade, without having missed essential fourth-grade content. If he has not yet acquired the reading ability to do fourth-grade work, he is given another year to gain the skills he needs. This procedure is based on the assumption that the pupil is capable of improvement in reading. If he is too mentally retarded to reach fourth-grade reading level at this time, he is given opportunity to learn in other ways — through visual aids, listening, and other activities. Plans similar to this one have been in operation in several school systems with apparent success.

One advantage of treating the primary grades as a unit rather than making a decision to fail or to promote a child each year, as is the usual practice, is that it gives the slow-maturing children and those from homes affording little intellectual stimulation a chance to catch up with the other children and to take advantage of the school opportunities for learning.

These special Language Arts Core Classes, like the remedial reading classes in junior high school and the special reading sections of English class in high school, give pupils with potential reading ability the instruction and practice in the basic language arts skills which they have not yet acquired. In these classes the pupils get instruction in word recognition skills, in sentence and paragraph comprehension, and other skills, in addition to the developmental skills appropriate to the grade and subject. In most schools the amount of special reading instruction, especially at the junior high school level, is inadequate to meet the needs of large numbers of pupils.

It would be most helpful if each teacher would pass on to the next teacher information about the books that the pupil has read, his special needs and problems. Thus each teacher would not have to start from scratch in ascertaining the reading status and needs of each new class. Such a record would be based on the preceding teacher's knowledge of the reading skills each pupil had acquired, the books he had read, his attitude toward reading, the needs that reading serves in his life, and what he gets out of the books he reads.

Oral Reading

Reading aloud has a real place in the total language arts program (28). In beginning reading it helps children to associate printed words with spoken words and it helps a sensitive and astute teacher to detect mechanical difficulties. This diagnostic function, however, should generally be exercised privately as the child reads to the teacher alone. Moreover, slow, laborious sounding of the words is not oral reading. There are special skills required in oral reading over and above the essential comprehension of the passage through silent reading. Occasionally adults have opportunity to read aloud, and should be able to phrase correctly; use tone, pauses, and stress effectively; and be keenly aware of the ability, needs, and expectations of the audience.

An Example of Reading Instruction in the Fifth Grade

In one fifth-grade class the teacher was concerned with the growth of every child as a person and tried to help each to succeed. The reading grades of pupils in the class were from four years, eight months, to seven years, six months. To provide for these differences in reading ability, this teacher's class was divided into three groups, each sitting around tables that had been moved together. The teacher was with one group while the other two groups worked independently.

The group of superior readers was reading a book on the sixth-grade level (*Stories to Remember*, Lyons and Carnahan). The pupil leader was a gifted boy who until that year had been a retarded reader. Serving as chairman gave him opportunity to bring out the ability of others as well as an incentive to comprehend the selection thoroughly himself. He began by saying, "Our story is *The Forty-Niners*." Then he pulled down the map and showed where pioneers had found nuggets of gold in 1848. He pointed out how the news got to the East in 1849, and told how many people went West to find gold.

Then he asked the other pupils to answer the questions they had raised in the beginning of the period and for which they had been reading silently to find the answers. For example:

Chairman: How long did it take news to travel from the West to the East?
Pupil: There were no telephones. One person told the news to another — like gossip.

The lowest group in reading ability was reading interesting facts about the koala bear in a fourth-grade reader (*Roads to Everywhere*, Ginn and Company). *Koala* was a difficult word for them to pronounce and trying to use the diacritical marks in the dictionary seemed too complicated for them. The teacher first associated the story with an experience the children had recently had — a visit with a lady from Australia. Pupils in this group, too, had chosen definite questions to answer during the

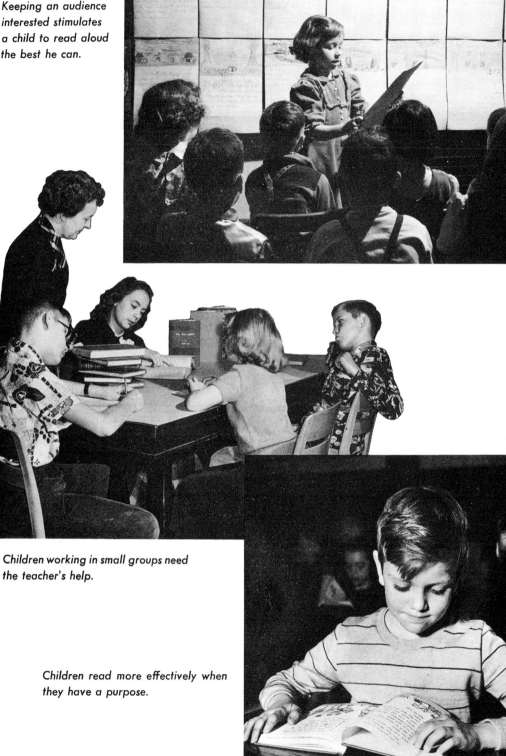

Keeping an audience interested stimulates a child to read aloud the best he can.

Children working in small groups need the teacher's help.

Children read more effectively when they have a purpose.

time when they were "on their own" reading silently. Some of the questions were:

"How does the mother bear care for her baby?"

"Find the paragraph that tells what the koala bear eats."

"Why are these bears so well liked?"

The group of average readers were using their fifth-grade book in a similar way. Since each group was reading different stories, they had the added incentive of gaining information to tell the whole class the most interesting things they had learned. This brought into play some other communication skills. The successful reading in this class may be attributed to the teacher's skill in group work and in methods of teaching reading skills and to the suitable reading material.

The skillful teacher encourages each pupil to practice initiative and to seek help when needed. He does not interfere with the children's enjoyment of the story by interrupting with irrelevant remarks as they read. For example:

Joan *reading:* A flash of lightning showed the great beast ready to spring. . . .
Teacher *interrupting:* Joan, don't hold your book so close to your eyes. Stand up straight.

Materials for developing basic reading skills must be of genuine interest to the pupils. The story or the information itself should pull even the reluctant reader along with it; he should be eager to find out what happens next or the answers to specific questions or problems. Being of immediate interest to pupils, the content can be interpreted by them in the light of their previous experiences. Much of the reading material should have the characteristics of children's classics — genuine emotion, true-to-life characters and plots, a fine style which is actually easier to read than a stilted, poorly simplified style.

Reading in the Content Fields

Teachers of social studies, science, and other subjects complain that pupils can read stories but not study-type of reading. The skills they have learned from reading the short stories in their basal readers do not seem to carry over to the textbook and reference reading they have to do in the upper grades. This condition need not exist. As soon as children have gained some basic word recognition and word meaning skills, they can begin to use these skills in reading in varied content fields and for various purposes. Aside from general instruction and practice in basic reading skills appropriate to this level, such as following directions, searching for the main idea, looking for details, and anticipating coming events, the elementary school teacher deals with reading problems unique to each of the subjects. Reading in the content fields is being emphasized more and more in reading programs.

In each subject the children will be faced with special difficulties. The teacher helps by showing pupils how to find and state worthwhile problems, by building a background of experience before beginning to read, and by clarifying key words. In a supervised study period the pupils learn effective methods of reading and ways to overcome difficulties they encounter. Such instruction precedes independent reading of new material in any subject.

Reading an arithmetic problem

Consider the kind of instruction a fourth-grade teacher would give his class in reading the following arithmetic problems:

He might first show snapshots or a picture of boys on a camp-out. Then he would introduce problems in campfire cooking, such as the following:

1. You can see the measuring cup the boys use for cooking. Tom said, "When we bake beans, we'll need $\frac{5}{8}$ cup of molasses." How could they measure $\frac{5}{8}$ of a cup?

Is $\frac{5}{8}$ more than $\frac{1}{2}$? $\frac{1}{2} = \frac{?}{8}$

Is $\frac{5}{8}$ less than $\frac{3}{4}$? $\frac{3}{4} = \frac{?}{8}$

How could they measure $\frac{3}{8}$ of a cup? $\frac{7}{8}$ of a cup?

2. The boys want to broil half a tomato for each boy. How many tomatoes should they order for 2 boys? 4 boys? 8 boys? 10 boys? 20? 24?

Can you make a rule for finding how many tomatoes they should order for any number of boys?

3. They buy $\frac{1}{4}$ pound of meat for each boy when they make meat balls. How many pounds of meat should they order for 4 boys? for 8 boys? 12 boys? 16 boys? 20 boys? 21 boys? 22? 23? 24?

4. If the boys need $\frac{1}{2}$ pound of butter for pancakes and have only $\frac{1}{4}$ pound, how much more should they buy? (4, p. 274)

To help his class read problems in arithmetic the teacher might follow these procedures:

1. He would probably build a readiness for these problems with some actual measuring and weighing activities. He would establish a felt need for the problems and would set a purpose for reading them.

2. He would need to remind his class that a slow rate is appropriate when reading mathematics and that often, as with these problems, reading requires visualization of the situation.

3. He would need to determine whether the special mathematical vocabulary of these problems would be a stumbling block.

4. He might need to give help to individuals on specific aspects of the problem. Poor readers would need help in reading the problem and in inserting in the example figures for the words given in the problem.

Reading a passage in fifth-grade science

Now note the difference in reading problems presented in fifth-grade science. What kinds of reading instruction should the fifth-grade teacher offer? Suppose the class were to read the following assignment:

ELECTROMAGNETS

Have you ever seen a magnet as large as the one in this picture? This magnet picks up very large and heavy pieces of iron and steel. You can see that this magnet is not shaped like any of the magnets you have worked with before.

It is different in another way too. This magnet is made by using electricity. It is called an electromagnet. If you would like to find out more about electromagnets, you might make one.

To make an electromagnet, you will need these things: a dry cell, a large nail, a switch, and about three feet of insulated copper bell wire.

Wind the central part of the wire smoothly around the nail. Fasten the end of the wire nearest the head of the nail to the middle screw of the dry cell. Cut a piece about six inches long from the other end of your wire so that you can put a switch in your circuit. The switch should go between the dry cell and the nail. You may use a knife switch like the one in the picture below, or you could use a push-button switch.

Put some tacks near the nail. Will the nail pick up the tacks? No, of course not. The nail is not a magnet.

Now press down the switch so that electricity flows through the copper wire. Now try to pick up the tacks with the nail. Do they jump toward the nail? You have made an electromagnet! (5, pp. 251–52)

In teaching pupils to read this science assignment, the science teacher might do these things:

1. He would build a readiness for reading this passage by establishing not only an interest in but a need for reading it.

2. He would recognize possible vocabulary difficulties as presented by such words as *electromagnet, insulated, switch,* and *circuit* and would clarify their meanings through pictures, diagrams, and the objects themselves, as well as by words.

3. The teacher would discuss the appropriate rate and purpose of reading for this selection before the pupils began to read.

4. A demonstration of the importance of prereading a set of directions might be given.

5. After the prereading, which would give an overview to the action

eading signs and rections has ersonal meaning r pupils.

Visit a Radio Station
Things to look for:
News Room
Master Control Room
Control Room
Engineer
Director
Actors
Announcer
Sound Effects Man
Sound Effects Table
Microphone
Radio Hand Signals

Preparing for a field trip introduces new words which will become rich in meaning.

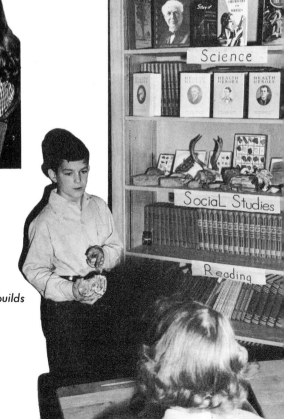

Science

Social Studies

Reading

First-hand experience builds science concepts.

necessary in making an electromagnet, the procedure would be a step-by-step reading. The final steps would be to carry out directions, reread the directions, and recheck the action.

**Reading in the social
studies field**

Below is a passage from a sixth-grade social science book. Contrast the reading difficulties and the reading instruction that would be needed in this instance with that of the two examples given above.

THE FIRST MINE

Their search for flint started men digging in the ground. Perhaps the oldest mine in the world is a place in Belgium where some of these early miners dug for pieces of flint. Not so long ago, when modern men explored this ancient mine, the bones of one of the miners were found deep in the ground.

Centuries and centuries ago that miner had crawled in there to dig out flint. The ceiling of the mine had caved in and he had died there. Beside the bones of this miner of long ago were some pieces of flint he had dug out of the rock. And lying there, too, was his pick that was made from a deer horn.

Since those early days, centuries ago, men have dug many mines, some of them thousands of feet deep. Men have drilled wells, some of them several miles deep. They have done this work to find minerals that people could use. They have discovered many things about the outer part of the earth, the part which is called the earth's crust.

The crust of the earth seems thick to us. But compared to the rest of the earth it is thinner than the skin of an apple. The crust we know about is really only a small part of the earth. Even the deepest mines and wells do not go far into it. Men have drilled wells about three miles into the crust of the earth. But they would have to drill about four thousand miles to get to the center of the earth. That isn't very likely to happen. (12, p. 146).

In this social studies selection, a teacher might take these steps:

1. In building readiness for this passage the social studies teacher would relate the present passage to the material which preceded it.

2. He would also arouse an interest in and establish a purpose for reading.

3. He might suggest a rapid glance, an overview or prereading, to find the main idea.

4. Before a detailed reading he would give help with time and place concepts.

5. He would also give whatever help this particular class needed with vocabulary (such as *flint, Belgium, explored, centuries, discovered, compared*) and with new concepts.

6. He might guide the interpretation of the author's message by asking questions to guide the pupils' silent reading.

7. Through discussion he would help the pupils evaluate the selection and make application of the material read.

**Reading for various purposes,
including pleasure and personal
development**

In reading for different purposes many children need the encouragement that teachers can give. To read to be a spokesman, to read to work with a group, to read to gain certain knowledge and understanding, or even to read to be able to criticize or differ with someone's opinion are purposes which appeal to youngsters of this age level.

The following list of purposes for reading might be the beginning of a comprehensive list made by the pupils:

1. Reading to share knowledge with a group.
2. Reading to work with others on small group projects.
3. Reading to gather all kinds of information.
4. Reading to understand the world in which we live.
5. Reading critically to question a presentation.

Equally important is wide reading for pleasure and personal development. Children generally reach a peak in their voluntary reading between ten and thirteen years of age. After that the amount of recreational reading tends to drop off, especially in senior high school. Much encouragement and guidance should be offered pupils in the intermediate and upper elementary grades in reading for fun and reading for personal growth. The school librarian and the children's librarian in the public library, as well as the classroom teacher and parents, stimulate, encourage, and make available the ever-expanding and fascinating field of children's literature. In this "extensive" reading program, as it is often called, youngsters may form a reading club, dramatize stories, give puppet shows, engage in musical and art activities, and participate in innumerable creative activities as a result of recreative and personal reading. A famous children's librarian, for a Wednesday afternoon program, decided to play the first in a series of records on the Newbery prize books. Knowing that her audience of from sixty to eighty children would expect to see as well as to hear something, this librarian supplemented the record on the book, *Wheel on the School*, by Meindert DeJong, with a movie on Holland.

Recreational reading has gained in importance and in scope in the reading program with the current emphasis on personal development through reading and with the expansion of the children's book field. An elementary school youngster today reads what he is interested in reading or what he needs to read as a member of a working committee or a larger group. His selection is made from a wealth of material assembled either in his own homeroom or in the school library. His world of books includes not only fiction but also information about the world in which he lives and the people in it.

Mrs. Camilla Anthony, Reading Clinic Teacher, Dallas Independent School District, makes good use of traffic signs for reading material that is interesting and purposeful for older boys. While driving along one of the turnpikes it occurred to her that many boys do not read fast enough or perceive quickly enough to read all the informative signs along the highways at the speed permitted on our new modern expressways. She jotted down all the signs as she rode along and later primer-typed them on cards for use in the individual tachistoscope:

> Do Not Pass When Yellow Line
> Is on Your Side
> Traffic Signal Ahead
> Slow — Merging Traffic
> Service Station and Café 1 Mile
> One Way — Do Not Enter

It was her idea to use these cards for perception training but she found them to be far more valuable as an "interest-getter." Large boys coming to the clinic are all aware of the written test required for a driver's license and immediately see this as a chance to learn to read for that purpose. From this beginning she moved into the driver's safety manual furnished by the state police, using the traffic words to teach word analysis.

For guidance in his own school, the elementary school pupil has his teacher and a children's librarian. Following his own interests and needs under guidance, the pupil reports his reactions and findings. This rarely takes the form of the traditional "book report" of other years. Enthusiasm for reading can be transferred from one reader to another in more interesting and more appropriate ways. Pupils in the elementary school are often seen writing informal reactions to books, school news articles, radio and television scripts, as well as talking, dramatizing, and making tape recordings and still and motion pictures about the books they have read.

In one school a book report took the form of a small mural which attracted much attention and favorable comment. Another book report, consisting of 35 mm. slides, was so popular it was repeated several times. Pupils sometimes prefer to write their own reading material. One teacher of retarded readers with a meager supply of suitable reading material, frankly shared his problem with the pupils. He said, "I know you will not like these books; you'll think they are too childish. But they are all we have. So why don't you write your own books about the things in which you are interested. I'll have your stories duplicated so everyone can read them." This idea appealed to the group and they wrote or dictated a wealth of material, high in interest, in their own vocabulary and language patterns.

A fifth-grade boy who was reading erratically at a second-grade level, took great delight in telling Miss Hettie Dougherty, Reading Clinic Teacher, Dallas Independent School District, that he read "by the pictures" and never looked at the print, "even to make book reports." He had so thoroughly convinced himself of this that, even after careful motivation, the reading clinic teacher was unable to get him to take more than a glance at the print and a guess at the content. He was so completely "space" and "gun" oriented that the clinic had little interesting material to offer him. The teacher suggested that he write his own stories. He took to the idea enthusiastically and began writing a serial about "Rocky Valley and the Space Raiders." He dictated the story to the reading clinic teacher, who acted as his secretary (which pleased him), and she typed the story word-for-word on the primer typewriter. He then read it back to her. This pupil always asked the reading clinic teacher to read it to him, and his usual comment was, "Say, that's pretty good!" After the third chapter he insisted on calling in his mother and reading it to her. He seemed completely absorbed in the project, read his own work with extreme care, and seldom missed a word. Interestingly enough, he had never missed difficult words such as *disintegrating, robot, raiders, rangers, suction,* or *bombs.*

Before starting another chapter he was asked to reread the last one aloud "so he'll know exactly where he left off." Occasionally he illustrated his story with a finely detailed pencil drawing. Although he liked to draw and claimed to be "the best drawer in the class," he seemed more interested in the story than in the illustrations. The first two chapters of his story follow:

SPACE RAIDERS

Chapter One

One day Rocky Valley was going down the lane and saw some enemy space ships. He went and told the crew and they got their space guns out. Then they got in their fort. Then Rocky got the disintegrating rifles out.

The space men attacked, and they had some robots. Then Rocky had to get in the rocket to get some gas bombs. The ship caught on fire before Rocky could get out.

Chapter Two

```
    The Space Rangers saw the ship on fire.  Tom and Joe got
the suction machine out.  Then they had to get some aid
powder.  The fire started going away.  When Rocky awoke he
ran for the gas bombs, but they were all gone.  He tried to
get the gas spears, but the gas wasn't very strong.  The
robots started in the ship.  Rocky tried to get the spears
before the robots got them, but the robots broke them with
their rays.
```

All these activities are above and beyond the "skills" program of the school and emphasize the richness and extensiveness of reading experiences offered to boys and girls of the elementary school today. Experience has shown that rapid progress in reading depends a great deal on the pupils' purpose and on the vital content of the reading material.

Concluding Questions

What is reading?

As stated at the beginning of this chapter, reading is much more than word pronunciation; it is more than word recognition; it is more than getting the meaning of individual words. It is the complex process of getting the meaning of words in combination and knowing what the author is trying to communicate — "What is the author saying to me?" Reading, in the broadest sense, goes beyond comprehension to the use or enjoyment of what is read. "Reading," said a gifted person, "is to me *one* means by which I can find out as much, or as little, of what I choose to know or learn about any given thing."

A teacher may be able to teach word pronunciation perfectly if he is concerned exclusively with it. When children have confused word-calling with reading, they may pronounce a passage perfectly but have no idea of its meaning. This sometimes happens.

On the other hand, when children have learned to read to comprehend, they welcome any method of word recognition that will help them attain that end. We cannot be indifferent to the thought process in reading. As E. L. Thorndike said many years ago, "reading is reasoning." Experience, interest, motive or purpose, an understanding of spoken words, and a sense of language structure all enter into the reading process.

The definition of reading offered by Edgar Dale emphasizes the active participation of the reader:

> Reading, we must remember, is a process of getting meaning from the printed page by putting meaning into the printed page. Reading taste and

ability are always tethered to past experience. But reading itself is one way of increasing this capital fund of past experience. Reading, therefore, must be seen as more than *saying* the word, more than *seeing* the sentences and paragraphs. Good reading is the way a person brings his whole life to bear on the new ideas which he finds on the printed page. It is reading the lines, reading between the lines, and reading beyond the lines (6, p. 2).

More specifically, we may describe reading as follows:

Reading builds on experience.

Reading is one form of experience.

Reading is a method of learning.

The reading process involves:

seeing the words clearly

recognizing their meaning

understanding sentences, paragraphs, and the

passage as a whole

appraising ideas critically

seeing relations among them

using these ideas in various ways, as in the

solution of practical problems

Reading makes possible the selection of material from a vast and permanent store. It facilitates thoughtful interpretation and deliberation. The reader can pause and reflect at any point. He can turn back to review what has been said. He can read what he wants when he wants it. Reading is thus a means of withstanding the propaganda constantly and insistently blared forth by radio, television, and motion pictures. To resist this barrage, one has a special need for critical reading.

**What is the relation
of words to reading?**

Words are labels for experiences relating to an object or action. They help to organize our experience; they are tools for thinking. Words help us to tell others about our experiences and to understand the experiences of others. The child sees words on signs, on television, in movie captions, in his own books, and in his father's newspapers. He begins to identify letters and their combinations in words. Gradually these words take on meaning; they evoke appropriate ideas. This process begins in various ways, as children themselves will tell you when they think back to the time they learned to read. Some associated a word with a picture or object; others recognized certain words in the stories their mothers or fathers read to them. Some learned by sounding out a word and still others by seeing it in an experience story they had dictated to the teacher. When words are seen in a meaningful context, children learn to relate one word to another. This is the natural way to deal with words.

Many words have more than one meaning. The best way to learn this is to read words in different contexts. In this way the child begins to realize that the meaning is more important than the word form. Once he has acquired this idea, he welcomes instruction in word recognition skills as a means to an end. He has a purpose: To discover, through reading, something that has personal meaning and interest to him. One difference between good and poor readers is that the errors made by good readers indicate that they are trying to get the meaning of the passage. For example, the good reader may read, "They went to the *farm*" instead of "They went to the *fair*," if the first makes sense, whereas the poor reader, struggling with pronunciation only, may read *fair* as *first*, without any concern for the meaning.

**What is the purpose
of instruction in reading?**

The purpose of reading instruction is to teach children how to read so that they will be "on their own in reading," like to read, read voluntarily, and apply the ideas gained in reading to the solution of practical life problems. To accomplish this purpose the teacher must understand the individual child and supply the experiences he needs when he needs them. Individual needs may be met by subgrouping within a class and by individualizing instruction in other ways. The teacher is concerned with the growth in reading of *each* child and may use a *variety* of methods to achieve this end. But the child must do his own learning; the teacher can create conditions conducive to learning but cannot "make him learn."

**Do pupils read more poorly
than they used to?**

Taking into account changes in promotion policy, and in the school population, it seems clear that, on the whole, boys and girls today read as well as or better than they did a generation ago — even though a larger number of less able children are attending school. This conclusion is based on a comparison of the scores of reading tests given in the same schools over a period of years. Judged by the increase in reading material for children and adolescents, they do more voluntary reading than they used to do. The number of books published for juveniles has more than doubled since 1925 and teen-age books are beginning to bridge the gap between children's and adults' reading interests.

However, there is room for improvement. Not all teachers at all levels

Reading is reasoning; pupils should take time to think about what they read.

Children read widely today.

are teaching reading as well as they can. Although the average achievement is encouraging, it is not evident in all schools. Also on the negative side are the facts that students do not read as well orally as they used to, and that their reading interests and tastes are in serious need of improvement. Since emphasis on oral reading has decreased during the past twenty-five years, it is only natural that proficiency in this kind of reading shows a slump. And since other mass media of communication are changing young people's values and standards, these changes would obviously be reflected in reading tastes.

Parents will probably continue to complain about the teaching of reading in our schools, as they did in 1845, when the Boston Grammar School Committee lamented that "a large proportion of the scholars in our first classes, boys and girls of 14 and 15 years of age, when called on to write simple sentences . . . cannot write, without such errors in grammar, in spelling, and in punctuation, as we should blush to see in a letter from a son or daughter of their age." Language arts problems are widespread and persistent, but interest in these problems is high and improvement is possible.

**What variety and progression of reading
experiences do children need?**

To develop reading proficiency, children need a variety of experiences. They need to listen to stories of a higher interest level than they can, at the time, read for themselves. Through listening to the teacher or parent read, children will glimpse "the delight that lies between the covers of books." They will gain many types of information and may develop new interests. They will become more familiar with the language patterns of books. They will learn to listen and use ideas gained in this way. In the discussion of books read, they will practice effective speaking.

Occasionally children will read to the teacher. This is a way for the teacher to get diagnostic information. It is also an incentive for a child to find and read something of particular interest. Children will often read to other children in an audience situation. This furnishes a strong incentive to find something of interest to the group and learn to read it well enough to win their classmates' appropriate response and approval.

As they grow older children read more and more to themselves. They especially enjoy free reading periods, when they may select the kind of reading they want, the kind they respond to. They want books that make reading rewarding, books with a real story interest, books that are "suspenseful," as one youngster said, books that amuse, books that give them insight into the meaning of life. Sometimes they want to read to solve a problem or to answer a question in any of the content fields. In this kind of reading they learn to locate the facts they need and to present them in a meaningful way.

Underlying all of these experiences is the need for instruction in the basic skills of word recognition and comprehension. When and how to give such instruction has been discussed in the previous pages. Many of the procedures described will be useful, in adapted form, for high school teachers.

We have seen that growth in reading ability as fostered by the elementary school is a developmental process, that there is nothing haphazard about it, and that when carried forward without complications, it brings the elementary school pupil to the high school years with an optimum of skill, ability, and appreciation. Elementary and high school teachers are partners in promoting this continuous growth in reading. When considered all together, these skills, abilities, and appreciations provide the readiness needed to undertake with pleasure and profit the experiences planned for the high school years. However, not all pupils arrive at this level with the same backgrounds, experiences, and capacities; their reading achievements vary widely, their needs are different, and adjustments to individuals must be made in materials, curriculum, and methods of instruction.

REFERENCES

1. ANDERSON, IRVING H., and DEARBORN, WALTER F. *The Psychology of Teaching Reading.* New York: Ronald Press, 1952.
2. BETTS, EMMETT ALBERT. "What about Phonics?" *Education,* Vol. LXXV, No. 9 (May, 1955), pp. 547–59.
3. BURROWS, ALVINA TREUT. "The Conflict over Phonics Is Still Raging." *The Reading Teacher,* Vol. VI (May, 1953), pp. 12–17.
4. CLARK, JOHN R.; JUNGE, CHARLOTTE W.; and MOSER, HAROLD. *Growth in Arithmetic,* Grade Four. New York: World Book Company, 1952.
5. CRAIG, GERALD S., and HILL, KATHERINE E. *Working with Science.* Boston: Ginn and Company, 1950.
6. DALE, EDGAR. *News Letter.* Columbus: Ohio State University, October, 1954.
7. DOLCH, E. W. "Recognition of Long Words." *Education.* Vol. LXXV, No. 9 (May, 1955), pp. 604–608.
8. FERNALD, GRACE. *Remedial Techniques in Basic School Subjects* (Revised) New York: McGraw-Hill Book Company, 1943.
9. GATES, ARTHUR I. *What Research Says about Reading.* Washington, D.C.: National Education Association, 1954.
10. GRAY, WILLIAM S. (Editor). *Classroom Techniques in Improving Reading.* Chicago: University of Chicago Press, 1949.
11. GRAY, WILLIAM S. *On Their Own in Reading.* Chicago: Scott, Foresman and Company, 1953.

12. HANNA, PAUL R.; QUILLEN, I. JAMES; SEARS, PAUL F.; and CAMPBELL, EDNA FAY. *Our World and How We Use It.* Chicago: Scott, Foresman and Company, 1953.

13. HARRIS, A. J. *How to Increase Reading Ability* (Third Edition). New York: Longmans, Green and Company, 1956.

14. HILDRETH, GERTRUDE. *Learning the Three R's.* St. Louis: Educational Publishers, 1947.

15. HORSMAN, GWEN. "Developing Independent Word Attack in Junior and Senior High School," *Basic Instruction in Reading in Elementary School.* Chicago: University of Chicago Press, 1948.

16. KIRK, SAMUEL A. and WINIFRED D. "How Johnny Learns to Read." *Exceptional Children,* Vol. XXII (January, 1956), pp. 158–60.

17. KOTTMEYER, WILLIAM. *Handbook for Remedial Reading.* St. Louis: Webster Publishing Company, 1947.

18. *Learning Methods Test* kit including one manual, four levels of picture-word cards on the primer, first, second, and third-grade levels, and two test record forms, available from Robert E. Mills, Reading Laboratory and Clinic, 310 Anderson Hall, University of Florida, Gainesville, Florida.

19. MANEY, ETHEL. "How to Help Children Sound Out New Words They Meet in Their Reading." *The Reading Teacher,* Vol. VII (October, 1953), pp. 42–46.

20. MCKEE, PAUL. *The Teaching of Reading in the Elementary School.* Boston: Houghton Mifflin Company, 1948.

21. MCKIM, MARGARET G. *Guiding Growth in Reading.* New York: The Macmillan Company, 1955.

22. MONROE, MARION. *Growing into Reading.* Chicago: Scott, Foresman and Company, 1951.

23. NATIONAL SOCIETY FOR THE STUDY OF EDUCATION. *Reading in the Elementary School.* The Forty-Eighth Yearbook, Part II. Chicago: University of Chicago Press, 1949.

24. NATIONAL SOCIETY FOR THE STUDY OF EDUCATION. *Report of the National Committee on Reading.* The Twenty-Fourth Yearbook, Part I, p. 24. Chicago: University of Chicago Press, 1925.

25. OLSON, WILLARD C. "Child Needs Aid the Curriculum." *Educational Leadership,* Vol. VI, No. 4 (January, 1949), pp. 195–99.

26. *Promoting Growth in Reading, A Teacher's Guide for Use in Secondary Schools.* Tulsa, Oklahoma, 1948.

27. Reading Number, *Education,* Vol. LXXIV (May, 1954), pp. 523–84.

28. ROBINSON, HELEN M. (Compiler and Editor). *Oral Aspects of Reading.* Supplementary Educational Monograph, No. 82. Chicago: University of Chicago Press, 1955.

29. SERVISS, TREVOR K. *Reading and Child Growth,* American Library Association Bulletin, Vol. XLVIII, No. 2 (February, 1954), pp. 72+.

30. STRANG, RUTH; MCCULLOUGH, CONSTANCE; and TRAXLER, ARTHUR E. *Problems in the Improvement of Reading.* New York: McGraw-Hill Book Company, 1955.

31. STULL, EDITH G. *Janie Learns to Read.* Washington, D.C.: National Education Association, 1954.
32. *The Reading Teacher.* "Phonics in Reading Instruction." Vol. IX (December, 1955), pp. 67–106.
33. WILLIAMS, GERTRUDE H. "What Does Research Tell Us about Readiness for Beginning Reading?" *The Reading Teacher,* Vol. VI (May, 1953), pp. 34–40.
34. WITTY, PAUL. "Phonic Study and Word Analysis, I." *Elementary English,* Vol. XXX (May, 1953), pp. 296–305.
35. WITTY, PAUL. "Phonic Study and Word Analysis, II." *Elementary English,* Vol. XXX (October, 1953), pp. 373–79.
36. WITTY, PAUL. *Reading in Modern Education.* Boston: D. C. Heath and Company, 1949.
37. YOAKAM, GERALD A. *Basal Reading Instruction.* New York: McGraw-Hill Book Company, 1955.

DIVERSITY OF READING ABILITY
AND INTEREST

TEACHERS ARE WELL AWARE of the diversity of physical development, social maturity, mental ability, and family backgrounds represented in junior and senior high school classes. The diversity in pupils' reading ability and interests is just as wide. To provide experiences that will encourage and stimulate some but not discourage and inhibit others is a challenge to every teacher.

Retarded Reader, Defined

A "reading problem" has been variously defined. Certainly it is a problem for both student and teacher if a student cannot read the books he is expected to read in his grade. Even if he is reading up to his grade level but not up to his mental capacity, he may be considered to be retarded in reading. A "retarded reader" has been defined as an individual with average or superior mental ability but a specific weakness in the language arts area; or, more specifically, his mental age is one or more years higher than his reading age. There is still another kind of retardation: that of the student who can demonstrate good reading ability on a test but does not use this ability in his day-by-day reading. In other instances, the student's average reading score is satisfactory, but further analysis shows he is very deficient in certain reading skills. All of these types of difficulty may properly be considered reading problems or a form of reading retardation. Instead of using the label "retarded reader," it would be better to speak of persons who are having "difficulty in achieving their reading potentialities."

Range of Reading Ability

Various estimates have been made of the percentage of pupils in our schools today who cannot comprehend the books they are required to read. This percentage ranges from 10 to 40, depending upon the sampling of pupils and the criteria, with the emphasis falling on estimates between 10 and 15 per cent of elementary school children. In a study of 19,063 eighth graders who were given a reading test, it was found that 20 per cent were reading below the seventh-grade level. The range of reading grade in this sampling was from third grade to college level. However, the factor of intelligence must be taken into account; some students are reading as well as they can even though they are reading below grade level.

Individual teachers have discovered wide ranges in the reading levels of their pupils. One high school teacher who became interested in this problem surveyed her tenth-grade class with results which were amazing to her. According to standardized tests she had three students reading at tenth-grade level, seven below, and sixteen above. In this particular class *seven* grade levels of reading ability were represented.

Another teacher surveyed her eleventh-grade class using standardized reading tests. She discovered a range of *fourteen* grade levels. In IQ as measured by group intelligence tests the range was 36 points. As judged by test results, some were retarded while others were reading better than their intelligence test scores would indicate.

Before testing their classes, these teachers answered certain questions about their students. Both considered their students high in economic background, high in meaningful experiences gained outside of school, and average in intelligence as far as they could judge from classroom observation. According to teachers' rating these two classes were considered superior. Yet these students with superior backgrounds read on many reading levels; they were not all superior readers.

In the upper grades of some senior high schools the range may not be so great, because many of the poorest readers have dropped out of school. There is evidence that low reading ability is related to premature school leaving. A study by Penty (18) showed that of 593 tenth-grade students whose reading scores were in the lowest quarter of their class, more than half dropped out of school before graduating, whereas, of an equal number whose scores were in the highest quarter of their class, only slightly more than an eighth dropped out of school before graduating. Of those who dropped out of school, about three fourths had the potential ability to read up to or above the seventh grade. These facts emphasize the need to help boys and girls improve their reading skills so that they will make the most of their school years.

Individual differences in reading may be increased by education and guidance; those who do not have the mental ability to read better will not be expected to do the impossible, while those who are reading below reasonable expectation will be helped to attain their potential. In a developmental college reading class made up of college freshmen from Arts and Science and graduate students, standardized reading tests showed a range of *twenty* reading grade levels.

A wide range of differences will be shown not only in general reading level but also in proficiency in different reading skills. Some students will be low in speed, high in comprehension, and average in vocabulary. Others will be high in speed, low in comprehension, and low in vocabulary. Still others will be average in speed, high in comprehension, and high in vocabulary. In the more advanced skills of drawing conclusions, making inferences, applying reading, interpreting what is read, reading creatively, reading critically, and reacting to reading, the range for individuals as well as for groups is tremendous.

Recognition of Diversity by Teachers

High school teachers take a step forward in solving reading problems when they ascertain the reading level of each student. If trained testers are not available, with a little expenditure of time and effort, most teachers can administer a standardized reading test (see Appendix, page 345); score it; and change the raw scores into grade level scores, using the tables given in the test manual. Study of grade level scores will show the number of students below grade level, the number above, and the number at grade level. Many teachers are startled by the wide range of reading ability represented in their own classes.

Even more enlightening are the results from an informal test using selections from the books that teachers will be expecting their pupils to read.

The following is an informal test that was given to 150 eighth-grade pupils in an urban industrial community (27):

Name _____ Age _____ Grade _____

Here are three paragraphs and a verse for you to read.
Read them as you usually do. Then turn the page upside down
and answer the questions.

1

Fear, like anger, stops the flow of the digestive juices.
In India a test was once used to tell whether or not a
prisoner was guilty of a crime. The man was given a handful
of dry rice to put in his mouth. He was told to keep the
rice in his mouth a few minutes. If the prisoner had committed a crime and was very much frightened, his saliva would
stop flowing and the rice would remain dry. If he was not
guilty and had no fear of being punished, his saliva would
flow as usual and the rice would be wet.

Answer the questions below.

3. What is the main idea of the paragraph?

2. What is saliva?

1. What did you get out of the paragraph you have just read?
Tell all you remember.

2

For centuries Puerto Rico belonged to Spain. The Spaniards
erected two stone forts to guard the entrance to the bay of
San Juan. These forts protected the city from pirates and
from the English "sea dogs," such as Sir Francis Drake.
Spain had to struggle to keep her island possessions in this
region, which was called the Spanish Main.

Answer the questions below.

3. What was Spain trying to do?

2. To what country did Puerto Rico belong?

1. What did you get out of this paragraph?
Tell all you remember.

3

The carrying of goods by land is the story, first of the
use of humans, then of animals, then of wheels, and then of
tracks. Perhaps today we might add, "wings." When the
earliest man traveled, it was by "shoe leather express,"
except that perhaps he had no shoes. Man carried goods on
his back or on poles over his shoulders. After a time he
made animals, such as camels and donkeys, do the carrying.
Then wheels were invented. They could go more easily and
rapidly and carry more goods than the heavily laden pack
animals, except over snow, and then sledges could be used.

Answer the question below.

1. Draw a picture to show the ideas you got from this
paragraph.

4

There was an old man with a beard
Who said, "It is just as I feared!
    An owl and a hen
    Four larks and a wren
Have all built their nests in my beard!"

Answer the questions below.

3. How do you think the author felt when he was writing
this verse?

2. What does larks mean?

1. What does this mean to you? Tell everything that you
thought of as you read it.

---

1. What kind of books do you like best?

2. Make up a title for a story boys and girls of your age
   would all want very much to read.

3. Now write as much of this story as you can before the
   end of this period.

On this test, some of the pupils showed practically no comprehension of the paragraphs presented, while others comprehended the main idea and the supporting details of each paragraph in their proper sequence. The test results showed very clearly lack of instruction in relating ideas and arranging them in order. The majority of pupils confused the illustration with the main idea in the first paragraph. Instead of stating the main idea — "Fear like anger stops the flow of the digestive juices," they said, "There was a test of guilt in India," and went on to describe it, usually quite accurately. Similarly in the social studies paragraphs, they reported scattered details without showing their relation or sequence. Their response to the Edward Lear limerick was most amusing and showed the need for instruction in identifying the author's mood, intent, and purpose. With almost no exception these pupils took seriously what the author intended to be funny and tried to make sense out of what he intended to be nonsense (27). One youngster wrote, "The old man should have taken better care of his beard," and another said seriously, "It is very unusual to see an old man with a bird's nest in his beard." Informal tests or practice exercises of this kind not only show the diversity of reading ability but also the kind of reading instruction pupils need to succeed in the reading tasks of their grade.

Reading Interests

Diversity of interests

Students' reading interests are as wide as their reading achievement. The variety of backgrounds and abilities in part accounts for the wide diversity in reading interests. In fact, teachers are more concerned with interests that require reading than with reading interests. In most high school classes there will probably be students who apparently have no need for reading in their lives — except to meet school requirements. Their out-of-school hours are filled with remunerative work or home or farm duties requiring little or no reading, with auto riding, sports, social activities, listening to radio and looking at television, going to the movies, and "just fooling around." They do practically no voluntary reading. It is difficult to motivate these pupils to improve their reading.

Then there are pupils who do some voluntary reading. But it is not high quality reading. Their reading is limited to the comics, sensational stories in newspapers, sports news, and *True Story* and *True Confessions* type of magazines.

Another group of pupils read somewhat better magazines and teen-age stories. The Teen Age Book Club (29) and teen-age magazines make a strong appeal to this group.

Other pupils will have quite mature reading interests and tastes. They have probably been brought up in bookish families, where reading good books was a matter of course and plenty of good books were easily available. Depending on their age and mental ability, they will be reading some biography and informational types of books as well as fiction, and will begin reading adult books, often with sound critical appraisal.

Many early adolescents fluctuate between childish and adult reading interests. One day they will be reading a popular juvenile series and the next day a play by Bernard Shaw or an adult best seller. This represents a normal fluctuation of feelings in this "in-between period." Growth in reading parallels students' interests and developmental needs: familiar experience, exploring a wider world, concern with their personal development and problems and their relation to others, looking to the future, and specialized fields of study.

A few students may be using reading as an escape mechanism. Not having been successful in their social relations, they retreat into books. Or not having the affection they crave they seek solace or recognition from their reading. Some teachers tend to encourage these students in their excessive reading, without realizing that this may be undesirable from the standpoint of their total personality development.

Common interests

Robinson (21) summarized the following research findings regarding reading interests:

Interests of boys and girls, as groups, begin to diverge during the intermediate grades.

Primary children like narratives about other children and animals; preadolescent boys "turn toward adventure stories, descriptions of 'how-to-do-it,' hero-worship and science," while girls prefer fantasy and stories about home and family life; adolescent boys are most interested in mysteries, sports, recreational activities, and comics, while girls prefer romance and stories of teen-age problems.

Adolescents' actual reading interests fall short of their potential interests. Their general interest in self-improvement and self-realization, including interest in finding and progressing in a job, is reflected in their reading interests. They want to identify themselves with characters who are vigorous, brave, sincere, kind, helpful, successful. The older adolescents are more likely to recognize that a happy ending is not always compatible with another quality they like in books, namely, being "true to life." Senior high school students are also more interested in the thoughts and feelings of the characters, whereas the junior high school youngsters, first of all, want action.

Youngsters enjoy some common reading experiences.

Individual interests motivate reading.

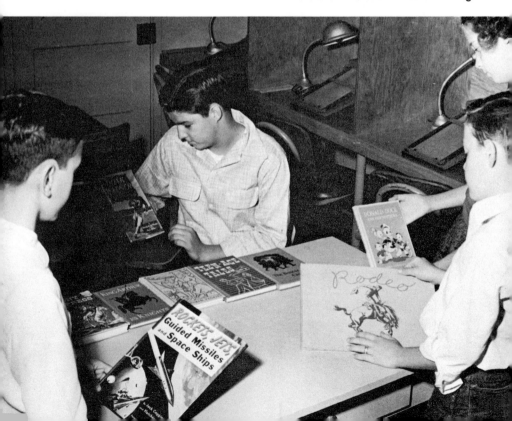

**Relation of television
to reading**

It is difficult to generalize about television. According to their own statements, some adolescents are practically addicted to television; they cannot tear themselves away from it. Others can take it or leave it, and are selective in the programs they view. They see positive values in these programs in giving a background of experience for reading and in stimulating further reading. A few express general dislike of television, especially of the commercials.

What to do about television in relation to reading interests is a question in the minds of many parents and teachers (31). This is certain: Television is usurping a large proportion of children's leisure time. A large percentage of children (92 per cent in a recent study) have television sets in their homes. Children in the primary grades view television on an average of four hours a day, while children in the middle grades average about three hours daily, and high school students slightly less. We find conflicting reports as to whether the amount of time youngsters spend viewing television is increasing or decreasing. When the television set was new, reading did fall off for a while. But despite the increasing number of television sets and programs, reading, too, as judged by the number of newspapers, magazines, and books bought, is increasing. In 1956, it was estimated that people were buying about 55 million newspapers a day, 58 million magazines a week, and around 800 million books a year.

Where is this time coming from? Is it time that used to be devoted to radio, movies, comics? Or to outdoor recreation and social activities? Or to home study? Or to sleep? Or to reading? The teacher who has established a friendly relation with his class can get this information from the twenty-four hour schedules which he can ask his pupils to keep. By discussing these schedules in the group and by having individual conferences with teachers, pupils may work out a better balanced daily schedule for themselves. Such a schedule would include time for outdoor recreation, sleep, social activities, reading, and study. Into this well-balanced daily program, they can fit their favorite radio and television programs.

What these programs will be, depends partly on the school's consideration of the television offerings. The children should be encouraged to discuss and appraise the programs they like and dislike. They will be influenced by the comments of their classmates, which, we hope, will tend to be in the right direction. In general, the vivid murder, crime, and horror stories should be replaced in the children's choices by more wholesome programs such as "Mr. Wizard," "Zoo Parade," "Super Circus," "You Are There," and other favorites.

There is evidence, as Larrick (12) has pointed out, that "more children are reading more books than ever before." Public libraries report millions of books taken out by children each year, and the percentage of books taken out is increasing each year. More children's books are being published each year — around eleven hundred new children's books in 1952 as contrasted with 532 new titles in 1935. Some of the most popular children's books have sold over one hundred thousand copies, while the sales of some of the 25 cent books have been extensive. The *Little Golden Books*, for example, which are sold in supermarkets, drugstores, and newsstands, since 1942 have sold over two hundred million copies.

**How to study
reading interests**

None of the methods used in studying reading interests are entirely satisfactory. If students are asked to check titles they have read, they may unconsciously try to make a good impression by checking more than they have really read. If books withdrawn from the library is used as a criterion, it is possible that the books may have been withdrawn but not read. If students are asked to write the names of books they have read, inaccuracies may enter in here, too. The best method of studying reading interests is through daily observation supplemented by the informal interview or freely written type of report guided by a few questions.

A teacher knows students — their attitudes, interests, abilities, experiences, and their environmental setting. A good librarian knows books — their content, grade level, and their readability. A knowledge of both is necessary. Hence cooperation between teacher and librarian is a necessity.

To discover the diversity of reading interests in high school classes, the teacher may ask students to keep a record of their outside reading for a week. If the teacher has a good relation with his class and presents this assignment as an opportunity for students to gain an understanding of themselves, and if he assures them that they will not be marked on the quality of their reading, he should get sincere and fairly accurate reports. These will show the range of reading interests and habits, and also serve as a basis for individual conferences and group discussions.

Although this informal method does not seem as precise and complete as questionnaires and inventories of the check-list type, it may supply more authentic information. To obtain more detail about the kind of books students like or dislike, teachers may use the form opposite.

These few simple questions will yield a wealth of information (26): You will find that adolescents have many reading interests in common.

TO THE STUDENTS

Year in school _____ *12* _____ Boy _____ Girl *x*

You need not sign your name unless you want to. ~~~~~~~

You have right now the best possible information about what high school students like to read. Will you share it with us by answering as thoughtfully and fully as possible the following questions:

1. What do young persons like you most want to read about?

Adventure with romance involved. Mystery and suspense.

2. What kind of a book or article would you choose to read above all others?

Novel with the characteristics stated above.

3. Suppose you were going to write a book or article that persons of your age would all want to read, what would be its title?

Adventure is my hobby.

4. Write a paragraph or two showing how you think this book should be written to appeal most to the boys and girls in your class.

First of all I think it should be written about young boys and girls. It should be written so that young people can understand it, not with the longest words in the dictionary. Not too fabulous so that it won't sound too adventurous or impossible.

5. Think of the books or articles you have read this year that you just couldn't stand. What was it in them that made you dislike them so much?

Confidential Agent: stupid story about espionage. So confidential and confusing. I couldn't understand it until I saw the movie. Too many characters involved with just the first initial of their name given.
Brainstorm: written about a person who went insane. Written by insane person only made to seem that someone else was writing all mixed up.

6. Think of the books or articles you have liked most this year. What was it in them that made you like them so much?

Captain from Castille — adventure and romance. Leave Her to Heaven — interesting and full of suspense Last Week End — Told how the author thought an alcoholic neurotics mind works.

7. Which book or article that you have read during the last year interested you most keenly? Give the author *Hugh Walpole*, title *Fortitude*, magazine or publisher _____, and date _____ (if you remember it). Then write as much as you can about the article and why you liked it so much. (Use other side of page.)

When asked what kind of book they would choose above all others, the following replies were typical:

"Anything exciting."

"Baseball."

"Books about people around my age."

"A short story, preferably a mystery."

"Historical novel or biography: character studies."

"A vocational story by which I would arrive at a better understanding of vocations and how I'm equipped for them."

"Adventure with romance involved; mystery and suspense." Here we have adolescent reading interests in a nutshell.

They go further into the reasons they enjoyed their favorite books:

"The people were real and things that happened to them really could happen."

"Poe's *Pit and the Pendulum* made me feel as though I was in the story myself. It was interesting and full of suspense."

One youngster said, "What makes a good interesting story varies according to the mood I am in."

They dislike books that are "written in a monotonous, uninteresting fashion," that are "very stuffy and drag a lot," that "have too much description and are depressing," that "have too many words which are long and hard to understand." When asked what makes a book easy to read many say, "When it's interesting." They will sometimes take a book we think is too difficult for them and read it eagerly. Books that are crammed with facts and lacking in human interest will not hold their interest. This is the trouble with many textbooks. They need to be supplemented with interesting detail and exciting incidents. The film strips and records based on the *Landmark Books* published by Random House furnish excellent enrichment material for social studies classes.

One youngster wrote, "Books with not much conversation and a lot of description are sometimes tiresome and hard on the nerves, especially if the book is compulsory and must be read." Another dismissed the problem of uninteresting books simply in this way: "When I come across something I dislike I don't bother to read it."

The interests of gifted children are not very different in kind from those of other children, though they are usually a year or two ahead of the others in their interests. They earlier become interested in specialized reading, such as biography, science, and other fields. One bright sixth grader said, "My daddy's a science teacher. From the first to the fourth grades I read the books that they had in school. I would take daddy's books to school to read when I got ahead of the other children. Sometimes I couldn't read them, but I liked to look at the pictures and sometimes I could read parts of them. In the fifth and sixth grades I liked aviation books and now I am interested in nuclear physics."

One way that students may broaden their reading interests is to keep an objective record of their reading pattern. They may do this very simply by listing together the books read in a given area and conferring with the teacher from time to time about the development of their reading interests. A published form, *My Reading Design* (on the next two pages), uses one page for listing the books read and another page for picturing the reading design in the areas of adventure and exploration, aviation, sports and games, poetry, comics, humor, animals, and others. It is published in Forms A, B, C, D, for each three grades from 1 to 12.

Having discovered the students' interests, the teacher will try to provide books and magazines on their reading levels and in the areas of their greatest interests.

High School Students' Need for Reading

The most difficult students with whom to work are those who seem to have no interest in or need for reading. Yet actually, reading is important to them. The needs of high school students for reading may be illustrated by the following analysis made by a teacher * :

1. Every young citizen is expected to be able to fill out certain information blanks. These include employment forms, school information blanks, government questionnaires, post office forms, and the like. Oftentimes the adults of the family, unable to read or write the English language, ask their children's help with other, more complicated forms.

2. In these days a good deal of necessary information comes in the form of pamphlets, newspaper articles, and printed material. For instance, the announcement came out one fall that boys and girls could be excused from two weeks of school if they would work on the farms and would fulfill stated requirements as given in printed directions. There are literally scores of such everyday needs calling for an ability to read and understand directions.

3. Everyone who travels is expected to be able to read simple road signs, bus signs, danger signals, and other directions to carry on normal living. For a motorist a road map is a convenience only if he can interpret it. Even the menu cards in the restaurants and drugstores demand a certain amount of reading ability.

4. In school, of course, the demands upon students' reading ability increase. For their social science classes, they must be able to read and interpret not only their textbooks, but newspapers and magazines, encyclopedias, and supplementary books.

* Contributed by Mrs. Amy Dahlgren Fenner, formerly teacher and librarian in McCarver Junior High School, Tacoma, Washington.

THE BOOKS WHICH I HAVE READ

Sample: 1A *Wagons Westward*

1. Tales of Shakespeare
2. The Robe
3. The Crisis
4. Freedom Road
5. Black Boy
6. The Uncommon Man
7. Sixty Million Jobs
8. Green Pastures
9. Of Mice and Men
10. Idiot's Delight
11. Emperor Jones
12. Winterset
13. The Adding Machine
14. Plays of Democracy (6)
15. The Faith and Fire Within Us
16. Let Us Consider One Another
17. The Merchant of Venice
18. Strife
19. The Lively Lady
20. Ethan Frome
21. Twenty Modern Americans
22. I Remember Mama
23. Angel Mo and Her Son, Roland Hayes
24. Aeneas Africanus
25.
26.
27.
28.
29.
30.

31. In this high school students were permitted to read any books of their own choice. It was not a part of the required work. It was reading for sheer enjoyment and enrichment.

33. The reader, entirely independent of the teacher, determined the categories of interest in which the books should be placed.

36. She determined that book No (I) is about *Romance, Adventure Detective Mystery, Drama & Poetry, Humor and Comics,* and in each of these four categories near the center of the design the reader placed the No (I) and drew a circle around it.

40. In a similar manner she recorded each book indicating the interests as she determined them. The design then becomes a reflection of the reader's active interests and at the same time it reveals the areas of human achievement in which she is a non-reader.

45. It becomes a matter of skilful guidance to cause the reader to explore books in categories in which she is not manifesting interest. The suggested sub-areas on the back page may help in this regard.

49. As readers compare designs they are often stimulated to expand their interests.

51. It is a matter of common experience that readers find great pleasure in developing their reading designs.

53. As the design grows it becomes increasingly important to effective teaching and proficient guidance.

MY READING DESIGN

TO THE READER: — Here is an unfin-
ished design. You may make it yours if you
complete it as you read and enjoy the books you
like. You may wish to build YOUR DESIGN in
this way. (1) Find the book you wish to read.
(2) Read it and write the title on the opposite
page. (3) Discuss the book with your teacher or
librarian, with your parents or friends to find
the parts of the circle in which the book be-

longs. If you examine the subtitles on the back
page it may help you find the correct parts.
(4) Put the number of your book in a small circle in each of the parts where the book belongs.
(5) Then trace those small circles with your
pencil. SEE SAMPLE. Very few books belong
in more than three parts. If you read many
books and record each book as you read, it will
be fun to watch your pattern grow.

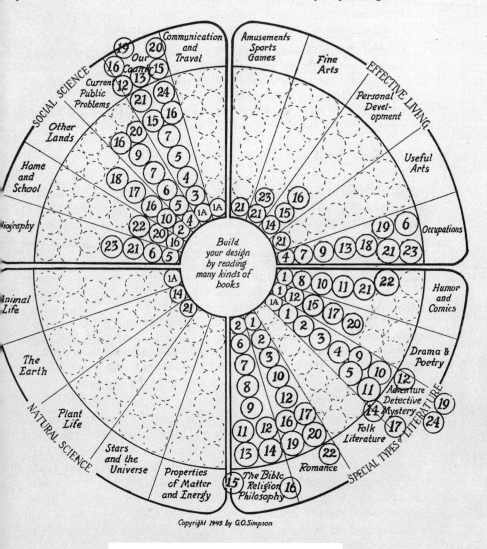

Copyright 1945 by G.O.Simpson

From *My Reading Design* by Glenn O. Simpson.
By permission of the publisher, Reading Circle, Inc.,
North Manchester, Indiana.

5. In science, a required course for the majority, students are expected to read difficult factual material.

6. In English, students need the skill to do extensive outside reading as well as the required class selections.

7. Typewriting involves comprehension of the material to be typed. Music demands ability to read and interpret the words. Mechanical drawing and woodwork shop require a certain familiarity with specifications made in printed form. There is scarcely a subject in the curriculum, unless it be gym, in which there is not a daily need for reading skill.

Recognizing students' needs, teachers have set teaching goals for themselves. One junior high school teacher stated his goals as follows:

I expect my eighth-grade students to read silently and orally with some degree of appreciation and comprehension. I expect them to increase their knowledge of vocabulary and analyze, along lines necessarily not too complicated, the structure of certain types of literature and the behavior of the characters. I always hope to develop at least the first step toward critical analysis of literary matter. My aims along these latter lines, however, are realized only in a few cases. Most of the students are unable to understand eighth-grade literature; a few cannot pronounce a printed word as simple as *majority*.

Another teacher, who has spent much time directing plays in school and has helped one of his English classes to organize a radio program, another to compile a book of short stories, and a third to edit a class magazine, wrote as follows:

My hope in teaching reading in junior high school has always been to broaden the reading interests of my students. I attempt to "expose" them to types of literature with which they are either unfamiliar, or in which they have had no interest, and, through class reading and discussion, to incorporate these into their already established interests. I hope to develop certain standards and sound criteria on which my students will base their choices. I have never used comic books as illustrations of poor reading matter, but have rather tried to suggest, through discussion of other types of adventure and action stories, that one may progress with pleasure beyond the comics.

Despite the recognition of students' needs and the good intention of many teachers, these needs are not being adequately met. More than three fourths of the poor readers in a good senior high school said that they had received no help in high school in finding material they could read, in improving their reading, in accepting certain limitations in their reading capacity, or in making the best use of their other abilities. The large majority wanted help in reading. To quote their words: Some help in reading "would have made all the difference in the world to me." "If

I had had help in reading, I could have understood history better and enjoyed it more."

The following longer quotation from the composition written by a sixteen-year-old girl probably expresses the feelings of many retarded readers:

Now that I'm a junior in high school I really think I could have gotten more out of grade school. For one thing, I think the teachers were too old. They were pretty crabby most of the time and too bossy. For all I know they are probably still teaching, in fact I'm sure they are. The kids in grammar school don't like a teacher that is mean. If a teacher is easy to get along with and wears a smile (like all kids are told to do) the whole class will be happier, and I'm pretty sure the kids would get more out of going to school.

In grammar school we were really never taught how to study, so we would get something out of the subject. We were told to read an assignment and we did. The next day the teacher would ask questions about it and no one would know the answers. That was because we read the assignment quick and didn't know what we were reading. The teachers never went into detail about something if a student, that was slow in learning, didn't understand it. Then when the teacher would ask a question the next day and the student didn't know, all the kids would laugh and make this person feel very embarrassed. I remember very clearly that that happened a lot in history, and there were a lot of children that hated the subject for that reason. I think if the kids were taught not to laugh when someone else makes a mistake everyone would be better off whether the answer is right or wrong. If the answer is wrong, the right answer should be explained more clearly. I know if the kids didn't laugh at the wrong answers in grammar school, I would feel more free to answer a question in class now.

High school students have mixed feelings about reading. Penty summarized the attitudes of the poor readers, both drop-outs and graduates, whom she interviewed after they had left school, under these headings:

(1) "I enjoy what I can read and understand," (2) "I would like to read, if I could read better," (3) "I like to read now but I disliked to read in high school," (4) "I am still trying to learn to read better," (5) "I have trouble with reading, so I dislike it" (18, pp. 38–39).

Kinds of Readers in Any Class

Among the pupils entering junior or senior high school are some gifted children who are reading far above their grade level. There are also gifted children who are falling short of their reading potentialities; they are above the average for their age and grade, but below their mental age. They have not matched their unusual native endowment with correspondingly high accomplishment. Many of the pupils are reading at about grade level, but not wisely and well; their reading tastes run to cheap fiction and sensational news stories. The retarded readers, according to our definition, have the mental ability to improve. Some of them need the instruction they have missed in the lower grades; some have emotional difficulties that make it impossible for them to put their minds on reading until some of their inner conflicts, fears, and anxieties have been lessened and until their concept of themselves as persons who cannot read has been changed. Finally, there are the slow-learning pupils who do not have the capacity to read at grade level, but can make some improvement. They require other avenues of learning besides reading.

Reading of Gifted Students

Gifted children are able learners who are usually reading above their grade level. On intelligence tests they score 130 or above. About half of the gifted children in Dr. Terman's famous study (30) had learned to read before they came to school. Many of them maintained their superiority throughout school and college years.

They learn to read by many different methods. When gifted children were asked to try to recall how they had learned to read, they mentioned the following methods:

As I remember, the way I learned how to read was by sight: (1) look at the word, (2) know its meaning, and (3) remember it.

In the first grade, after learning the basic words such as *it*, *was*, *were*, *have*, *mother*, *father*, and others, I zipped right along.

I learned by very small words and sentences. Also by syllables and the letter's sound.

I think phonics has helped me very much in sounding out new words. In the second grade my teacher implanted a love for reading (25, pp. 36–37).

The methods these gifted children mentioned in order of frequency were: sounding out words; use of flash cards; memorizing common words and learning words at sight, thus building up a basic vocabulary; associating word with picture; learning words in simple sentences, booklets, newspaper headlines, signs, self-teaching workbooks, first-grade readers.

**Identify gifted
children early**

Gifted children should be identified early. This is not difficult. Their intellectual superiority usually shows up in any standardized reading or intelligence test. Observation in the classroom may confirm the results of tests or it may identify pupils who have not shown their true mental ability on the test. The intellectually gifted usually have a superior vocabulary, learn quickly, have a good memory, see relationships, and solve both abstract and practical problems more readily than the average. Teachers' observations may be supplemented by questions concerning their favorite radio or television programs, books, magazines, plays, and other leisure activities. Their answers to these questions will often identify individuals with mature interests.

Give gifted children reading experiences they need

If the gifted children in a class are identified early, the development of poor attitudes and habits of reading and study may be avoided. The teacher should try to give them free time to read, suitable reading material, as much instruction and guidance as they need, and encouragement to use their ability. Instead of drills and exercises that they do not need, instead of requiring them to listen to the halting reading of other pupils and to unnecessary explanations, they can work independently or go to the library to read according to a plan they have made in conference with the teacher. They can keep their own reading record and confer with the teacher about it from time to time. They can accept special assignments, often to get information needed by the class or to present an advanced aspect of the subject in a form that the rest of the class can understand and enjoy.

Although the gifted children need relatively less attention from the teacher in comparison with other groups within the classroom, they do need skillful guidance and instruction. Important as interest and motivation are, a teacher needs to do more than merely "make the pupils happy and surround them with books." Such a theory can be detrimental even to able readers. The gifted usually need a quick check on basic skills. Some of the teacher's instructional jobs with able learners are as follows: planning an individual reading program with the student; showing him how to check his plan; helping him to raise his standards; guiding his choice of reading; teaching him higher-level skills of locating information, critical reading, and interpretation of literature; and showing him ways and means of sharing his reading experiences.

It is usually easy to interest gifted students in the history of words. They are intrigued by the idea, for example, that *school* originally meant *leisure*, and enjoy studying books such as the following:

Joseph T. Shipley, *A Dictionary of Word Origins*. New York: Philosophical Library, 1945.
Wilfred Funk, *Word Origins*. New York: Wilfred Funk, Inc., 1950.
Charles E. Funk, *Thereby Hangs a Tale*. New York: Harper and Brothers, 1948.

Margaret S. Ernst, *More about Words.* New York: Alfred A. Knopf, 1951.

Margaret S. Ernst, *Picturesque Word Origins.* Springfield, Massachusetts: G. & C. Merriam Company, 1933.

Gifted students also become interested in studying common roots, and how prefixes and suffixes modify their meaning. They also will respond to the subtleties of good literature and go more deeply into the science of semantics than the average student, becoming keenly interested in figurative language and in the way the context affects the meaning of words.

**Give gifted children opportunities for
service, all-round development, and
creative work**

The contributions that gifted students can make to any group are limitless. If a classic in its original form cannot be read by some members of the class, able learners can dramatize or read parts of it orally. They may give enjoyment to the group as a whole by reading poetry aloud. They may share with the class the most interesting parts of English selections which are involved, lengthy, and dull for many students. Audience reading situations help to increase the listening vocabularies of the pupils in the entire group and greatly enrich the experiences of every listener, as well as the readers.

One teacher in developing a unit on Medieval Life distributed the reading jobs according to the ability of her students. The poorer readers assumed responsibility for locating books pertaining to the Middle Ages and for collecting simple facts pertaining to dress, habits, and customs of that day. The average readers contributed information from books written at their grade level. The gifted students ranged wide and far in their contributions. After making a plan with the teacher, they searched through many kinds of adult literature to obtain details that would round out the description of medieval life. They rechecked their plan, reporting back to the teacher, evaluating their progress, and sometimes modifying their plan in the light of their discoveries. In the end they had created an original play based on life in the Middle Ages and, with the help of others, it was presented to an interested audience.

Engaging in group projects involving creative, intellectual, and service activities is the best way to avoid excessive bookishness. Occasionally a gifted child will use reading as an escape from social situations with which he has not learned to cope. The result is very high reading achievement, but a one-sided development, and often real unhappiness in not being able to relate himself to others and to enjoy normal social activities.

Reading leads to further
activity such as
dramatization of a story.

Interest in a topic leads
to a search for more
information on it.

Reading should illuminate life, not be
used as an escape from reality.

We can make pupils too bookish. Like all children, gifted children have other needs. They should have opportunities to develop physically, socially, and emotionally. The gifted enjoy as much as other children games and sports that have social as well as health values. The class can suggest projects in which a wide range of ability is needed — a class newspaper, an original play, an assembly program, a community service, or school improvement project. Many of these activities call for "research reading," for creative writing, for skill in social relations. If they are successfully accomplished, all the pupils will get satisfaction from the success of the group; it will give them a "we" feeling and discourage an undesirable kind of competition. These are kinds of experiences that challenge intellectually gifted children to develop their reading potentialities for social purposes.

**Ask gifted children
for suggestions**

When asked what advice they would give to teachers, some bright sixth graders said:

"Give the bright children special assignments — for the whole week sometimes. They could make a report of some sort to the class. It should be interesting to the class."

"Give them some assignment while they are waiting for the rest of the class to catch up. Perhaps they could have a library period. I just love library periods."

"The teacher could have two groups, a fast and a slow one. She could work with the slow ones and the fast ones could just go along by themselves."

"The children who get through their work could work on hobbies and have a hobby show. If the teacher let the fast children do this, it would make the slow children work harder so that they could do it, too."

The advice to teachers given by a group of older high school students may be summarized as follows:

Start them with more interesting beginning reading.

Give them opportunities to use their abilities.

Give them encouragement for good work and not so much criticism.

Teach them vocabulary — the roots of words and how words are built.

Teach them how to read a book.

Know each student so that you may guide him.

Have a classroom library of different sorts of books suited to their reading level.

Encourage them to do more reading on their own; stretch their reading interests.

**Reading difficulty
among the gifted**

Some retarded readers have high intelligence. Although they may be up to grade level in reading, they are reading below their potential ability. These children have been neglected in our classrooms. For example, consider Harry, an eighth grader. When standardized tests were given to his class, Harry scored at the eighth-grade reading level. Many teachers would think, "Harry is reading at the eighth-grade level. I don't have to worry much about him. He's an average reader." But Harry had a teacher who believed in encouraging youngsters to achieve according to their ability rather than according to their grade placement. Her classroom observation of Harry led her to believe that he had high intelligence. She checked the office records on intelligence tests and found that, according to a group intelligence test, Harry had an IQ of 150. In the light of this information Harry could be considered a "retarded reader" even though he was reading at grade level. He was retarded because, according to his mental ability, he *should* be reading two or three grades *above* the eighth-grade level.

Harry's teacher not only was aware of the relation of intelligence and reading but also knew the importance of checking other factors that might be preventing Harry from realizing his reading potentialities. Accordingly, she asked and answered as best she could these questions: Does he have any physical handicaps? What about his vision? And his hearing? Has he been severely ill at some time in his life, and, if so, when? Are there environmental factors which would enter into this problem? Are there emotional involvements? Or is Harry's case one of lack of stimulation or deprivation of educational opportunities?

There are a number of reasons why many gifted pupils are not reading so well as they could. Some have been disillusioned about reading and about school. The books they have been given to read were dull and lacking in the information they wanted. They have been forced to mark time waiting for other pupils to catch up. Often, too, they have been given drills they do not need and must listen to explanations with which they are already familiar. Sometimes a social factor enters in; if they read more difficult books than the average pupil, the other pupils may not like them and call them "a brain" or "a square." Consequently, they tend to suppress their natural interest in reading.

They need some reading instruction with the other pupils. It is a mistake to let them be completely on their own. But "enough is enough," and teachers should be sensitive to their readiness to go ahead by themselves as soon as they have learned effective reading methods.

Most important is the provision of suitable reading material — books that tell them something new, books that stir their imagination, books that enable them to make an intensive study of some problem, books that broaden their reading interests and improve their reading tastes.

Others Reading below Their Potential

Many average and below average students also have unrealized reading potential; that is, they have the mental ability to read better. For example, a student with a mental age of twelve who is reading at the fifth-grade level *should* be able to read on the sixth- or seventh-grade level. Mary is an attractive girl of fifteen, whose mental age is fifteen. Her reading level should be ninth or tenth grade, but instead it is eighth grade. Likewise, Tom, an eighth grader with a mental age of thirteen, should be reading at the seventh- or eighth-grade level. Tests, both formal and informal, however, show Tom reading at fourth-grade level.

Some students cannot read well enough to get meaning out of the high school books they are expected to read. These Bullock (3) has called "non-reading pupils." A few individuals are able to read easy technical material in which they are highly interested when they apparently cannot read the literature or textbooks required in their grade.

Appraisal of poor
readers' proficiency

Unfortunately, helpful as standardized tests may be with most pupils, as Bullock (3) has pointed out,

they are often misleading and unreliable with pupils of low reading ability. These pupils with their poor working habits and their expectation of failure, are often quite unable to put their best efforts into test performance, so that such ability as they do have may not be truly represented. Rather than attempting to read, many such pupils prefer to guess. And at the lowest end of the scale of reading tests, scores are greatly influenced by guessing. . . . A non-reader who chanced on the rather plausible expedient of marking all the first answers could still not read a second grade book, although he scored at grade 2.4 in total reading. Valuable as such a test may be for pupils who can read at somewhat higher levels, it is misleading when applied to non-reading pupils. Vocabularies of these pupils, moreover, may be so limited that representative sampling is not possible. Non-reading pupils, too, may have such poor study habits and so little independence in the type of work required by group tests, as to make difficult any true demonstration of ability in such tests. . . .

In studying the non-reading pupil, the teacher must not be misled by poor working habits or distractibility. A pupil who does not read is not necessarily one who cannot read, although his presence in the secondary school certainly does not warrant any assumption that "he could if he only would." How

Use the card catalogue to locate suitable reading material.

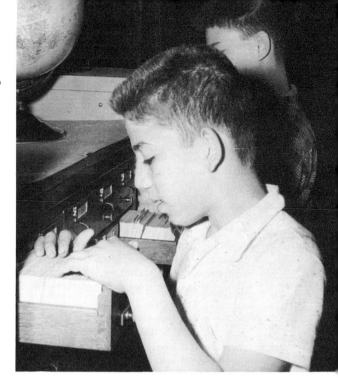

How do your students read? Observe them in the library.

then to distinguish between those who can't and those who won't? The answer is found in observation of the pupil's attempts to read under supervision and with high positive motivation. . . .

The sampling [of reading] itself could begin with a discussion of various common signs a pupil might encounter in his daily life, such signs as EXIT, NO SMOKING, PUSH, PULL, MEN, WOMEN, the names of streets frequented by the pupil, and other everyday reading experiences. The worker would print these on a sheet of paper, all capitals as usually found on signs. Generally a pupil would find some success in this type of reading. The sampling would go on to brief simple sentences, printed upper- and lower-case, involving the pupil's name and facts known about him by the worker. "Jim is here"; "Jim lives on 63rd Street"; "Jim goes to Lincoln Junior High School"; or even as highly motivating a sentence for reluctant readers as one beginning, "Jim loves ——," waiting for him to finish the sentence one way or another. Any of these serve the purpose of encouraging the pupil through the use of words familiar or easily guessed, in a familiar context; they show the pupil that he really can read something. The only pupils to fail this part of the sampling in the worker's experience were an apathetic, psychotic thirteen-year-old girl who was always drifting off into reverie and a sixteen-year-old farm boy of obviously limited ability who had never been in school before in his life.

The next step in the sampling came in attempting to read from a book. There was always a variety of attractive books strewn about the table, some very easy, some more difficult but included for their interest value. If a pupil would express interest in any of the books or would pick one up, the worker would let him leaf through it to find a place which seemed to interest him. The worker would then begin reading to the pupil slowly, directing the pupil's attention always to the words being read, and occasionally pausing so the pupil could read a word he might know or guess from the context.

If the book seemed too difficult for the pupil, or if he had selected no book on his own initiative, the worker would presently pick up easy graded material, such as the easiest edition, third grade, of *Reader's Digest Reading Skill Builder*, and give the pupil opportunity to select a story from it. If the pupil would make no choice, the worker would select one he thought would interest him and suggest that the pupil attempt reading it by himself. The pupil would not be permitted to lose the thought of the story by puzzling long over any word, help being given promptly where needed. If the pupil had a very difficult time with this, the worker would stop him after a sentence or two, or read on if the pupil showed interest in the content of the story. Should the pupil seem upset by his unsuccessful attempt, the worker would immediately put the book aside and change the subject, after reassuring the pupil that he wasn't expected to be able to read everything. If the pupil seemed to find this material simple, the worker would try him similarly on the fourth-grade *Skill Builder*, and perhaps even the fifth-grade booklet. . . .

As may be apparent, the process of sampling the reading ability of non-reading pupils was calculated, as far as possible, to build confidence and motivation for reading, with close observation and supervision. Colorful, illustrated books of obvious interest value and the attractive *Skill Builders*, with their intriguing pictures and stories to appeal to a wide range of ages and interests, seem to arouse less anxiety than standardized test material . . . which is, however, valuable with non-reading pupils, in providing opportunity for testing under close observation. While the informal and less standardized method described here does not yield a reading score, that is no disadvantage unless numerical ratings are required for statistical purposes. It can be advantageous, when a very anxious pupil seems to be worrying unduly as to his reading grade level (3, pp. 9–13).

If non-language or individual intelligence test scores and reading scores are available, a reading expectancy estimate may be made. This is useful in indicating each student's reading potential. The following figures are from a reading expectancy table made by Quinn (19) in his class for children of retarded mental development:

Name	Chronological Age		Binet IQ	Mental Age		Reading Grade	Reading Expectancy
	Yr.	Mo.		Yr.	Mo.		
A.M.	14	0	61	8	5	2.0	3.0
C.D.	15	10	75	11	3	2.3	5.0
F.M.	14	8	60	8	4	3.1	2.0
K.L.	14	0	63	8	8	2.0	4.0

It will be noted that three of these individuals, low as their measured intelligence is, should be able to read better; one, F.M., seems to be achieving above what would be expected from his present mental ability score.

Understanding how poor
readers feel

Most of these retarded students, as Bullock (3) has pointed out, have had at least seven years of experience of failure in school. For some, this experience has resulted in a fear of reading and an inability to put forth the effort needed to improve. As they grow older, they feel more and more ashamed of their inability to read. When asked about reading, they often change the subject to something they can do. They need a feeling of success somewhere in their lives. For others, however, especially the younger teen-agers, hope may spring eternal; some have an irrepressible optimism and look forward to the new experiences in junior high school. Even a little progress is encouraging to these. Each time they succeed, they lose a little of their fear of and resistance to reading.

Essential always in the learning situation is an understanding adult. Some teachers, counselors, and clinicians are gifted in building rapport between themselves and their pupils. Especially do severely retarded readers neêd consideration, time, and sympathy. For the first time in their lives here may be the person who will listen, will not criticize, will lend aid and encouragement.

Consider Charles, for example. His was a severe and complicated case, though there are many with his attitude because of years of defeat, frustration, and even cruelty. This boy was interviewed by Harrison Bullock in the High School and College Reading Center of Teachers College, Columbia University. He was

an unprepossessing client of a welfare agency with a long record of truancy, referred to the worker for help in reading. Half an hour after the time for the scheduled interview, the worker had almost given up hope of seeing the boy when the secretary ushered in a sullen-looking junior high school boy and a determined-looking girl of about seventeen. She said, "I'm his sister. He wasn't going to come, so I brought him." In reply to the worker's question, Charles said Mr. Simpson had told him to come to the Reading Center. At this point the sister left and the interview continued as follows:

Worker: Well, now, why did Mr. Simpson tell you to come here?
Charles: I dunno. He told me to come here to learn, you know, both speaking and how to read.
Worker: I see. Have you been having trouble with both speech and reading?
Charles: Yeah. I have like hoarse, like a hoarse voice.
Worker: Yes? How did it happen?
Charles: I don't know. . . .
Worker: Well, how about reading?
Charles: I don't know how to read big words; I just know how to read four-letter, three-letter words.
Worker: Always had trouble?
Charles: Yeah. Since I started school.
Worker: What grade are you in now?
Charles: Seventh.
Worker: Seventh. Let's see, thirteen. . . . You missed one year somewhere. Which year was that?
Charles: Last year I was in the seventh, you know, I didn't go to school and I used to play hooky and then I got back to the seventh again.
Worker: I see, last year. And how's your attendance been this year? A little better, or about the same?
Charles: Same.
Worker: About the same. Is it because you don't like school? Or are there things outside that you'd rather do?
Charles: School.
Worker: Tell me about school.

Charles: Like I don't know how to read, so the teacher gives us a test and I don't like to go when they give a test. Sometimes they give you a reading test and I don't know how to do it, I just sit there.

Worker: I can see why you wouldn't like that. . . . Tell me some more about school.

Charles: I like to do arithmetic, but sometimes like when they give a test on arithmetic, they give like fractions, and I don't know how to do that and I sit down, and then the teacher comes around and sometimes he hits me and sometimes scolds me.

Worker: Does that happen often?

Charles: Like sometimes when the class is reading, so the teacher tells me to read, and like I don't know how to read, he tells me, "What was you doing, playing?" And then he hits me. . . .

(*Charles tells about liking arithmetic and some science periods.*)

Worker: You like that because you can do it. How do you feel about English?

Charles: No, I don't like that.

Worker: Why?

Charles: The teacher doesn't show you how to read. They just give you the book and then they tell you to read.

Worker: They just tell you to read?

Charles: Yes.

Worker: What sort of books do they give you?

Charles: Like fifth-year books, you know, but they have big words, nine, eight letters, like that.

Worker: Some of the words are hard. Do they tell you what they are?

Charles: No.

Worker: Do you ask the teacher what the words are?

Charles: He says, "You should know."

Worker: Do your friends tell you?

Charles: Yeah, like if the teacher sees my friends tell me, the teacher come over, you know, hit my friend.

Worker: Oh, for talking. That's too bad. . . . Well, how about social studies?

Charles: I don't like that either.

Worker: What is it about?

Charles: Anything like, you know, about Christopher Columbus and ex-plorers and all that.

Worker: And what do you do in that class?

Charles: The teacher takes the book and writes, you know, on the board, and then we take and copy it in the notebook.

Worker: You don't mind that so much?

Charles: No, that I like, you know. I like to write (3, pp. 45–49).

Charles's description of his various classes and teachers showed how hopelessly confused he was about school and how completely unable he was to meet the demands made upon him. He also revealed his embarrassment and feeling of inferiority when called upon to read. As he perceived the situation, he was punished for his failures but not taught how to avoid failure.

Although on the surface, many of these students seem "just lazy," they express satisfaction in working and are encouraged by any progress they make. Perhaps this is why they rate drill lessons, spelling books and lessons, and lessons from the newspaper as their favorite procedures in reading class (19). The most important factor in their success seems to be encouragement and emotional satisfaction in their home and school environment.

Providing suitable reading
material and other experiences

Many teachers are ingenious in finding suitable reading materials for the non-reading students in their classes. One teacher encouraged an adolescent who was reading on the first-grade level to dictate simple sentences about each member of her family, to find pictures to illustrate them, and to make an attractive book, which was easy beginning reading material for her. Other teachers and librarians have obtained very easy books and magazines from which these students may choose (see Appendix, page 348). Often books are chosen from the *American Heritage Series*, the *American Adventure Series*, the *First Book Series*, the *Film-Story Books*, the *Reader's Digest Skill Builders*, or *English as a Second Language Readers* (1). Interesting, simple stories or articles from various sources — readers, magazines, etc. — are cut out and placed in folders, one to a folder, together with questions to check comprehension. In this way, a poor reader is confronted with something that is relatively short and is able to see that there might be a possibility of completing the story. Also, this material is not labeled as to grade placement. The teacher's aim is to help students avoid reading situations in which they fail again.

Since these students have the mental ability to comprehend concepts above their reading level, certain children's books have been skillfully used for this purpose by Mrs. Doris Coburn, a reading teacher in the New York City junior high schools. The following are a few examples of books of this kind — Young Scott Books, published by William R. Scott, New York:

Heavy Is a Hippopotamus by Miriam Schlein.

This book introduces the concept of absolute and relative weight and leads to a discussion of different kinds of scales and different meanings of the word *scale*, e.g., a scale in music, fish scales. It also has personal

Reading may lead to making things, doing experiments, or carrying out directions.

The teacher can help the student to find suitable reading material.

Reading may be a rewarding search for knowledge.

meaning, which one youngster summed up by saying, "*Heavy* is anything that is hard for *you*."

How Big Is Big? by Herman and Nina Schneider.
This book starts with the child, and develops the concept of *big* from the universe to the atom.

What's Inside? by May Garelick.
This book consists of fine photographs showing the birth and first days of life of a gosling. It has an element of suspense and may lead to a discussion of some of the problems of sex and family relations, about which young adolescents are concerned.

What's in a Line? by Leonard Kessler.
When asked what a line meant to them, some junior high school pupils gave as illustrations: "What's your line?" "Jim has a good line with girls," a "fishing line." In reading the simple text, the pupils also got the idea that a line is within your control — you can make it do anything you want it to. Similarly, other things are under our control — an important concept for the child who feels shy and insecure.

Often teachers try to present reading matter to retarded readers in forms other than books since these students have already experienced so much failure with books. One gifted teacher asked the small group she was teaching to write some simple directions on slips of paper. These were then exchanged. Each pupil silently read the direction he had received, carried it out, and let the others check his slip to see whether he had read it correctly. Some of these were humorous, such as "Walk round and round with a paper cup on your head." This made the reading period a jolly one, and all pupils received practice in reading simple directions.

Another creative teacher, Jean Rennolds, at the High School and College Reading Center, wrote stories specifically for a low IQ boy with whom she was working, using his language, and expressing his feelings of hostility and aggression. Because books had always been pushed at him until he had developed a general resistance to them, she wrote these stories on colored 2″ x 4″ cards with one sentence on each card. He enjoyed these stories greatly and read them with expression quite different from his usual monotonous word-by-word reading.

More and more teachers are using all kinds of audio-visual aids (see Appendix, page 347) to stimulate interest and to enrich experience relating to the reading. This new and different approach one teacher used with a small group of retarded readers by presenting a social studies film strip. Although this film strip was originally prepared for elementary school use, its subject matter — daily life of a tugboat — was of interest to these high school students.

Description of a
skillful teacher

Bullock (3) described a successful teacher of retarded readers as follows:

Mrs. Russell was an energetic, humorous, friendly, resourceful teacher. Her classroom was always a beehive of activities, with pupils working individually, in pairs, in groups, or with the teacher. About the room was a variety of examples of pupil work of all sorts: pictures, maps, posters, notebooks, collections, or displays of every imaginable subject. Officially she taught the social sciences, and while there was plenty of evidence that her teaching was not bound by artificial subject matter boundaries, there was also plenty of evidence that she taught her subject in an interesting and vital way.

Mrs. Russell was so individual in her treatment of all pupils that a retarded reader presented no special challenge to her. Her attitude toward him was well expressed in her own words:

"First, by some definite motivating device, a movie, a play, a film strip, get him to accept the class as important. Ask him some questions you are sure he knows. Then pose a problem you are sure he can work on. Put him with someone whom he respects. Have them work together. As he accepts the class and his place, give him increasingly difficult problems, along with other duties and jobs he thinks are important. To keep such duties he will work on things he might deem unimportant.

"It seems to me that the challenge to the teacher is to make the subject matter interesting enough to get the boy's attention. Make him realize that the goals are worth working toward. Then tackle the problem as to *how* each person may attain these goals."

Treat him as a member of the group; avoid making him feel different; give him opportunity for assured success in front of his classmates; help him to feel useful and needed; keep him interested in the subject content of the class. It is unlikely that a retarded reader would feel entirely isolated and futile in a class operated on these principles. Perhaps the two most important principles Mrs. Russell mentioned were the ideas of insuring success — asking questions you are sure he knows — and of building up the class as something worthwhile in his mind for reasons he already understands.

She pointed out, too, an important consideration in assigning pupils to work together, either in groups or in pairs: "Put him with someone he respects." With non-reading pupils assigned to work with reading pupils, this is particularly important. As Mrs. Russell said, assigning a partner to work with a non-reading pupil

"might be a good idea if one is careful that the proper relationship exists between him and his helper. Must be someone whom he likes and wants to have help from."

Obviously, assigning a partner whom the retarded reader does not like, or who does not like him, is to invite friction; likewise, assigning someone who is his good friend, but an undependable or irresponsible pupil, is to encourage trouble.

Mrs. Russell also had ideas on how the subject teacher should approach the specific problem of reading. She was not in favor of attempts by the teacher to introduce this:

"Let him listen awhile. Help him get ready to read. Move slowly with him."

A personal reminiscence illustrates how she helped individual retarded readers in her class:

"I once had a boy in a social studies class who was a non-reader until by some chance he happened to speak to me about magic. I got him a book on magic, even though it was much too hard for him to read and the class he had with me was social studies. He read the book, seemed to get quite a lot out of it. We looked up some more material on this subject. He made a talk to the class on magic, got status with the class, got an A from the teacher. He kept up with magic, failed English consistently, is now a magician of some note — TV and such. Made his way through high school doing magic. Took public reading, etc. He seems to read enough for what he wants.

"Had another who got started reading in the seventh grade because he got interested in snakes while we were studying Brazil in social studies. Etc., etc."

The et ceteras are Mrs. Russell's. She had discovered the idea that if a pupil's reading disability is a matter of poor habits, attitudes, or an emotional block, and provided he has a basic sight vocabulary, he may do surprisingly well in reading material which strongly interests him for some reason. Magic, as mentioned here, can strongly motivate a pupil to read to find out how he can mystify others, even as they sometimes mystify him with academic exploits which he cannot hope to equal! A somewhat older boy can be motivated to read material which will tell him how to fix his jalopy, because that is so important to him. Nearly any pupil will be motivated to read what is said about himself in the columns of the school paper — particularly in the gossip column.

This principle is so useful, however, that it occasionally can lead a teacher to expect the impossible. There must be at least a minimum sight vocabulary before a pupil can read even something he is strongly motivated to read. More than one non-reader in the armed services, for example, has been miserable at not being able to read letters from his girl back home.

Mrs. Russell, too, had a way of detecting incipient restlessness and putting the emerging energy to constructive use. She might send a pupil on an errand of some sort, or even put a retarded reader on some physically active task involving reading. She might tell him the title of a book and have him find it in the bookcase. Or she might send him out with pencil and paper to copy all the signs he could see on the street facing the school and have him learn to read these signs.

Mrs. Russell was, of course, a highly gifted and imaginative teacher. Not every secondary school teacher has the training or the energy to keep so many different activities going in the classroom at one time. Teaching each child as an individual according to his own special needs and capacities is an ideal toward which all teachers should aspire. When such an ideal is reached the non-reading pupil will not present nearly so difficult a problem as he will when class activity is standardized on a level with which he cannot conform (3, pp. 76–79).

There are, however, various forms of reading by which even severely retarded readers can learn. By recognizing numbers, picture clews, and the few words they know, they can frequently, with a little help, gain information they need. A retarded reader was able to get considerable information from a handbook put out by the State Department of Motor Vehicles for people learning to drive. The illustrations, reproductions of road signs, and numerals, combined with a basic reading vocabulary on the automobile — motivated by a burning interest in that vehicle — helped him get much more information than he could have acquired by straight reading of the material in text form. Another severely retarded reader was able to locate essential information regarding the care and feeding of his pets and to assimilate it with a minimum of help. Interest and motivation can influence a retarded reader to exercise all his ingenuity to get information from printed matter. Once these students feel the need for reading and want to improve, they usually make progress.

Helpful as interest can be in motivating a retarded reader to put his efforts into learning to read, the teacher must not be misled into thinking that reading disability is simply lack of motivation. The disability is real and no amount of motivation can *in itself* overcome it. It can only be overcome by effective practice and instruction, facilitated by interest. Freedom from physical defects, emotional readiness for reading, and skillful instruction are three essentials of effective work with retarded readers.

The word *remedial* is being used less and less even for special cases of reading difficulty. There are two reasons for this. One is the stigma sometimes attached to any kind of remedial work. "Something must be awfully wrong with me," some youngsters may think, "if I have to be in a remedial class." Another reason is that the developmental point of view seems much sounder. Even work with retarded readers is essentially developmental because the worker starts where the reader is and helps him, from that point, to move forward along *his true* developmental growth curve.

Slow-Learning Students

Among the students in any grade who cannot read well enough to get the information the teacher expects of them are some who are slow learners. These are different from the retarded students who are reading below their potential ability. Not as much growth in reading can be expected of them. The slow learners, to be sure, need to have a minimum of reading ability in order to meet the demands of life — to find their way around, to read notices, to avoid danger, to get a job. Some employers will not hire workers with reading ability below fourth-grade level. But the slow learners also have as many other needs as any students. And they can learn in other ways than by reading. Many of them like to talk things over with the teacher and with fellow pupils; they enjoy discussion periods. They learn from carefully planned and conducted discussions, from films and film strips, from excursions, from selected television programs, and from many other kinds of experience.

The role of the teacher with slow learners

Effective learning depends a great deal on the relationship between student and teacher and among students — a relationship that is friendly, accepting, encouraging. The teacher has a smile just for him, listens to what he wants to talk about, shows genuine pleasure in his success.

Next in importance is the task of creating conditions in which a simple kind of reading is important and necessary to the student. For example, he may need to read certain road signs or a letter from a friend or an application blank for getting a part-time job.

It is also important to pace the slow learner's progress correctly. One or two new words are enough to introduce at a time with daily reviews in many different contexts, and no new words on some days. Learning these words can be made an enjoyable, successful experience. For example one teacher of junior high school age youngsters introduced a game called "Places to Go." As they suggested words they had already learned — home, country, city, store, etc. — she wrote them on the board. One mischievous girl, Patty, suggested other places like jail, up a tree, etc. Then the teacher would say, "Sally, go home," and Sally would go to the board and point to the word home. When the teacher said to Patty, "Go to jail," Patty went up and correctly pointed to the word, to the merriment of the whole group. This group also made picture books using the words they were learning in simple sentences under each picture. Very simple stories and directions using the same words gave additional practice in reading these words in context.

Some teachers make the mistake of pushing the slow learners beyond their capacity. This may increase their resistance to reading and their dislike of school and teacher. It is no fun to be confronted day after day with impossible tasks. None of us would stand it very long, except under compulsion. Pressures placed on these slow-learning adolescents are sometimes unbelievable. In one reading clinic twin girls were brought in for a diagnosis and for remedial help. The diagnosis revealed a great difference in the ability of the two girls, yet the same achievement was demanded of both. For the quick learner, school work was easy, but for the slower twin it was drudgery. All day long she was asked to perform impossible tasks and then in the afternoons and evenings her parents kept her home hard at work to the exclusion of all recreation. The result was, of course, frustration and emotional disturbance — just short of the breaking point. If these slow learners are compelled to remain in school until they are fifteen or sixteen years of age, then the school must provide suitable experiences for them.

Other teachers make the mistake of underestimating the slow learners' ability to learn. Consequently, they often let them sit doing busy work — drawing aimlessly, copying words and sentences, tracing maps. To all appearances they are doing a semblance of academic work, even though it has little meaning or use to them. The skillful teacher knows that *some* progress is possible. He first tries to find out what kind of progress each student can make. He realizes that some of the reasons for lack of progress are beyond the help of the school. For example, he cannot do much to change the effects of conditions of birth, certain home conditions, or unfavorable parental attitudes. He may, however, help the student to discover and correct defects of vision and hearing, understand and accept his strengths and weaknesses, and encourage him to achieve along the lines in which he is most capable.

Procedures that have worked
with slow learners

Having a real immediate need for learning certain words. One boy before leaving on a visit to his uncle in New York learned to read a menu and many of the signs that he would see there. A girl, bored with drill on words and sentences, became eager and happy and competent when she was the "teacher," testing others on these words and correcting their mistakes.

Interesting repetition of words to be learned. One girl with an IQ below 50 spoke about her dog one day. The teacher pointed out the word *dog* for her and suggested that she make a picture book of dogs. She found many pictures and made a simple heading for each page — three dogs, a white dog, a big dog, etc. For her, this was splendid achievement. She was very proud of the first book and made others similar to it, using the words she had learned. These books made by the pupils should be used to build an excellent beginning reading library for slow learners. Some of the books will be about automobiles, boats, airplanes, travel, men at work, and other subjects of interest to the older students just learning to read.

Seeing the progress they have made. "Nothing succeeds like observed success." A card file of words they have learned to spell or to read is tangible evidence of growth. The mark 100% on a paper conveys to them the feeling of accomplishment. The teacher's spontaneous praise for any genuine progress spurs them on to further achievement. In many experiments praise has been shown to be more effective than blame and criticism. Yet we so often tell pupils what is wrong with them instead of what is good about them. Any individual who has experienced a great deal of failure and rejection needs an overdose of approval and affection to restore his self-confidence and self-esteem.

One teacher of children of retarded mental development, Thomas J. Quinn (19), used the following procedures for helping a slow-learning boy in junior high school improve his reading. From informal tests of his oral reading ability, the teacher learned that Jack had a limited sight vocabulary, ignored punctuation, seldom used context to gain the meaning of unfamiliar words, and was weak in letter sounds and common phonograms. He depended upon guessing and noting the striking features of the word for recognition clews.

The teacher began with activities in which Jack was interested — shop work and drawing. Out of these activities grew interest in making a picture dictionary of the names of tools and articles in the shop. He was then ready to spend several weeks with the Dolch materials starting with the Picture Reading Game, Picture Word Cards, and Basic Word Cards (see Appendix, page 348). The Dolch games used in small groups motivated him to build a basic sight vocabulary. To help Jack gain word recognition skills, the teacher assigned to him a workbook, *Phonics We Use* (see Appendix, page 349). It was not long before he expressed a liking for a spelling book, entitled *Spelling Today* (13). When he had finished books three and four in this series and the phonics workbook he made a grade score of 2.4 on a group reading test. This phase of the work covered a period of four months. During this time, he took part in the class discussion of newspaper articles and contributed drawings for the articles prepared for other groups. His election as class monitor further increased his self-esteem.

The drill books on which Jack next worked included *My Word Book; Standard Test Lessons in Reading*, Books 1, 2, 3; and *English Practice Exercises*, Books 1, 2, 3 (see Appendix, pages 348–350). He made rapid improvement once he saw that progress was possible and that he himself was of worth and had something to offer to the group.

Too much pressure often evokes resistance.

Praise for genuine progress usually increases effort.

Some drill on new words is desirable. Quinn (19) used the following steps:

1. Write the word in a phrase, using a different color for the word to be learned.

2. Pronounce the word and have the pupils repeat it.

3. Have the pupils copy the phrase on paper and underline the word to be learned.

4. Erase the word. Pronounce the word again. Have the pupils turn their papers over and write the word from memory.

5. Repeat the procedure until the words are learned correctly.

6. Dictate short sentences in which the words are used.

7. Check the sentences for accuracy.

All the language arts are involved in the communication of ideas — which is the main purpose of the reading program. Speaking more effectively is encouraged by having pupils suggest situations in which they feel at a loss as to what to say. Some of the common situations are "conversation on a date," "introducing friends," "interviewing an employer," "talking to a teacher or a school principal." After discussing the situation and playing the roles, the teacher may write on the board simple phrases and sentences appropriately used in such a situation. Then the sociodrama may be repeated and improvement noted. The students' vocabulary may be enriched by showing the object, by pictures, sketches, and demonstrations.

For slow-learning students, material from all the curriculum areas and current events and stories in which the pupils express special interest, need to be revised downward to the reading level of every member of the group. It is necessary to rewrite material of interest to those who are reading on first- and second-grade levels. When the books available are much too difficult for them to read, the teacher may tell them about a given topic, let them relate it to their own experience, and summarize orally what they have learned. As they tell what they have learned, the teacher may write it, giving them some guides to organization as they go along. Later he could have it typed and use it as the text for these students. They will be pleased to have written their own text for the subject.

The students may bring in newspaper and magazine stories and articles of special interest to them. The pictures are mounted and discussed. Several difficult words essential to the comprehension of the material are copied on cards for drill, using larger sheets or "oaktag" with the phrase or sentence in which the word occurred. A blank space is left in which to insert the correct word. This drill can be carried on as a game. The student with the most word cards correctly placed is the winner.

Another teacher, described by Bullock (3, p. 72), who taught junior high school classes for the mentally retarded, divided his entire class into groups of three to five. In each group he made sure there were at least one fairly good reader and someone with leadership ability. These groups would read a selection together, helping each other to comprehend it and to get information or entertainment from it. Sometimes they would find an amusing story or little play to read to the whole class. Frankly, he was surprised at how well these youngsters cooperated in group work and in helping one another.

Another procedure used by the same teacher was the group writing of stories. They would dictate the sentences and he would print the story in manuscript writing, keeping it essentially in their own language. They would then read this story after the teacher had anticipated difficulty with certain words and had taught these words before they read the story. This method had strong interest value for these students.

Ways to Individualize Instruction

Some specific ways of individualizing instruction have already been described. In view of the diversity of reading interest and ability represented in any class, individualization of reading instruction is imperative. Four main methods are being used:

One. The problem-solving or project method

In this method teachers and pupils plan a project or a unit centering around a problem of interest to them. They outline the main aspects of the problem. Each student chooses the aspect in which he is most interested. They discuss the place of reading in the total project, how to locate information on their topic, and how to work together in small groups. With the help of the librarian, teacher, and other students they find books and articles on levels of difficulty corresponding to the range of reading ability in the class. Then the committees go to work, with the teacher helping groups and individuals to select books they can read, to extract relevant ideas from their reading, and to present their findings in a clear, vivid way to the class as a whole. This method requires an excellent class library and a teacher with energy, initiative, and imagination.

Two. Grouping according to ability

This method requires knowledge of the reading proficiency of members of the class and books on several levels of difficulty. The groups read while the teacher helps each group with the comprehension and presentation of their material. This method, while superior to the one-book method, does not always sufficiently individualize instruction and provide for progression on the part of individual pupils.

Three. Multi-level material

The essential feature of this method is a range of practice material as wide as the range of reading ability represented in the class. With such material the individual student can progress independently, checking and charting his progress from day to day. This method gives practice in specific reading skills and satisfaction in seeing them develop. The individual work is supplemented by free reading, writing, and discussion to give practice in other communication skills (17).

Four. Free reading plus individual diagnosis and instruction

To use this method successfully, from fifty to seventy-five books covering a wide range of interests and difficulty and a class, preferably no larger than twenty-five, is needed. Each student chooses the book he wants to read. If he is not satisfied with his first choice, he may choose another. While the class is reading silently, individual students come up to the teacher and read a paragraph or two from their book. The teacher notes their reading difficulty and gives each student instruction and practice material to overcome the difficulties. This method provides for real individualization of instruction. Its success depends upon the students' ability to work independently or in small groups; the skill of the teacher in diagnosing the students' reading; the reading ability of the class — whether they can comprehend through silent reading of the books available; and a wealth of material for free reading and for practice on specific skills.

Concluding Statement

It is a step forward when teachers recognize that there are wide individual differences in the reading ability and interests of the boys and girls who enter high school classes today. Even though the elementary school teachers have done the best possible job of teaching reading, there will still be this diversity. Factors of native ability and home conditions are beyond the control of any teacher. Accordingly, each pupil must be accepted at his present reading level and at his own learning rate.

Further progress will be made when teachers take pains to learn more about the reading ability and interests of every student in their classes. This should be done as part of regular teaching, not as an extra task. The teacher may be encouraged to spend half his time studying his students as individuals and the rest of the time providing the experiences they need.

Some of the characteristics and needs will be common to all the students in the class. These may be met through common experiences. Such knowledge will help a teacher chart a course which will be valuable to

In a group project each student contributes according to his ability and interest. Here a student helps mimeograph the report of a group.

Students learn by making reading material for themselves and others.

all members of the group. But there will be characteristics and needs which will be unique to certain students. Likewise, then, the teacher must provide for the diversity of needs recognized. A fundamental oft-repeated principle for every teacher is that the most effective instruction in reading is based on understanding of the students and is geared into the developmental tasks of students of different ages. This involves recognition of readiness for different kinds of reading experiences. And reading experiences contribute most to growth and development when they are part of an optimistic, friendly, meaningful environment.

REFERENCES

1. BRACKEN, DOROTHY KENDALL. "Easy Reading Material for High School Students." *The Reading Teacher*, Vol. VII, No. 4 (April, 1954), pp. 236–39.
2. BRADDOCK, RICHARD. "Selecting Novels for Group Reading." Unpublished doctoral project. New York: Teachers College, Columbia University, 1956.
3. BULLOCK, HARRISON. *Helping the "Non-Reading" Pupil in the Secondary School.* New York: Bureau of Publications, Teachers College, Columbia University, 1956.
4. BLAIR, GLENN MYERS. *Diagnostic and Remedial Teaching.* New York: The Macmillan Company, 1956.
5. CUSHMAN, C. LESLIE, and GREEN, ROSEMARY M. "Philadelphia Schools Attack the Reading Problem." *Nation's Schools*, Vol. LI (May, 1953), pp. 52–55.
6. EDWARDS, MARGARET. "The Rise of Teen-Age Reading." *Saturday Review*, Vol. XXXVII (November 13, 1954), pp. 88–89, 95.
7. GATES, ARTHUR I., and PRITCHARD, MIRIAM C. *Teaching Reading to Slow-Learning Pupils.* New York: Bureau of Publications, Teachers College, Columbia University, 1942.
8. HEAVEY, REGINA. "High School Students Build Vocabulary." *The Reading Teacher*, Vol. VII (April, 1954), pp. 229–31.
9. KIRK, SAMUEL A. *Teaching Reading to Slow Learning Children.* Boston: Houghton Mifflin Company, 1950.
10. KIRK, SAMUEL A., and KOLSTOE, OLIVER. "The Mentally Retarded." *Review of Educational Research*, Vol. XXIII (December, 1953), pp. 400–416.
11. KOTTMEYER, WILLIAM. *Handbook for Remedial Reading.* St. Louis: Webster Publishing Company, 1947.
12. LARRICK, NANCY. "Helping the Child Find the Right Book." A Report of the Ninth Annual Conference on Reading, pp. 71–82. Pittsburgh: University of Pittsburgh Press, 1953.
13. LEE, J. M.; STINEBAUGH, V.; and MAY, D. *Spelling Today.* New York: Charles Scribner's Sons, 1950.
14. Los Angeles County. *Slow Learner in the Secondary School. Material for Use by Classroom Teachers, Counselors, and Administrators in the*

Secondary School. Secondary Curriculum Monograph M–70. Los Angeles, California: Division of Secondary Education.

15. MULLEN, FRANCES A. "The Slow Learner Needs Special Help." *The Reading Teacher,* Vol. VII (February, 1954), pp. 138–43.

16. NORVELL, GEORGE W. *Reading Interests of Young People.* Boston: D. C. Heath and Company, 1950.

17. PARKER, DON H. "The Multi-Level Approach to Meeting Individual Differences in Reading." *The High School Journal,* Vol. XXXIX (January, 1956), pp. 247–52.

18. PENTY, RUTH C. *Reading Ability and High School Drop-Outs.* New York: Bureau of Publications, Teachers College, Columbia University, 1956.

19. QUINN, THOMAS J. "A Reading Program for a Group of 14–17-Year-Old CRMD Pupils in a New York City School." Unpublished doctoral project. New York: Teachers College, Columbia University, 1955.

20. ROBINSON, HELEN M. (Editor). *Promoting Maximal Reading Growth among Able Learners.* Supplementary Educational Monographs, No. 81. Chicago: University of Chicago Press, 1954.

21. ROBINSON, HELEN M. "What Research Says to the Teacher of Reading: Reading Interests." *The Reading Teacher,* Vol. VIII (February, 1955), pp. 173–77+.

22. RUSSELL, DAVID H. "Cherishing Differences in the Reading Program." *The Reading Teacher,* Vol. VII (December, 1953), pp. 66–69.

23. SIMPSON, G. O. *My Reading Design.* North Manchester, Indiana: The News-Journal, 1946.

24. STRANG, RUTH. *Reading Diagnostic Record for High School Students* (Revised). New York: Bureau of Publications, Teachers College, Columbia University, 1952.

25. STRANG, RUTH. "Reading Development of the Gifted." *Elementary English,* Vol. XXXI (January, 1954), pp. 35–40.

26. STRANG, RUTH. "Reading Interests 1946." *English Journal,* Vol. XXXV (December, 1946), pp. 477–82.

27. STRANG, RUTH. "What Is Communicated?" *Educational Forum,* Vol. XVIII (November, 1953), pp. 15–19.

28. STRANG, RUTH; MCCULLOUGH, CONSTANCE; and TRAXLER, ARTHUR E. *Problems in the Improvement of Reading* (Revised and Enlarged). New York: McGraw-Hill Book Company, 1955.

29. *Teen Age Book Club,* 33 West 42nd Street, New York 36, New York.

30. TERMAN, LEWIS, and OTHERS. *Mental and Physical Traits of a Thousand Gifted Children.* Stanford University, California: Stanford University Press, 1925.

31. WITTY, PAUL. "Children's Reactions to TV — A Fourth Report." *Elementary English,* Vol. XXX (November, 1953), pp. 444–51.

32. WITTY, PAUL (Guest Editor). *The Reading Teacher,* Vol. IX (April, 1956), pp. 195–230.

ESSENTIAL READING ABILITIES

WE HAVE CONSIDERED thus far the development of reading in the elementary school and the great diversity of reading ability and interests represented in the students who enter junior or senior high school. This information serves as a backdrop for understanding the needs and for planning the reading program for students in grades seven through twelve. Such a plan should include the teaching of reading skills essential to all subjects.

Reading Development in High School

Every teacher would find it helpful to set specific goals for reading instruction: What reading development should my students achieve? What personal development can be accomplished through reading? These goals would vary somewhat with the needs and abilities of each class, but certain reading abilities are essential in reading any subject.

During the seventh, eighth, and ninth grades elementary reading skills should be extended in altitude and in breadth. The student should be able to get the main idea and related details — the author's pattern of thought — in increasingly difficult passages (altitude) and in a wider variety of reading material (breadth). He should be able to see sequences and cause-and-effect relations. Many eighth graders are deficient in these reading abilities. More and more the junior high school student needs skill in reading to make reports to the class, to solve real problems, and to communicate his new ideas effectively to others. He should also be developing increased skill in the interpretation of literature, taking advantage of clews to the understanding of the characters and the meaning of events in their lives.

Underlying these high-level reading skills is knowledge of the meaning of words. This knowledge usually cannot be acquired by wide reading alone, important as that is. Some attention to vocabulary building in connection with the reading of each subject is needed. Many students still need instruction in word recognition skills, especially with polysyllabic words (see page 35). Some students profit by work in the subtle aspects of semantics — how words shift their meaning in different contexts, how they arouse emotion, and how, in figures of speech, they may convey meaning far afield from their primary sense.

Personal Development through Reading in High School

"The heart of the matter," Frank Pierrepont Graves, formerly Commissioner of Education of New York State, once said, "lies in the development of intellect, of character, and of personality through reading activities." Reading may make an important contribution to the personal development of high school students. Old habits may be revised, new insights gained. On the positive side, reading should be viewed as one of life's most valuable experiences.

Failure in reading is a warning signal. It is often associated with delinquency and emotional disturbance. According to one report, three fourths of the delinquent youngsters brought to court were two or more years retarded in reading. Some were practically non-readers. This does not mean, of course, that every poor reader is headed toward delinquency. But just to be a poor reader among other boys and girls of the same age is often a source of emotional disturbance and dissatisfaction with school.

To promote personal development through reading, variety of reading material is needed. Especially helpful are stories and articles about other teen-agers. For example, students may gain understanding of what it means to be a good sport by reading about teen-agers who engage successfully in sports and also about those who fail to make the team or win the race. They may enlarge their understanding of themselves and their social environment by reading about other adolescents' difficulties and struggles in growing up and their problems of family relations and boy-girl relations. Career material acquaints them with the qualifications required and opportunities offered in different vocations, while readings in science and social studies help them to feel more secure — less, as Housman expressed it, "a stranger and afraid in a world I never made."

The high school student needs individual guidance in the choice of books to meet his needs at a particular time. He should have opportunity to share and discuss his reading with classmates and to make practical applications of the ideas gained through reading in creative writing or other activities.

Types of Reading Programs

In the high schools today we find many different programs for the improvement of reading. Some of these patterns will now be briefly described so that the reader may select and adapt the program that best fits his school.

1. Reading instruction may be integrated with the whole school program. Every teacher gives instruction in reading as it is needed in his classroom. This is theoretically sound and is the goal toward which we should work. But at present most high school teachers have had no preparation for the teaching of reading; consequently they do not even recognize opportunities for giving instruction in reading and if they see the need, they do not know exactly what to do. To be effective, this program would require:

(a) A wealth of suitable reading materials for each classroom.

(b) In-service education of all the teachers in reading methods.

(c) The guidance and services of a reading specialist in the school or school system.

It would also require curriculum modification to provide more meaningful learning and to incorporate instruction in reading in the curriculum as a whole.

2. Reading may be taught as a subject, along with speech and other tools of learning and communicating. Such a course in reading is taken by all students and carries regular high school credit. Although a specially prepared reading teacher should be assigned to teach this course, the other teachers are not thereby relieved of their responsibility for teaching the reading of their subjects.

3. A special section in English may be scheduled in large schools for

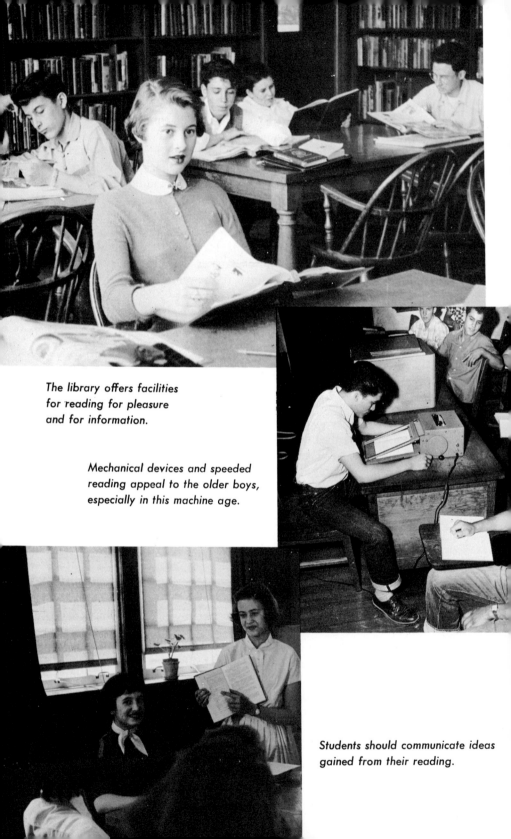

The library offers facilities
for reading for pleasure
and for information.

Mechanical devices and speeded
reading appeal to the older boys,
especially in this machine age.

Students should communicate ideas
gained from their reading.

students who are reading two or more years below their grade level on standardized reading tests, who have the mental ability to improve, or who have been recommended by their teachers for this special section of English. In such a class students would have a variety of experiences:

(a) Appreciation of the literature taught in that grade through films and records, by having parts read aloud or dramatized by the more able readers, and by reading simplified versions, if available.

(b) Reading for enjoyment stories and articles on their level of ability and interest.

(c) Discussion of books and articles they have read.

(d) As much instruction and practice in word recognition and word meaning skills, in sentence and paragraph reading, and in creative and critical reading as they need and can profit by.

These students, while getting intensive practice and instruction in reading, also should keep up with their regular English course of study so that at the end of the semester or a year they may go ahead with their class in English. An English teacher with special training in high school reading problems would be the best qualified to teach this kind of class.

4. Instruction in reading may be offered to students, on a voluntary basis, as an extra class without credit. These classes may be scheduled during the students' study periods and any student may sign up for the course. This plan, carried out by a reading specialist in the school, has proved popular with both able learners and retarded readers.

5. Instruction in reading may be required of all students who cannot profit by their regular classwork because of lack of reading skills. Students should be assigned to such a class on the basis of test results, teacher recommendation, and the students' felt need for help. It should be taught by a well-qualified reading teacher or specialist and geared in with the other subjects the students are taking.

6. Seriously retarded readers may be put in special classes with one teacher who provides all the experiences they need during most of the school day.

7. Complex reading cases may be referred for individual treatment to a reading teacher or specialist or to a counselor or psychologist with special training in reading.

The best pattern for many schools seems to be one that has these three features:

(a) Instruction in reading in every subject by the teacher of that subject.

(b) Special sections of regular English classes in which retarded readers may receive the extra instruction and practice in reading they need.

(c) Individual case work for complex reading problems. Every teacher should be acquainted with the total school reading program so that he may see more clearly his responsibility and the sources of help available to students in his classes.

How to Begin

To institute a reading program leadership is necessary. It may be the principal, a teacher, the dean or counselor, or the librarian who asks: "What are we doing to improve reading in our school?" Many other members of the staff have usually recognized the need; they cannot avoid seeing evidences of poor reading in their classes.

A few of the most interested members of the staff may get together and form a Committee for the Improvement of Instruction in Reading. They study the results of reading tests. By arranging the test scores for the students in each class from the lowest to the highest, they show each teacher the wide range of reading ability represented in each of his classes.

Next the Committee inquires, "What are we doing about it?" At a general faculty workshop, held one afternoon when classes have been dismissed early, they share their most successful methods. Several senior commercial students take notes, and later transcribe the teachers' reports. These are edited and organized by the Committee, then mimeographed as the Committee's first report. It is helpful to know the best methods other teachers are using to help students improve their reading.

But this is not enough. Teachers have many unanswered questions and they need some expert help. They want someone who knows more about the teaching of reading than they do — someone who has a good background in child development and the psychology of reading and learning, as well as training in testing and the diagnoses of reading difficulties. They want someone who has had experience under supervision as well as on his own in working with reading cases, individually and in groups, someone who is skilled in counseling. Most of all, they want someone who is friendly, understands teachers' problems, and can help them make reading instruction an intrinsic part of the high school curriculum. Perhaps the principal can persuade the board of education to employ such a reading specialist to work with them and with the seriously retarded readers whose needs the teacher cannot meet in his regular classes.

If the school board is not willing to appropriate money for a reading specialist for the school, the principal will try to get some consultant service (see pages 336–337). This may come from a person employed to serve the schools of a district or county. If no such person is available and only a minimum of aid is appropriated, a consultant may be invited to the school on a one-day-a-week basis for a half year or even for a few meetings with the school staff. Often staff members of reading clinics or members of schools of education in near-by colleges and universities serve as consultants to public school systems (see Chapter 6).

The school staff will use the reading specialist or consultant in various ways. They will have seminar-like meetings with him in which they will bring up pressing questions and problems for thorough, down-to-earth discussion. They will have clinical-type meetings in which they present information on a single reading case, interpret it, and make tentative recommendations. This is the case conference or child study approach. Everyone present learns more about reading problems in general from the intensive study of one case. Teachers may ask the reading specialist to demonstrate in their regular subject classes some techniques of helping students to improve their reading. This is different from the ordinary demonstration in that teacher and specialist share responsibility for the lesson. At first, the specialist takes major responsibility for teaching the class while the teacher observes and makes comments; then the regular teacher gradually takes over, while the specialist observes and makes helpful suggestions. Both learn from the experience.

Another feature of the continuous study program is the collection and preparation of reading material. A special committee may be interested in doing this. They may prepare informal tests and exercises in their subject (see Chapter 2). Some may enjoy making reading games for students to use individually or in pairs to improve certain skills in which they are weak. The ingenious teacher will invent reading games of interest and value.

If no consultant service at all is available in a particular school, the school reading committee can study the problem together, using books and magazine articles as a source of information and inspiration. Members may also visit schools where effective reading work is being done and report back to the group on what they have observed. Some members of the committee may take extension or summer session courses in reading and share their knowledge with the other teachers.

In these and other ways, and by means of continuous evaluation of the methods and materials used, every teacher will contribute to the school-wide reading improvement program. It takes time. But teachers and other staff members get genuine satisfaction from working together in a friendly relation and from seeing the results of their efforts.

Overview of Reading Skills

Teachers frequently ask, "What are the basic reading skills common to all subjects, which should be developed more fully during high school years?" We say "more fully" because all skills have their roots in beginning reading. Briefly, the common reading skills are:

1. To recognize words and their meaning.
2. To fuse separate meanings into ideas, relate ideas to one another and to previous knowledge and experience.
3. To respond thoughtfully, critically, or with appreciation to what is read.
4. To use the ideas gained.

These skills have been only partially acquired during the elementary school years. They must be refined and expanded during the high school period. Although these reading skills are needed more in English, social studies, and science than in some other subjects, every effort should be made to develop the basic reading competency useful in all fields. In addition, instruction in reading that is specific to each of the content fields is needed.

Reading on the secondary level makes specific demands upon the reader. He must be skilled in locating information. Once it is located he must decide on his approach to the material, the purpose for which he intends reading it, and the appropriate rate. Having located the material and decided on the approach, he needs many comprehension skills to enable him to master the meaning. These, as already stated, include capturing the main ideas, relating details, organizing and outlining, critically considering the material, and drawing conclusions. With some kinds of material, especially literature, skills of interpretation and appreciation loom large. And, finally, he will make application of the thoughts, ideas, and concepts gained as the result of his reading experience.

Learning to Get Information Needed

While elementary school pupils have had some instruction and practice in locating sources of information, it remains for the high school teachers to help students become more expert in this skill. Competencies in this area are not accidentally acquired; they are attained as a result of motivated instruction and practice. Students must be taught the use of the card catalogue; indexes such as the *Readers' Guide to Periodical Literature;* reference works such as encyclopedias and the *World Almanac.* They should become acquainted with the Dewey Decimal Classification, book lists, and the use of bulletin boards for finding book notices, reviews, and collections of books on a given topic. As is true with the teaching of any skill, the best time to introduce these skills is when the need arises in natural school or life situations.

For instance, one high school class was studying recreational opportunities in their neighborhood when someone suggested that the class needed more information. The teacher, recognizing that this would serve as an opportunity to develop skills in locating information, suggested that the next period might be devoted to looking for additional information in the library. A committee of students was delegated to ask the librarian if she could give them special help at that hour. Before the class was dismissed, the teacher had the students suggest key words which they would keep in mind as they explored the subject. These included *games, play, recreation, playground, commercial amusements, youth-serving agencies.*

During the following period this class met in the library and explained their problem to the librarian.

**How to find references
on a subject**

"Do you know how to use the card catalogue?" she began. "The card catalogue is the 'table of contents' of a library. The 'contents' are listed alphabetically on cards in three different ways. There are author cards with the surname first. For instance, this is an author card." She opened the drawer and showed the class a card which read:

795.54
P483 1   Peters, Raymond Russell, 1905–

Let's go camping [by] Raymond R. Peters,
illustrations by Brenda Hill. Elgin, Ill.,
Brethren publishing house [1945]

128 p. illus. 20cm.

Bibliography: p. 124–128.

1. Camping. I. Title.

SK601.P43   796.54   45-5834

O

Library of Congress   [4]

"Then," she continued, "there are title cards on which the first words in the title of a book are alphabetized. The exceptions to this are the titles which begin with *a, an,* or *the.* These titles are alphabetized by the second word in the title. Finally, there are subject cards which list books by subjects. To get the information you want now, how will you begin? By author, title, or subject?"

The class responded, "By subject," and one student added, "We don't know any authors who have written on this subject or any titles of books — yet."

The librarian went to the drawer marked "R" and opened it. Expertly she thumbed through the "R's" until she came to "Recreation." "Here," she said, "are all the cards on your subject. These cards list the books we have specifically on the subject. Each card has a number which indicates its classification according to the Dewey Decimal System. This is a standard classification system which is uniform for all libraries. To aid you in finding your particular volume, in case the librarian is busy, we have posted here a chart showing where different kinds of categories of books are located.

"But," continued the librarian, "there are other sources of information than single volumes." She walked over to the long tables in the center of the room.

"Here," she said, pointing to some very thick books, "is the *Readers' Guide to Periodical Literature.*"

"What's periodical literature?" asked one student.

"Magazines," another answered.

"Yes," affirmed the librarian. "This is an index of the articles which have appeared in the magazines that are listed here." And she pointed to the list of magazines in the front of one of the large volumes.

"Materials in magazines are listed in the *Readers' Guide* in the four following ways: by authors, articles by subject, stories by title, and poems under *Poems.*"

In a like manner the librarian pointed out the encyclopedias and gave some specific instructions on the use of these reference books.

**How to extract the
information needed**

Once the students had located the specific books, magazine articles, and paragraphs from reference books on the subject, the next problem was to learn to use the aids offered in the materials in extracting the information needed. As the teacher observed students who were skilled in the use of tables of contents, indexes, headings, and other aids, she suggested that they help other students to improve their techniques.

Later, more practice in these locational skills was given by such exercises as the following:*

How to Locate Information in an
Encyclopedia

You will learn a great deal while you are in school but you will forget some of the subjects you have studied. That is the reason why you should learn how to find information quickly and how to organize it intelligently. Then

* From "How to Use An Encyclopedia, The Look-It-Up Book Three." Copyrighted by Field Enterprises, Inc., 1949. Used by special permission.

you will have learned two of the most important lessons of your school life. Answer the following questions briefly, using an encyclopedia:

1. Under what pen name did Samuel L. Clemens write? _____
2. Who named the city of Philadelphia? _____
3. What is the motto of the Girl Scouts? _____
4. Is the tomato a fruit or a vegetable? _____
5. What President added the most territory to the United States? _____
6. Who invented the art of printing from movable type? _____
7. What dictionary was first published while John Quincy Adams was President? _____
8. On a baseball field, what is the distance between home plate and first base? _____
9. What are the three main cards in a library card catalog? _____
10. What traveler visited the court of Kubla Khan? _____
11. What is the main language spoken in Brazil? _____
12. Are diamonds mined in the United States? _____
13. How many justices are there in the Supreme Court? _____
14. Is a whale a fish? _____
15. What prize did Jane Addams win in 1931? _____
16. Where is the original Declaration of Independence kept? _____
17. What country produces the most petroleum? _____
18. What is the distance from the earth to the sun? _____
19. From what nation did the United States buy Alaska? _____
20. Who invented the air brake? _____

Using Cross References

The term "cross reference" means to "cross over" to another subject. Many things are known by more than one name. The daisy is a pretty flower, but in parts of the country where it grows wild in fields of wheat and corn, the farmers call it the whiteweed. If you look up "Whiteweed" in an encyclopedia, you will be referred to "Daisy." This "crossing over" is called a cross reference. Under "Daisy" you will find a complete story of this plant.

This plan makes it possible to locate any subject, no matter how many names it may have.

Look up the following topics. Each subject is followed by a cross reference. On the blank lines, write the name under which you can find the full story about the subject:

1. Black Alder _____
2. Antler _____
3. Plural _____
4. Table Manners _____
5. Decoration Day _____
6. Dermis _____
7. Johnny Appleseed _____

8. Devil Fish _____

9. Love Apple _____

10. Book Review _____

Sub-Topics

Major topics, or long articles, often take up many pages in an encyclopedia. Such subjects have divisions. These subheads in heavy black type will save time in locating the section you need in a long article. For example, the subject "Health" covers seven pages in one encyclopedia. Look up "Health" in your encyclopedia. Under what subtopics will you find information about the following:

1. Importance of food _____
2. Preventing disease _____
3. Community health _____
4. Importance of fresh air _____
5. Housing and health _____

Related Subjects

Most of us have relatives — such as cousins, uncles, aunts, and grandmothers. Not all of our relatives live in the same house with us. In the same way, certain subjects in an encyclopedia have "related subjects" in other places in the volumes. For example, the lark is a member of the bird family. At the end of the article "Bird" in one encyclopedia there are 266 "related subjects." "Lark" is one of them. It is related to the general subject of birds, because it is a bird. But "Lark" is important enough to have its own place on a page in the "L" volume.

A list of Related Subjects will be found at the end of many articles in an encyclopedia. You should look up many of these if you need more information about any given subject.

1. Look up "Transportation." How many related subjects beginning with the letter "O" do you find? _____

2. Look up "Silk." What plant is named as a related subject? _____

3. Look up "Tree." How many tropical trees are listed under related subjects? _____

4. Look up the article on "Immigration and Emigration." How many distinguished immigrants are listed in the related subjects? _____

Instruction from the librarian alone is insufficient, however. The teacher of each content field has a responsibility to follow up with motivated practice the librarian's instruction. Teachers in each subject can carry forward the development of these skills by planning interesting projects. Many students in one class mentioned with satisfaction the current events period in their social studies class. Each student had an opportunity to read to the class some news item he thought was particularly interesting and important. In another class students looked through the pages of the evening paper every day to find an item about the topic on which the class was working. If they were successful, they brought the clipping to school, told the class about it, and put it on the bulletin board. From time to time a rotating committee of students took responsibility for filing the articles of permanent interest and value. One boy attributed his large gain on the reading test to this reading of current events.

Many teachers instruct pupils in the following procedure in exploring a new book or in locating information on a topic:

When you first approach a textbook or other key book, read the title and put the probable content of the book in your own words. Find out who the author is and what he has done to qualify as an authority on the subject. Then look at the table of contents. Read each topic and any comments given after each topic. Try to put each topic into your own words. Note also the sequence of topics and how the author has organized them. Think of certain topics in this field that interest you especially. See under what headings they might come. Whenever you want to gain information on a new topic in an unfamiliar book, use the table of contents to find the page numbers and to locate the material, especially if the topic is one that is likely to be treated extensively in the book. Read the preface for hints of what the author intends to do in his book. This preliminary exploration will save time in the end.

Films will improve locational skills. Two good ones on library usage are by Paul Witty and Margaret I. Russvold (see Appendix, page 347).

Procedures of this kind motivate the students to acquire the skill they need in "locating references quickly, finding and selecting relevant items of information, and organizing data from different sources in terms of the problem under investigation" (13, p. 113).

Approaches to Reading

After a reader has located the material he wants to get information on a topic, to solve a problem, or to obtain pleasure, he should consider the proper approach to reading it. The approach will vary with the kind of reading material and the purpose for which he is reading it.

The teacher will learn much by observing students as they begin a reading assignment. How many spend a few minutes to consider thoughtfully how they should read it? How many quickly preread the selection? How many consider the purpose for which they will read or the approach required in reading a certain type of material? How many just begin to read without any deliberation?

What are some of the purposes for which students might read? To find a single fact? To get answers to specific questions? To learn how to do or make something? To get information needed to solve a problem? To ascertain in general what the author is trying to do? To get the author's pattern of thought or line of reasoning? To pass a true-false examination? To follow the plot of a story? To understand the characters and why they behave as they do? To learn the author's philosophy of life? To appreciate and enjoy his style of writing? To prepare to read a selection aloud? These are some of the purposes for which students may read. Each requires a somewhat different method.

Good readers are particularly skillful in adjusting their method and rate of reading to the purpose for which they read. They have a repertory of reading skills and use them as appropriate to their purpose and the material. They do not read a story in the *Saturday Evening Post* and their chemistry assignment in the same way. In fact, it is this flexibility in reading approach that most clearly distinguishes the good readers from the poor readers.

Good readers vary their method of reading with the kind of material as well as with their purpose in reading it. They ask such questions as: Is this merely a source of separate facts like a directory or is it material that will yield a general conclusion? Is it simple story material or material which contains great thoughts? Is it written in a direct newspaper style or in the more figurative language of poetry? Is it a popular magazine or a textbook? All in all, the way in which students approach any reading experience is governed both by their purpose in reading it and by the type of material.

Some students read everything rapidly; some read everything word by word. Each of these readers has only one approach to reading. But one approach is unsatisfactory. To read the advertisements, simple magazine stories, and easy fictional material word for word at a "snail's pace" is as inappropriate as merely to skim the editorial page, poetry, or the Bible. The expert reader adjusts, or "shifts gears," as he reads according to his purpose and material.

Students seem to be helped to see the reasons for adjusting rate of reading by a discussion of a chart such as the one below. One teacher first explains the advantages of choosing the right approach to each piece of reading material. Then she says, "If we could have only four rates of reading we might call them

1. the skimming rate (fastest),
2. the speeded-reading rate (fast),
3. the study-reading rate (slow),
4. the reflective-reading rate (slowest)."

Students need instruction and practice in how to read plays, poetry, and other types of literature.

Learning the meaning of abstract words is essential to effective reading of the news.

Then she lists on the board the purposes for which each rate may be used. After that she asks her students to name the kinds of material they should be reading at a given rate and for a specific purpose.

CHART OF FOUR DIFFERENT READING RATES

Rate	Purpose	Kind of Material
1. Skimming (fastest)	To locate information	Directory, dictionary, and any material which will yield a specific answer
	To skim for the main idea or to find out "what happened next"	Easy, simple material, newspaper, magazine, fiction
	To "survey" or get an overview and raise questions the selection can answer	Study material, difficult material, material that must be organized, textbooks, technical articles
2. Speeded reading (fast)	To read rapidly for certain details or main ideas	Any material on which main ideas *and* supporting facts are to be picked up — newspapers, magazines, stories, easy texts, etc.
3. Study reading (slow)	To read with maximum understanding Survey Raise questions Read Review Recite	Textbooks, technical articles, any material which you read in detail to organize, present to others, or for which you are held responsible
4. Careful and reflective reading (slowest)	To follow directions as, for example, how to make a cake or perform a chemistry experiment; to reflect on content; to evaluate; to enjoy; to read aloud to share an esthetic experience	Directions; any work which contains great thoughts, such as the Bible, etc.; some reports of current events; editorial pages of newspaper; poetry, drama, etc.; descriptive material; anything read orally

**Paragraphs illustrating
different approaches**

Later practice involves bringing to class sample materials that require various approaches, as illustrated by the following sample passages:

A Descriptive Paragraph: Reader's Purpose: to picture and appreciate a scene
The guests had arrived before the rain began to fall, and they were all now assembled in the chief or living room of the dwelling. A

glance into the apartment at eight o'clock on this eventful evening would have resulted in the opinion that it was as cozy and comfortable a nook as could be wished for in boisterous weather. The calling of its inhabitant was proclaimed by a number of highly-polished sheep-crooks without stems that were hung ornamentally over the fireplace, the curl of each shining crook varying from the antiquated type engraved in the patriarchal pictures of old family Bibles to the most approved fashion of the last local sheep-fair. The room was lighted by half-a-dozen candles, having wicks only a trifle smaller than the grease which enveloped them, in candlesticks that were never used but at high-days, holy-days, and family feasts. The lights were scattered about the room, two of them standing on the chimney-piece. This position of candles was in itself significant. Candles on the chimney-piece always meant a party (14, p. 170).

1. Answer the following questions about the paragraph:
   a. What is the aim of the paragraph?
   b. What is the main impression gained from the description?
   c. Make a sketch of the scene described.
   d. By what method was the paragraph developed?

An Expository Paragraph: Reader's purpose: to comprehend the idea presented and developed

Talk about an ideal democracy! In the realm of time there is no aristocracy of wealth, and no aristocracy of intellect. Genius is never rewarded by even an extra hour a day. And there is no punishment. Waste your infinitely precious commodity as much as you will, and the supply will never be withheld from you. My mysterious power will say: "This man is a fool, if not a knave. He does not deserve time; he shall be cut off at the meter." It is more certain than consols, and payment of income is not affected by Sundays. Moreover, you cannot draw on the future. Impossible to get into debt! You can only waste the passing moment. You cannot waste the next hour; it is kept for you (1, pp. 7–8).

1. Answer the following questions about the paragraph:
   a. What is the main thought?
   b. Where is the main thought found?
   c. By what method was the main idea developed?

A Passage with Hidden Meaning and Intent:
Reader's purpose: to catch the author's mood and intent by reading between the lines and beyond the lines

It was a crisp and spicy morning in early October. The lilacs and laburnums, lit with the glory fires of autumn, hung burning and flashing in the upper air, a fairy bridge provided by kind Nature for the wingless wild things that have their home in the tree tops and would visit together; the larch and the pomegranate flung their purple and yellow flames in brilliant broad splashes along the slanting sweep of the woodland; the sensuous fragrance of innumerable deciduous flowers rose from the swooning atmosphere; far in the empty sky a solitary oesophagus slept upon motionless wing; everywhere brooded stillness, serenity, and the peace of God (7, p. 137).

1. Answer the following questions about the paragraph:
   a. What does this paragraph mean to you?
   b. What is the author's purpose? What clews did you get of his humorous intent?
   c. How does he use words to serve his purpose?
   d. What kind of response does the author expect of the reader?
   e. Why are so many readers tricked into thinking that this paragraph is a serious description of nature?

The teacher may bring the class samples illustrating many different approaches to reading. Some may only require finding the answer to a single question; others may be best comprehended by visualizing a scene; still others demand the recognition and weighing of the ideas presented; and some will serve as a springboard to the reader's own creative thinking. For each passage the teacher should include suitable comprehension questions and specific suggestions as to how to read the passage. These exercises should all be approximately the same number of words in length. The teacher should have the students record the time for reading each but she should emphasize appropriate comprehension, not speed. In the discussions following the reading of each of these exercises the students will acquire a feeling for the variety of purposes for which they might read and the need to adjust their rate and method to their purpose and the kind of material.

Comprehension Skills

Comprehension is essentially reading for meaning, and reading for meaning is part of all reading. To develop this ability teachers should try to give reading personal meaning for the student. How can they do this? The best way is by creating conditions in which reading is necessary. Joan receives an invitation to a party, or a letter from a friend who has moved away. Naturally she wants to read this for herself. Bill sees a notice on the bulletin board about the baseball team's practice. What does it say? Dave wants to make a model plane. He needs to read the directions. Sally hears that the club sponsor has posted a notice about some change in the time and place of the party. She must find out what it is. Ted is fascinated by radar. He reads technical books to get more exact information. Experiences such as these build the idea that reading is one of many ways of satisfying our needs throughout life.

**Illustration of instruction
in reading for meaning**

Students need instruction in acquiring comprehension skills. Such instruction is given preferably whenever specific problems of comprehension arise. At such times the teacher may ask questions that direct the students' attention to certain clews and help them to anticipate and find meaning. Such instruction in reading for meaning may first be given in a group and then practiced individually.

The following account shows how a skillful teacher taught a group of retarded readers in high school to anticipate and look for meaning as they read. The selection chosen was "A Massacre and a Monster" (26).

The teacher began by writing *travel* on the board, saying, "About this time of year many people travel and they are called *travelers* (wrote it on the board under *travel*). This story is about travelers who went abroad and traveled in Scotland. In this story we will find they saw a sign which marked the place where a *massacre* took place. They saw *heather*. (Wrote it on the board. Since the word was unfamiliar to the students the teacher wrote the word *leather* directly under *heather*. This enabled the students to pronounce the new word. Some of them had heard this word and shared their experiences with it.) Another bush that was new to these travelers was *gorse*." (Teacher wrote, pronounced, and described it.) The word *monster*, which she next wrote on the board, was familiar to most of the students.

As she continued to talk about the story she wrote *moor*. "This word has three meanings, but in this book it is used in the sentence: 'They saw mountains, moors, and valleys.' From hearing the word in this sentence, what would you guess *moors* are?"

Student: Some kind of land.
Teacher: Yes. But if you said, "The Moors live in Africa," what would you guess Moors are?
Student: People.
Teacher: Right. But if you heard someone say, "The man *moors* his boat at the dock," what would you guess *moors* means?
Student: To fasten; to anchor.
Teacher: Good. You see we cannot really tell the meaning of a word until we know the context — the sentence or sentences in which it is used. As we read, we get the meaning of many words from their context.

As needed, the teacher showed other ways in which the pupils could work out the meaning of words for themselves. Occasionally she asked them to divide the word into syllables or used the phonic approach, as with *monster*, words they knew as soon as they could sound them out.

She used structural analysis, as in the word *Dutchman*, made up of two words they knew. She called attention to the force of prefixes as in *undecided*. They used the dictionary to look up *dinosaur* and agreed to bring in several books about prehistoric animals.

The purpose of this preliminary word study was to give meaningful practice in word attack skills as well as to prevent their stumbling over unfamiliar words in the chapter they were about to read.

Teacher: Now if you turn to page 33 in your book, you will find a chapter called "A Massacre and a Monster." Let's read the story about the massacre. (*The teacher asked questions to which the students found the answers by reading silently.*)

In what year did the massacre take place?

How did the Highland clan feel about the new Dutch king?

Who won the battle?

What did the king ask all the clans to do?

What did most of the clans do?

What did one of the clans do?

Two weeks after the soldiers came to live there, what happened to all the people in the valley?

When they reached the end of the valley what did they find? What did they do? What happened as a result?

Why might the massacre not have happened if the king had been there?

What did the girl traveler think as she looked at the peaceful mountains?

For stories of this kind, it is good to have photos, illustrations in travel books, or motion pictures that enrich the meaning of unfamiliar words and give the setting for the story. This kind of historical detail in a story setting helps to bridge the gap — make the transition — between fiction and textbook kind of material.

The next part of the story about the Loch Ness monster was taught in the same way. Some of the questions answered by the students as they read silently were?

Which of our travelers was most eager to go to Loch Ness?

Why were they so sure there was a monster in Loch Ness?

The next three paragraphs tell what people said about the monster. Find what the old Scotsman said about the monster. The Englishman? What did Uncle Tony think? What was the young Scotsman's story? What kind of person was the Englishman? What words give you clews as to the kind of person he was?

Read the rest of the page to find out how the Englishman's story differs from the other two stories told about the monster.

Read the rest of the story to find out what Uncle Tony thought.

Note the excellent variety of questions asked. Some could be answered by all the pupils, such as finding the date of the massacre. Some were clearly answered in the paragraph to which the students' attention was directed. Others called for the making of comparisons and the seeing of relations. Still others required finding clews to the personalities portrayed.

Asking questions of this kind as the students read silently to find the answers is a far better learning experience than merely taking turns reading aloud. The differences in learning values between these two methods may be summarized as follows:

Raising Questions to Be Answered by Reading Silently	*Merely Taking Turns Reading Aloud*
1. Everyone is active and interested.	Some do not follow the text but merely listen; the good readers are bored; the poor readers are embarrassed.
2. They read each part with a specific purpose.	They have no special purpose.
3. They learn how to recognize unfamiliar words.	No instruction is given in word recognition.
4. They learn to make comparisons and to draw inferences.	They do not get this kind of practice in thinking.

After students have had some group practice in reading for meaning, they may be given questions and read the entire selection independently. Later they may learn to ask their own questions and to find clews to meaning themselves.

Still more detailed instruction and practice is needed to help students choose the main ideas, relate details to the main idea and to one another, organize and outline, read critically, draw conclusions, and make inferences.

Paragraph comprehension

How can students be taught to find the main ideas of a selection? Teachers have been in the habit of teaching that each paragraph has a main idea, and that good writers state this main idea in a topic sentence at the beginning of a paragraph or in a summary sentence at the end. Students will find many paragraphs constructed in this way. They will be able quickly to grasp the main idea and, if necessary for their purpose, the supporting details or illustrations.

However, if students expect to find all paragraphs constructed in this way, they are bound to be disillusioned. The main idea may be stated anywhere in the paragraph, or it may not be stated at all; then the reader has to form his own judgment of the contribution the paragraph makes to the thought of the selection. Students will find many different paragraph patterns. Some will be nothing but a rewording of an idea previously expressed. Some will present two contrasting ideas, the second being introduced with a signal word or phrase such as *however, nevertheless, but, on the other hand.*

With a class of high school seniors in Newton High School, Newtonville, Massachusetts, the teacher, Henry S. Bissex, explored what was happening to the paragraph in contemporary writing. They have found many forms other than the classic paragraph. In some instances, the dynamics of thought defy classification. They used the following "pure forms" as guides to discovering the structure of paragraphs they meet in their reading:

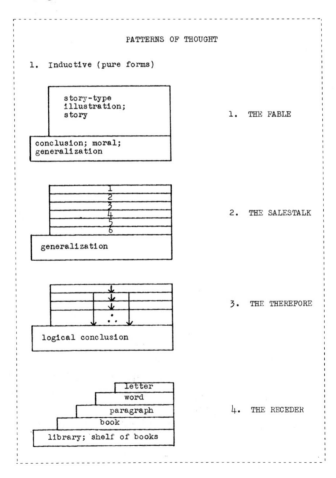

Deductive (pure forms)

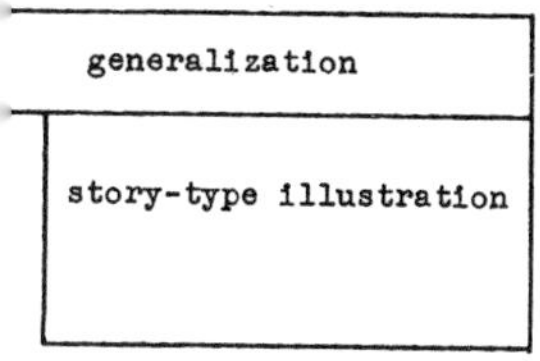

generalization

story-type illustration   5. THE FOR EXAMPLE

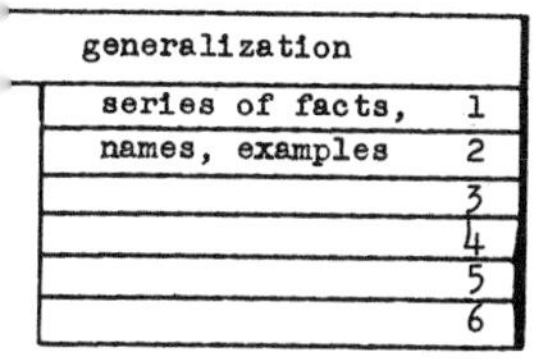

generalization

series of facts,	1
names, examples	2
	3
	4
	5
	6

6. THE COUNT THEM

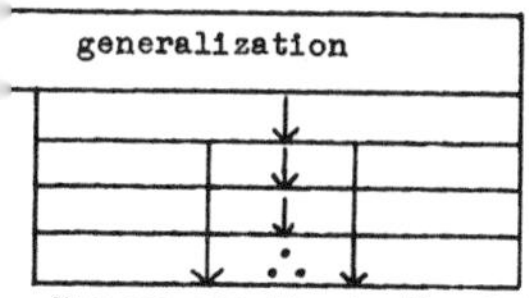

generalization

7. THE BECAUSE

Now we see the truth of the generalization
as a conclusion

generalization

more detail

still more detail

finer details

close-up

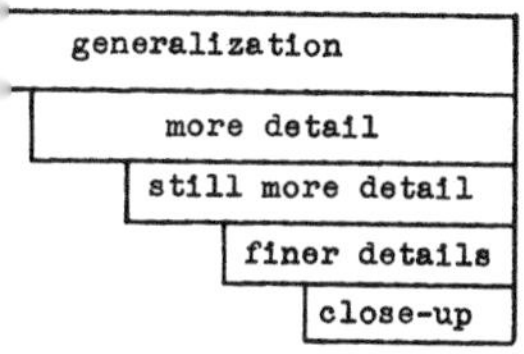

8. THE ADVANCER

3. Balanced (pure forms)

9. THE COME-ON

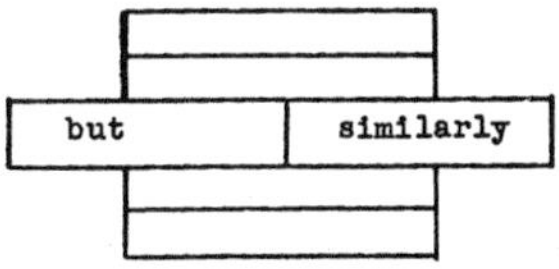

| but | similarly |

10. THE SWITCH

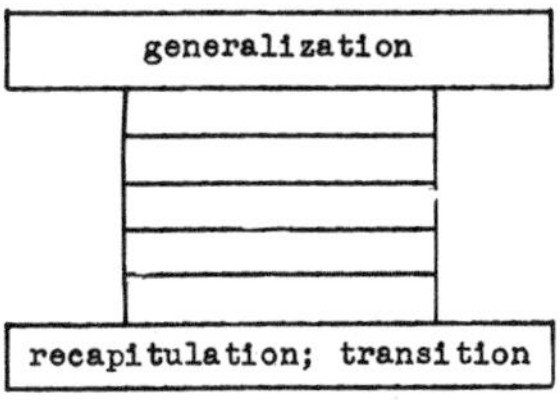

generalization

11. THE CLASSIC

recapitulation; transition

main idea implied
or stated in some
other place

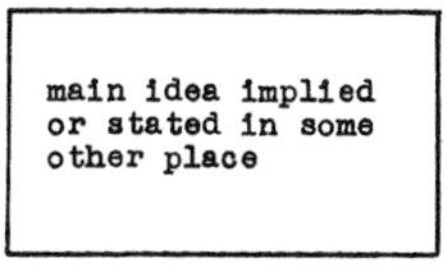

12. THE THINKER

To read paragraphs most effectively we should first find out what is the purpose of the paragraph, what its function is. Some paragraphs are introductory; they orient the reader to the article or chapter as a whole. Some paragraphs illustrate a point previously made. Other paragraphs follow the time-honored pattern of one main idea supported by details or illustrations. Once the reader senses the purpose and structure of a given paragraph, he can read it for the contribution it makes to his comprehension of the chapter or article. If we are to be realistic, we must study actual paragraphs rather than assume that every paragraph is constructed according to our preconceived idea of paragraph structure.

The kind of exercise on pages 120–122 calls students' attention to paragraph structure and gives students practice in comprehending different kinds of paragraphs. After they have done some of these exercises, they may look for examples of different kinds of paragraphs and state the purpose each serves in the selection in which it was found.

Stella Center (5, pp. 23–48) listed a number of different paragraph patterns found frequently in "the literature of knowledge":

1. Question — answer
2. Repetition
3. Conclusion — proof
4. Opinion — reason
5. Problem — solution
6. Fusion of details: description
7. Contrast
8. Specific instances
9. Free association
10. Events in sequence
11. Systematic organization of related details

Pupils may study mimeographed stories composed of well-constructed paragraphs to get a sense of the structure of each paragraph: its topic sentence if there is one; its main idea; or its function. They may then write original paragraphs using their knowledge of paragraph building.

Writing techniques

A study of writing techniques has been found profitable in improving comprehension. Good writers usually have some kind of paragraph organization in mind when they set down their main ideas, present the supporting details, draw conclusions, write descriptions, or develop a line of thought. The reader's job is to quickly identify the author's pattern in order to better understand, appreciate, or criticize the material. To do this he must bring his intelligence to bear on the pattern of thought with which the author has presented him. It is the writer's responsibility to start with the reader's interest, organize his ideas logically, and express them in a vocabulary and sentence structure that the reader can understand. Consider, for instance, the following recommendations given to students for improving their writing and note how a study of these writing techniques would improve reading comprehension skills:

Four Practical Suggestions for
Good Writing

1. Center Your Thinking
   a. Center your thinking on something you know.
   b. Center your thinking on a limited topic.
   c. Make the central idea clear to the reader:
      (1) by a topic sentence which states the central idea explicitly
      (2) by frequent references back to the topic sentence
      (3) by the avoidance of digressions and irrelevant material
      (4) by a conclusion that reminds the reader, either directly or indirectly, of the central idea

2. Organize Your Thinking
   a. Chronological Order
      (1) FICTION. In fiction (the short story or novel) the primary function of the narrative is to re-create experience for the reader in such a way that he can participate in it vicariously and see its meaning to the events of his own life. Good fiction is "pointed up" experience. . . .
      (2) HISTORY. In history, biography, and autobiography, the writer communicates a chronological sequence of events in such a way that the reader learns not only the facts but the time relation of the facts. Frequently in showing time relations the writer also attempts to show causal relations; that is, he reports that not only did event B happen after event A, but in his judgment event B was in part caused by event A. . .
      (3) EXPLANATIONS AND ARGUMENTS. In explanations and arguments, an incident or specific instance is frequently employed to make sure that the point is driven home . . . the writer's point is stated. The rest of the paragraph drives it home by use of a specific instance. . . .
      (4) DIRECTIONS AND DESCRIPTIONS OF PROCESSES. In directions and descriptions of processes, chronological order is clearly called for. The best communication occurs when the steps are not only evident but obvious to the reader. . . .
   b. Spatial Order
      If you will glance about the room in which you are now, you will understand what is meant by "physical arrangement," sometimes called

"spatial order." If you were to write a description of what you see, the order of details would be strongly suggested by the order and arrangements which you observe among the real objects. Your purpose would be to re-create the picture in the "mind's eye" of your reader. You would tell not only the size and shape of the various objects but also their spatial relation, one to the other. As in narrative, then, the writer gets his writing plan rather directly from his material. . . .

c. Logical Order
The word "logical" is used here, not in the strict sense in which a philosopher or logician would use it, but in the looser sense meaning "reasonable." Logical plans are the result of the application of reason to the material. . . . When all the supporting ideas involve elements of like nature, the result is a fairly loose relationship between parts. Figuratively the writer is simply hanging so many shirts on a line; literally he is simply enumerating. Whenever possible, material should be organized so that a tighter relationship between parts is achieved. These relationships vary so greatly with the material that they could not possibly be all listed here. But three basic orders can be mentioned: likeness and difference, cause and effect, problem and solution. . . .

3. Be Specific and Concrete in Your Thinking

a. Develop your ideas by specific facts, not vague approximations of facts.
b. Develop your ideas, whenever possible, with concrete details.

4. Present Your Thoughts Clearly and Precisely

a. Catch the reader's attention in the introduction and focus it on your central idea.
Type 1: "This is important, no matter who or what you are."
Type 2: "Here is something of unexpected interest."
Type 3: "There is something mighty wrong here."
Type 4: "There's more to it than appears on the surface."
Type 5: "Relax. You don't have to be serious all the time."
Type 6: "Now here is the situation I am in."
Type 7: "Here is the way it was. . . ."

b. Use paragraphs to signal main parts of your writing.
Paragraphing is a mechanical device to help the reader see, easily and quickly, the main parts of a paper. Many inexperienced writers, however, confuse the reader by indenting too frequently or, more rarely, not frequently enough. In the normal paper of roughly two to five hundred words, each of the following deserves a paragraph of its own: (1) the introduction if it is longer than a sentence or two, (2) each main division in the development of your central idea, (3) any transition between main divisions which is complicated or especially significant,

In speaking to a group students should learn to organize their thinking.

In writing a paper students should learn to
present their thoughts clearly.

and (4) the conclusion if it is longer than a sentence or two. It should be immediately emphasized that these represent only rough guides. . . .

c. Keep your sentences connected. (9, pp. 5–28)

The good reader will be sensitive to the organization and interpretation of what he reads. He will more readily see clews to the relationship and meaning of the author's statements.

Reluctance to write, or an apparent paucity of ideas, may be overcome in various ways. Some students enjoy writing a story about provocative magazine pictures. This can be done by the class or by individuals. Another device is to begin a story and let the students finish it. They are interested in reading their compositions aloud to the group, and comparing them with the original ending. A somewhat similar exercise is to give them a newspaper headline such as "Plane Crashes Off Labrador Coast," and ask them to write the newspaper account. A familiar parlor game causes much amusement: One person writes the first sentence of a story, folds over the paper and passes it on to the next person, who writes another sentence without seeing the one previously written. Even the most reluctant readers will insist upon reading the final product.

**Outlining and
organizing ideas**

The effective reader comprehends the author's pattern of thought simultaneously with his reading and keeps the organization in mind. You do not see him mechanically taking copious notes, with little intervention of thought. While he is reading he "takes note" rather than "takes notes." He is more likely to concentrate on reading a section short enough for him to keep in mind. Then he writes his outline, showing the relation between main ideas and supporting details. This method has several advantages:

1. To know he will have to outline later is a stimulus to concentrate and organize while he reads.

2. To give undivided attention to reading aids comprehension.

3. To write the outline gives an immediate review of the main ideas and aids his memory of them.

This is a sound procedure.

In teaching outlining it is a good idea first to give the students a partially filled-in outline of a selection they are to read. This skeleton outline tells them the number of main points and the number of subpoints under each. Some of these points are given; the students complete the outline. The next time fewer headings are given; then just the outline form; and finally the student constructs his own outline.

Instead of the outline form, a narrative summary may be suggested.

This has an advantage over the outline in that it enables the writer to show the central idea from which others may radiate. It also provides for emphasis better than the outline form. Students should frequently write or give orally the author's pattern of thought. This is important, for the reader's first obligation is to know what the author has said. Then he may give his own interpretation, agree or disagree, or make whatever applications appear desirable and necessary.

Word meaning

Comprehension of paragraphs and the reading passage as a whole is obviously blocked by the students' unfamiliarity with key words. Consequently the teacher must pay some attention to vocabulary building during high school years. The abstract words used in social studies need special study. Some students have not acquired the word recognition skills taught in the elementary grades (see Chapter 1). A small group within a regular class may want drill on these skills, which will help them to get the meaning of words that are already in their speaking vocabulary.

More useful are the word-meaning skills, which may be expanded and reinforced by incidental practice (see pages 123–124). Every class period offers opportunities to learn to get the meaning of an unfamiliar word from its context. For example, a teen-age student was guided to the meaning of an unfamiliar word, *bibliotherapy*, which she found in a book she was reading. She asked the teacher what it meant.

Teacher: Can you find out for yourself? What would you do first to try to discover the meaning?

Student: I'd guess, or look at the rest of the sentence.

Teacher: You're right. Use the context of the sentence to get any clew you can.

Student: Well, the sentence reads: "The teacher's use of bibliotherapy was admirable." Doesn't help much!

Teacher: If context doesn't help you, what else can you do? Does this word look like any other word?

Student: Not the whole thing.

Teacher: Well, then let's break it into parts. Does one part look familiar?

Student: Yes, the first is like bibliography and that means a list of books. This must have something to do with books, too. But what does "therapy" mean? I think I've heard doctors use it. Does it have to do with helping people get well?

Teacher: Yes, to get well in body or in mind. Let's see again how it was used — "The teacher's use of bibliotherapy was admirable." What might it mean in this sentence?

Students need to learn to divide words into syllables.

Word study is needed in mathematics, too.

Student: It might mean that the teacher used books successfully to help students get well — in their thinking, I suppose.

Teacher: Exactly. They might find out in books how other people handled problems similar to theirs. The use of books in this way is sometimes called *bibliotherapy.*

In books on science and social studies students will frequently find technical words defined by the author, as, for example, in the sentence, "The overweight person should count his *calories,* which are measures of the energy value of food." By attempting to puzzle out the meaning of the word as used in the sentence, students frequently become more adept in using context clews. They also learn that sometimes this method fails to give the correct meaning of the word; their guess is wrong. This failure to get the meaning suggests the need for other word-meaning skills. For example, those who study Latin will be able to identify Latin roots in English words and share their knowledge with other members of the class.

One teacher, Mrs. Hazel Horn Carroll, Assistant Director of The Reading Clinic, Southern Methodist University, uses the device of putting three new words on the board for each meeting. These are not always new words, but each one represents one of three main kinds of structural analysis: looking for parts of a compound word, looking for familiar prefixes, suffixes and roots, and dividing words according to their vowel and consonant patterns. These three words are kept in columns, one column for each method of word analysis. A new word is added to each column at each class meeting. Pupils look forward to this procedure. If for any reason she neglects to write the words at the beginning of the meeting, the pupils never fail to say, "Oh, Mrs. Carroll, you forgot the three words!" The following are examples of words for the columns:

battle field	un mind ful	flăn něl
over board	re pair ing	brā zĕn
pan cake	dis trust ful	ē vĭl

The words in the first column are compound words. The words in the second column are built from clearly recognized prefixes, suffixes, and roots; the words in the last column can be divided into syllables according to the rules stated in Chapter 1.

Occasionally the teacher may introduce special vocabulary study. One teacher did this by asking, "Can you think of any words that come from people's names?"

Ted: Pasteur. We *pasteurize* milk.

Teacher: Can you think of another? (*no reply*) *Listerine* — comes from Lord Lister, who was a famous scientist. Listerine is used for a mouth wash or for a sore throat. *Macadamized* — you know we have macadamized roads — comes from a man named McAdam who was a Scottish engineer.

A series of slide films on word origins (see Appendix, page 347) often arouses enough interest on the part of students to send them looking for origins of other words they meet daily.

Word study may stem from pictures and cartoons. In one group the students had brought in pictures or cartoons illustrating certain words. One had the caption, "She's surprised."

Teacher: What are some other words that mean the same as *surprised?*
Dave: *Startled.*
Sally: *Amazed.*
Teacher: These words describe. What do we call words like that?
Ted: Adjectives.
Teacher (*showing two poses of a black dog*): What words would describe this dog?
Students: Black, little, long haired, watchful, patiently.
Teacher: *Patiently* tells how he sits. What kind of words tell *how?*
Mike: Adverbs.
Teacher: Can you tell us what a noun is, Sally?
Sally: It's the name of something.
Teacher: Tell me all the nouns you can use to name things you see in this room.
Mike: Pencil, table, book, chair.
Others: Earrings, pocketbook, bracelet.

There is a certain fascination in keeping a vocabulary file of new words learned. On one side of each card is written the word; on the other side, its definitions, the part or parts of speech it is, and a sentence or two using it. The student may review these cards from time to time by looking at the word and giving its meaning, then turning over the card to see if he was right.

A class-illustrated dictionary may be made on various subjects. Each student contributes one or more pages which are held together with rings so the pages can be easily alphabetized. On each page is printed the word, as a whole and divided into syllables; its definition, sentences using it, and a clipping or drawing illustrating it. Students enjoy leafing through these dictionaries, curious about the words others have contributed and proud of their own pages. Miss Martha Ferguson, English teacher in Sunset High School, Dallas Independent School District, encouraged the members of her class to make such an illustrated dictionary. Each pupil chose the word he wished to study and printed the information he found

Dictionary Reference and Illustration of Precipitate

d: precipitate

rce:
der, Thornton, The
idge of San Luis
4, Grosset and
nlap, New York, 1927,
5.

tence:
Friday noon, July
twentieth, 1714,
finest bridge in
Peru broke and
ecipitated five
avellers into the
If below.

ay
Moore

4. Reason for Reference:
I choose to look up the
word precipitate because
I could not fully under-
stand the sentence
without this word. I
knew one meaning of
the word but not the
one as it was used
in the sentence.

5. Example:
After the airplane
exploded, pieces of
metal precipitated
to the earth.

7. Illustration

---

garet Stricker

Dictionary References

Word: Nimbleness
Source: Silas Marner - George Eliot - Houghton Mifflin - Cambridge - Page 286
Sentence: "Talk o'nimbleness, look at Mrs. Osgood."
Reason For Reference: I wanted to check the meaning of the word
Example: Nimbleness is required to be a good dancer.

Nimbleness (nim'ble ness) noun, Middle
English - nymel, Old English - nyman
1 active and sure-footed: light and
quick: quick-moving 2 quick to understand and reply: clever — Synonyms-
agile, lively, spry, brisk — Antonyms - slow
and heavy.

about it on a large sheet of tagboard. Students illustrated their words in a variety of ways. Some students used cutout drawings; some used single line drawings. One youngster illustrated her word with figures made from toothpicks and yarn. Illustrations of two of the pages of this dictionary are given on the previous page.

Vocabulary games are not too childish for high school students as the widespread adult interest in *Scrabble* attests. Some of the games may be made by the students. For example, a game of matching words with definitions is made by printing the words in oblong spaces on a card, shellacking the card, printing the definitions of these words on similar blocks, and cutting the blocks apart. The separate definition cards are put in an envelope on the back of the word card, ready to be matched with the word. A key enables the students to check their accuracy without bothering the teacher.

To provide her superior seniors with vocabulary practice exercises, one teacher tore from copies of the *Reader's Digest* the section entitled "It Pays to Increase Your Word Power." These she numbered and mounted separately on thin cardboard with answer keys on the reverse side, and a rating scale at the bottom of the key. Her superior students were thus provided with challenging vocabulary exercises. As the students worked through these sheets, they wrote those words which were new to them in their individual dictionaries. To find these words used in context for illustrative sentences to add to their dictionaries required wide and rapid reading.

To help high school students build vocabularies, Regina Heavey (15) used headlines as a springboard for word study. She asked each student to bring in ten headlines and to tell orally in class what the headline meant. They were unable to pronounce many of the words, much less grasp their meaning. Next, they tried to identify the unfamiliar words, to ascertain their meaning and to substitute synonyms for them. The students then pasted the headlines on sheets of paper, underlined the unfamiliar word or words in each, and listed the following items:

1. A guess at its meaning from the context or from the first sentences of the news story

2. The pronunciation as given in the dictionary

3. The part of speech and the meaning as they apply in the headline

4. An original sentence using the word

The same general method can be used with advertisements or with sentences from any subject. This kind of study of words makes the student aware of unfamiliar words currently used in the world about him and the obstacles that they can be to comprehension.

These are a few of the simpler devices for building vocabulary knowledge. They are not a substitute for wide reading and experience, which is the way most readers have improved their word knowledge. Nor do they take the place of incidental word study in each content field. (For other aspects of teaching word meaning, see pages 177–182.)

**Comprehension
through skimming**

Suppose a teacher has discovered that most of the students in his class are word-by-word readers; they have never learned how to skim. A few students think it is wrong to skim — they have the idea that "to read" means "to read every word." Others skim everything; they need to learn when skimming is appropriate and when it is not. Even some adults, who should know through experience that some writers as well as speakers are, like the nurse in *Romeo and Juliet*, afflicted with total recall, read every word an author writes; they have not learned to let the dead wood lie.

There is more than one kind of skimming. We use skimming:

1. To locate items such as numbers, names, answers to specific questions.

2. To survey, as the first step in the study-reading formula, SQ3R (*S:* to see what the author is trying to communicate and relate the new material to what one already knows or wants to know; *Q:* to raise questions that can be answered by the passages; first *R:* reading carefully; second *R:* review, to see if one has the answers or the information he needs; third *R:* recite it in the form one will be likely to use.)

3. To capture the main ideas or the general trend or pattern of an author's thought.

The first is the most rapid skimming; the second and third, a slower skimming pace.

The best way to teach skimming to locate specific information is to give students practice in skimming for different purposes. The teacher may begin with the easiest kind of skimming — finding a name, a date, or other specific figure or formula. He might say to the class: "Turn to page 27 in your social studies book. On this page you will find the date when the Declaration of Independence was signed. See how quickly you can find it. Write the date in your notebook as soon as you have found it; then raise your hand." The teacher will note those who put up their hands first and have correctly located the date. Then, when most of the class have found it, he may say: "Ted, read the sentence in which you found the information you were looking for and show us where it is." Then he may ask several who found the date most quickly, "How did you find that date so quickly?" They may be able to tell the class some effective shortcuts in skimming. Most of them will probably say that they zigzagged down the page until their eyes caught a figure; then they stopped to see if it were the figure they were looking for. But they will say this in their own words and their classmates will understand the method better than when it is stated in the teacher's language. This exercise should be repeated with other pages and other books until all the students have gained proficiency in this kind of skimming. Similarly they can learn higher levels of skimming — looking for specific facts or answers to questions such as, "Who won the race?" "What are the chief exports of Peru?" "What are calories?"

To find out what the author is trying to do and the general structure of the article or chapter requires the kind of skimming suggested in the study-reading formula. This, too, should be taught. The teacher might say, "When you have an article or chapter to read, what do you do?" Some students will say, "Just start in reading." Others will suggest better methods. The teacher should summarize the best ideas before the students begin to practice this method: "Look at the title. What do you think the chapter is about? What do you already know about this subject? How does it relate to your life today? If you were writing the chapter, what would you say? Now skim to find the main topics that the author is including and the questions he is trying to answer."

After the students have done this, let them compare their lists of topics and questions. Ask those who did this well in the shortest time to explain the skimming method they used. The film "How Effective Is Your Reading?" (see Appendix, page 347) may be used to picture the method after the pupils' first attempt and before their second period of practice of this kind of skimming.

To see the author's pattern of thought requires more careful skimming. The method is to catch main ideas "on the fly" and to relate them as one reads. Here knowledge of paragraph structure and the clews the author gives of main ideas is important. The reader will note statements such as, "There are three main reasons . . . ," center headings, side headings, italicized words, charts, and diagrams.

Each of these methods of skimming should be described, practiced, discussed, and used again and again until mastered. Practice alone is not enough, for one may practice errors. Instruction is needed to improve practice. One of the most effective kinds of instruction is to have the students tell one another the best methods they have used.

Speed of comprehension

Most students want to read faster; this is their most commonly mentioned difficulty. Some who want to speed up have got into unnecessarily slow habits of reading, although they have a good vocabulary and can comprehend what they read. For students who have no serious educational or emotional involvements, a mechanical stimulus to read faster may be helpful; it may help to bridge the gap between the rate at which they actually read and the rate at which they could read.

There are several mechanical devices which will aid in speeding up reading. The Reading Rate Controller, the SRA Reading Accelerator, the Reading Pacer, the AVR Rateometer, and the Shadowscope Reading Pacer (see Appendix, page 358) put pressure on the individual to read faster. The Rate Controller, Accelerator, and the Rateometer operate on the principle that the reader must read faster than the shutter which moves down the page of print. The pushing device on the Reading Pacer is a pointer, while on the Shadowscope the "pusher" is a shadow.

Selection of materials to use for practice on any mechanical devices is important. To increase the reader's motivation, books or articles should be suitable to his needs and ability. The selections should be relatively easy because speeded reading is *not* appropriate for unfamiliar material, technical material, poetry, drama, or selections containing thoughts that invite deliberation.

There are several reasons why mechanical devices are helpful to some students. They center the reader's attention. Progress in reading usually follows an improvement in concentration. There may also be a gain in quickness of association between seeing and comprehending, between eye and brain. Mechanical devices interest high school and college students and adults; they usually like to use these gadgets. They are not like the methods students may have previously used unsuccessfully. The poor reader may think: "Here is something new and different. Maybe I can learn to read now."

Consider, for example, the case of Nick, a seventeen-year-old senior. Tests showed Nick to be in the upper 10 per cent of entering college freshmen in intelligence, in the sixteenth grade in level of comprehension and vocabulary, and in the upper quartile in word attack skills. In speed, however, he fell within the lowest quarter. Here, then, was a superior youngster with efficient reading skills in all areas except speed. By means of appropriate instruction, practice on speeded exercises, work on the reading pacers and tachistoscopes, Nick, in three weeks, raised his rate of comprehension 24 per cent on one type of material and 36 per cent on another type.

Several factors operated in this success story. Nick, with his high intelligence, was quick to put into practice the principles which his teacher gave him. He was highly motivated because he planned to enter college the following fall and he felt a real need for speeding up his reading. Also, Nick was a student who worked to attain the goal he had set for himself. The record of progress, which he kept himself, appealed to him and he took great pride each day in "competing" with his own previous record. He found the mechanical devices interesting and worked with them conscientiously. Nick gave the mechanical devices credit for his progress. "The instruments did it," he said. "They really make you read faster."

The tachistoscope or flashmeter (see Appendix, page 358) which Nick used in addition to the reading pacers, flashes forms, figures, words, phrases, or sentences at a fraction of a second for groups. The students are shown where to look, the operator gives the signal, the word is flashed, the student tells or writes what he sees. At first, it was thought that this device was useful in increasing the individual's perception span. But research has shown that the average adult can *see* short sentences of four words at 1/100 of a second. This means that we already can perceive printed words at the rate of about twenty-four thousand words per minute; there is no need to increase the *perception span!* The problem is *how to increase the attention and thinking span.* The flashmeter may be useful in training attention and concentration, and in making more rapid the association between what the eye sees and what the brain comprehends, i.e., in increasing the speed of associating the word with its meaning. The Timex, a newer machine which operates on a slightly different theory, is used for the same purpose. It uses rolled film rather than glass slides. Any practice of this kind should be given in small doses as part of a well-balanced, individualized reading program.

For use with individuals there are small tachistoscopic devices. After some work in a group there will be those who will profit more from individual training. The individual flashmeters (see Appendix, page 358) use the same principles as the larger machines and offer the advantage of individualized training.

Another mechanical device is the reading film (see Appendix, page 347), the Harvard Films for the Improvement of Reading for college-ability students, and the High School Reading Training Films (Iowa), which are more appropriate in content for high school and some college freshmen. Instead of flashing separate words and phrases, the films flash them in a connected meaningful content. The films begin at a slow rate and increase their speed as progress is made through the series. Students' comprehension is tested by multiple-choice questions on inferences and conclusions as well as on main ideas, details, and vocabulary. These films give practice in concentration and in getting the author's pattern of thought simultaneously with the reading. They may also shake some students out of the habit of word-by-word reading.

Another instrument which is used for this purpose is the Controlled

Reader (see Appendix, page 358). A line at a time is flashed on the screen and a shadow moving from left to right directs the eyes of the reader. Materials for all age levels, from the reading readiness period to college level, have been developed for the Controlled Reader. It would seem that the Controlled Reader would be particularly useful in giving directional and re-directional training.

Still another instrument, the Perceptascope (see Appendix, page 358) is a 16 mm., multi-function projector which synchronizes a film with words and another with pacing slots. It is electronic with remote control. This two-film principle would seem to make possible every projection technique in a single device.

A word of warning is necessary here. Mechanical devices should be used cautiously. Although they seem to help many persons improve their rate of comprehension, at least for the time being, a few readers decrease in rate and comprehension. One student explained his lower scores by saying that he had become so aware of the reading process that he could not concentrate on the content. He compared this mechanical kind of practice in reading to a golf swing when one is trying to apply too many suggestions or to the confused centipede who did not know which foot to put forward first!

These pressure devices are not suitable for individuals who lack basic comprehension skills. Like the rats and sheep that become neurotic when subjected to too great difficulty, some students may become confused and disturbed when pushed by mechanical devices to read faster than they are able to read with the skills they have thus far acquired.

Teachers should always remember that reading is thinking; it is not a mechanical process although it has mechanical aspects. Accordingly, they should approach the reading problem first from the standpoint of improving the student's motivation and background for reading and his basic comprehension skills. Many students are reading within the limits of their possible speed of comprehension.

A controlled experiment (30) conducted with sophomore high school classes was set up to compare five methods of developing reading skills: the use of the tachistoscope and accelerator, direct approaches to reading skills other than mechanical devices, guided free reading, and the usual course of study. Members of the two classes that participated in the guided free reading program used a great deal of initiative in choosing their own reading material. Each student kept a cumulative reading record which he evaluated at intervals with the teacher, taking into consideration the variety of books selected, the amount of reading, the growth in maturity of reading taste and interest in reading. Individuals and small groups shared their reading experiences with their classmates by means of oral and written compositions, skits, panel discussions, and book reviews. As judged by results of the Iowa Silent Reading Test, Advanced Form, and the Diagnostic Reading Test (Survey Section), administered at the beginning and end of the experiment, the guided free reading group, in general, made adequate progress; it was surpassed significantly by the accelerator group on the rate of narrative-type reading. The final conclusion of the study was that, for the majority of tenth-grade high school students of the general ability represented in the experiment, the guided free reading, with systematic vocabulary study and accelerator training as needed, would be most interesting and effective.

Often teachers and administrators become excited about new mechanical devices and substitute them for a sound all-school reading program. This is understandable but very undesirable. It is relatively easy to operate a machine according to instructions in a manual; it is far more difficult to discover individual needs and provide educational experiences to meet those needs. Instruments often impress the layman, but educators should put mechanical aids *into their proper subordinate place* in the reading program. If they have a limited budget, it would be better to spend it for suitable reading material than for these gadgets.

Interpretation of meaning

The meaning of words has wide significance (6). It has personal importance; without words we cannot think or act as human beings. It has national significance; much conflict and disagreement might be avoided in our national life if people understand what they are talking about — if they "keep the line of communication open." Interpretation of meaning also has international implications — it would prevent peoples of the world "shouting at each other over seas of misunderstanding."

On the deeper levels of interpretation, we try to find the meaning behind words. This systematic study of meanings is called *semantics*. Semantics makes us aware of the multiple meanings of abstract words. To see how varied the meanings of abstract words are, a teacher may ask his class in history or social studies to write what *democracy*, *communism*, or some other abstract words mean to them. He will get as many different meanings as he has students in his class. Then he may help them try to get at the meaning behind the abstract words: How did the word originate? How has it acquired different meanings? To what persons, actions, things does it refer? How does the idea it represents operate?

There are all degrees of interpretation of meaning, becoming progressively deeper as the reader becomes more mature. The study of semantics can begin when the child is about ten years old. He can then distinguish the difference between fact and opinion, if the subject is within his experience. From then on students have many opportunities to make this distinction. Stuart Chase (6) illustrated the difference between a fact, an inference, and a value judgment by these three statements:

1. This train is going at the rate of 50 miles an hour. (fact)
2. If this train continues at the same rate, we will get to Washington by three o'clock. (inference)
3. The trains on this railroad are never on time. (value judgment)

Students like to write similar examples and see if the rest of the class can tell which is fact, which is inference, and which is value judgment.

Another aspect of interpretation of meaning is to detect the "reading blocks" to communication. These are most clearly identified in advertisements and the headlines of partisan papers. Students may look for the following kinds of devices used to distort meaning:

1. Associate something that is of questionable value with something that is much desired or has prestige value. For example, alcoholic beverages are associated with roses, orchids, thoroughbred horses and dogs, aristocratic settings, sports, and even the values of courage and homely virtues.

2. Associate something desirable with something low in prestige value or with ridicule. For example, a musical comedy associates a sincerely helpful organization such as the Salvation Army with ridicule; a story or play invests immorality with unrealistic glamour.

3. From among all the characteristics a person or group may possess, select one that is undesirable with which to identify the person or group. For example, stinginess is sometimes emphasized as the main characteristic of Scottish people.

4. Characterize a person's action as completely good or completely bad with no middle ground or examination of motives.

This kind of interpretation can best be taught as a word or phrase or passage calls for deeper understanding. As a result, students gradually get an appreciation of the jobs words do, how we can make words work for us, and how other people are using words to enlighten or influence us.

The skill of reading between the lines and beyond the lines — comprehending a selection in which the meaning is inferred or implied — can be given more systematic attention. In the reading of poetry, for example, analyzing cartoons may serve as a springboard to reading plays and interpreting poetry. The teacher tries to help the students comprehend meaning more fully, and relies on the poet to arouse the overtones of appreciation and depth of feeling.

This fuller comprehension is necessary to develop the highest appreciation of what is read. It is a means of getting more pleasure from reading. Such appreciation is possible only from reading; radio, television, and motion pictures do not permit this time-consuming search for hidden or implied meaning and for as much exercise of imagination.

The study of meanings may also be undertaken as an extra-class activity, such as that described by Hogan (16). Junior high school pupils who became interested in the study of word meanings in science class formed a semantics club. In this club they learned about interesting word origins and shifts of meaning. For example, *broadcast* once meant "to scatter seed" but now the most common meaning of the word is "to speak messages over the radio." They learned that a word often has many meanings, that the dictionary records the various meanings, and that the reader must select the one that fits the context or the situation.

To see for themselves that "Gossip Can Be Dynamite" they worked out the following experiment: A pupil in the first seat looked at a picture for forty seconds and then tried to repeat what he had seen to the next person. This was repeated down the row. The last person told what he had heard. The results were both amusing and impressive. The pupils realized the unreliability of second-hand information. The unreliability of evidence was further demonstrated by the varied reports of an accident which eyewitnesses had observed.

Advertisements came in for their share of analysis. The pupils found examples of fallacious logic and of other devices used to induce customers to buy their products. Similarly, they learned that illusions may be created by politicians, who gear-in their statements with people's wishful thinking.

The differences between inference, judgments, and reports were also studied by finding examples of each. The students learned to separate reports and inferences in their thinking and to report specific facts. "The group decided that inferences are statements about matters which are not directly known, made on the basis of what has been observed" (16, p. 490). Instead of saying, "He thought a lot of himself, and he was frightened by girls," they substituted, "He seldom spoke to subordinates in the office. I saw him at a dance and he only danced when a girl asked him" (16, p. 490).

The study of semantics will give students increased awareness of how words are used and how they influence people.

Critical Reading

Reading makes possible selection of information from a vast and permanent store. It makes possible thoughtful interpretation and deliberation.

Learning to read the news critically is a crucial skill.

Small interest groups work busily.

The reader can pause and reflect at any point. He can turn back to review what has been said. He can read what he wants, when he wants. Critical reading is a means of combating the propaganda which is found in the radio, television, and motion pictures.

Critical reading, creative reading, and critical thinking are inseparable. A simple kind of critical reading should be taught in the lower elementary grades; more complex aspects in high school. Since a certain amount of maturity is necessary, many high school students are markedly deficient in critical reading.

Johnson (19) described three levels of thinking:

1. A parrot-wise acceptance of whatever a student hears or reads.

2. A critical appraisal of the plausibility of his specific statements — a tendency "to check at least roughly on the validity and usefulness of his remarks."

3. An ability to appraise generalizations and abstract statements and to select the most valid of specific statements.

To develop this higher level ability, the individual must learn to ask, over and over again, these two questions:

"What do you mean?"
"How do you know?"

Misinterpretations and false conclusions may arise from many different causes. The "hunt and peck" or "hit and run" method of reading makes it impossible to weigh evidence or even to get enough fragments out of the context to reconstruct the author's meaning accurately. Another cause of misinterpretations is taking figures of speech literally, and interpreting seriously what the author intends to be humorous. Lack of skill in recognizing clews to interpretation — key words and key lines — is another cause of misinterpretation, as is also the inability to relate main ideas and details in patterns or in sequence.

Critical thinking is stimulated by having vital problems to solve. This creates a readiness for critical thinking which cannot take place in a vacuum.

To introduce the idea of the difference between fact and opinion, Dr. Nancy Young began by asking her students to copy the words *all, everybody, everyone*, and to spell *fact* and *opinion*.

Teacher: Albany is the capital of New York. Is that a fact or an opinion? (*Students agree that it is a fact.*)

Teacher: California is the most beautiful state in the Union. Is that a fact or an opinion?

Ted: That's a fact.

Teacher (*laughing*): You must come from California, Ted. Some might think Texas or some other state is the most beautiful.

Mike: Then it's an opinion.

Teacher: Right. Make up a few statements you think are facts and a few that you think are opinions and bring them in tomorrow. Then you may ask the other students which they think is fact and which is opinion and see whether they agree with you.

Systematic instruction in critical reading and listening may begin with statements heard over the radio or seen in advertisements: "Nine out of ten people smoke Mildo," or an advertisement of a patent medicine such as the following:

Picture of a man in a white jacket such as those worn by physicians in hospitals; the caption: DOCTORS HAVE WORKED MANY MONTHS IN THEIR LABORATORIES TO PERFECT THIS MEDICINE WHICH IS ENDORSED BY NUMEROUS HOSPITALS. Below is a picture of people in agony before taking the medicine and another picture of people smiling and happy after taking the medicine. Below the pictures is the note: These pictures were posed by professional models.

Students may be asked: What do you think of these statements? Which are unwarranted, unsupported generalizations? Which mislead by giving a partial truth? Which illustrate reasoning by analogy? Why do people make such statements?

Different parts of a newspaper also offer a fertile field for teaching critical reading. To judge the authenticity or possible bias of an article, students should consider:

What questions should we ask about the author or speaker?

Who is he? What are his interests? What is his occupation? What are his experiences?

What background does he have in the subject?

What methods did he use to gather his information?

Why is he writing this book or article? What seems to be his intent?

Is his reasoning sound?

What evidence does he offer to support his conclusions or generalizations?

What indications, if any, of prejudice do you get?

Is the writer fair-minded?

Class discussion or writing about questions of this kind might well follow each period of serious reading and listening. This would not only bring out the meaning of words, phrases, and sentences, but also give practice in critical thinking.

Another exercise is to read two versions of the same news story and let the class describe their different feelings and impressions of the two stories. Then the class analyzes words, phrases, and placement of ideas that created these impressions.

Although there is no substitute for practice in lifelike problem-solving situations, the problem of developing critical reading may be attacked more systematically. First an informal diagnostic test in critical reading may be given, such as the one developed by Kay (20). This would be followed by practice exercises in forming conclusions oneself, checking conclusions against those of the author, comparing treatments of the same topic by different authors, discovering misleading omissions and inaccuracies in the articles. Discussion of each exercise helps to highlight the process of critical reading — each sentence is carefully weighed to see what it adds to the support of the premise or solution of the problem. Partial conclusions may be formed while reading and these may be condensed into a final summarizing statement. Along with special exercises in critical reading, opportunities for practice may be found in the books students are reading on different subjects.

The techniques used by those who would influence thinking and action should be well known by all mature readers in America today. The critical reading skills are of importance to the life and health of our nation if an understanding of issues and conditions is to be gained by the voters of our democracy.

Often readers are misled by propaganda because they fail to identify it as such. Here are the seven devices which the propagandist uses:

1. "Name Calling" is a device to make us form a judgment without examining the evidence on which it should be based. Here the propagandist appeals to our hate and fear. He does that by giving "bad names" to those individuals, groups, nations, races, policies, practices, beliefs, and ideals which he would have us condemn and reject. . . .

2. "Glittering Generalities" is a device by which the propagandist identifies his program with virtue by use of "virtue words." Here he appeals to our emotions of love, generosity, and brotherhood. He uses words like truth, freedom, honor, liberty, social justice, public service, the right to work, loyalty, progress, democracy, the American way, Constitution defender. These words suggest shining ideals. All persons of good will believe in these ideals. Hence the propagandist, by identifying his individual group, nation, race, policy, practice, or belief with such ideals, seeks to win us to his cause. As Name Calling is a device to make us form a judgment to *reject and condemn*, without examining the evidence, Glittering Generalities is a device to make us *accept and approve*, without examining the evidence. . . .

3. "Transfer" is a device by which the propagandist carries over the authority, sanction, and prestige of something we respect and revere to something he would have us accept. For example, most of us respect and revere our church and our nation. If the propagandist succeeds in getting church or nation to approve a campaign on behalf of some program, he thereby

transfers its authority, sanction, and prestige to that program. Thus we may accept something which otherwise we might reject. . . .

4. The "Testimonial" is a device to make us accept anything from a patent medicine or a cigarette to a program of national policy. In this device the propagandist makes use of testimonials. "When I feel tired, I smoke a Camel and get the grandest 'lift.' " . . .

5. "Plain Folks" is a device used by politicians, labor leaders, businessmen, and even by ministers and educators to win our confidence by appearing to be people like ourselves — "just plain folks among the neighbors." . . .

6. "Card Stacking" is a device in which the propagandist employs all the arts of deception to win our support for himself, his group, nation, race, policy, practice, belief, or ideal. He stacks the cards against the truth. He uses underemphasis and overemphasis to dodge issues and evade facts. He resorts to lies, censorship, and distortion. He omits facts. He offers false testimony.

7. The "Band Wagon" is a device to make us follow the crowd, to accept the propagandist's program en masse. Here his theme is "Everybody's doing it." His techniques range from those of the medicine show to dramatic spectacle. He hires a hall, fills a great stadium, marches a million men in parade. He employs symbols, colors, music, movement — all the dramatic arts. He appeals to the desire . . . to "follow the crowd." *

It is well to teach high school students these steps in critical reading:

1. Recognizing the author's intent. What is the author trying to say or to do? Is he trying to influence the reader in one way or another? What might be his reason for doing this? How do you know you are right in your opinion? Sometimes an author tells the reader his purpose in a preface or elsewhere; the newspaper man usually does not. The reader's choice of a book or article is often determined by what he considers the author's mood, intent, and purpose to be. He will choose one book to be amused; another book to be informed.

2. Exploring the scope of the selection. What questions does it answer; what topics does it cover; what use is it to the reader?

3. Reflecting about biases, attitudes, and other factors in one's own background that may influence one's interpretation of the selection. Does one feel so strongly one way or the other that he notes and remembers only such details as support his point of view, or is he open-minded enough to get the author's point of view?

4. Comprehending accurately what the author said. Does one grasp the author's main ideas and supporting details? This is basic to the acceptance, rejection, or application of the ideas gained from reading.

5. Appraising the soundness of the author's ideas and assumptions.

* From "How to Detect Propaganda" by Clyde R. Miller, originally published in *The Publications of the Institute for Propaganda Analysis*, Vol. I, November, 1937.

The reader asks: Does the author have the background of experience and education to think straight in this field? Are his sources of information reliable? What evidence does he offer to support his statements? Is he consistent in his statements?

6. Relating and synthesizing the ideas presented in the book or article, in relation to the wider field of which they are a part. This process may go on simultaneously with the reading.

7. Applying ideas gained from critical reading. The reader should test the ideas by experience. Do they help to clarify today's personal and social problems?

Critical reading can be taught on different levels; but we cannot expect all students to attain the highest level of abstract critical thinking. There are limiting intellectual factors and personality patterns. An individual's reading reflects his personal problems and life pattern; but improvement in the clarity of his comprehension, in turn, is likely to have a beneficial effect on his personal development.

Application of Reading

Using ideas gained from reading is essential to learning. In fact, immediate use for the ideas read is one of the best motivations for reading and one of the best means of remembering what has been read. The idea of writing a diary of their reading appeals to some adolescents. They choose the books they want to read, give the title and author and their own responses to and reflections upon the book. Instead of the boring book reports written as a homework assignment, which students have come to dislike, reviews written for a purpose are far more appealing. They may be written as "sales talks" to give in class or assembly. They may be contributed to the Book Review column of the school paper or to the library file that other students consult when they come in to choose a book. Group discussion of books read can be very lively and stimulating. One class spent two days in guided reading in the library and, on the third day, came back to discuss the books they had read. Many of these students later wrote of this experience with enthusiasm. When the discussions are informal, they resemble conversations about books in life situations. One girl became interested in reading for the first time when she was able to make use of it in her social relations.

The teacher may help students to make creative responses to reading. One teacher told her class that they could choose a book, read it, and share their reading in any way they wished. The results were most interesting. One student read a biography of a musician and as a result composed a short piece in imitation of the musician's style, played it for the class, and had the class guess whom she had read about. Another drew

Students want to share reading experiences.

a frieze depicting the important events in the novel she read. Two boys who read the same space-fiction book took the class on an imaginary trip to a planet. Several girls who chose the same book dramatized a portion of it for the class. This kind of "book reporting" proved to be the most popular way of sharing their reading with others.

If a class is working effectively and congenially in committees, each group may be motivated to get the information they need on their topic and present it dramatically to the class. Those interested in taking part in plays — and most high school youngsters are — will work hard on learning to read their parts in a dramatized reading of a story or a play.

Another immediate use for reading is in carrying out directions and learning how to make and do things. One mentally handicapped girl began to make progress in reading when she applied it to the cooking and housekeeping she liked to do. A country boy was highly motivated to read better by his interest in finding out from the agricultural bulletins how to plant strawberries and how to raise a prize pig.

Reading to learn how to play a game is another immediately useful kind of reading. The directions for playing the game *Fowl* or *Bird* were given to some students:

Teacher: What is a fowl? (*No one knew.*) Mike, will you look it up in the dictionary. (*He looks it up and reads the meaning.*)

Teacher (*to test their comprehension of the game*): Ted, what should you do when the leader says, "Monkeys fly"?

Ted: Keep your hand down.

Mike: What do you do when the leader mentions something that does fly?

Others: Wave your arms as if you were flying.

Having checked their understanding of the rules, they then actually played the game.

These are only a few examples of immediate applications which motivate reading and invest it with meaning, use, and purpose for the student. When a poor reader realizes, sometimes for the first time, that books have personal meaning and value to him, he begins to make progress in reading.

Planning a Balanced Reading Program

Achieving a balanced reading program in the context of one's daily activity sets the stage, as it were, for the best functioning of the specific reading skills already described. A balanced reading program includes biography, informational books, poetry and plays, essays and speeches, as well as fiction (see *My Reading Design*, pages 72–73). A balanced daily program includes outdoor exercise, wholesome social activities, some home duties, enough sleep and rest, and time just "to sit and stare" as well as time for reading, radio, and television. Social experiences so important to adolescents may be combined with reading in the form of reading clubs or book clubs, poetry groups, informal dramatic clubs, listening and discussion groups for selected radio and television programs. These may be made both enjoyable and educational.

Concluding Statement

Every junior and senior high school can have a good developmental reading program. It builds on the basic vocabulary and word recognition skills acquired in elementary school. Such a program increases proficiency in paragraph comprehension and expands the fields in which the students read. Locating the books and articles they want, finding the information in them they need, comprehending what the author says as a basis for interpreting, appreciating, applying — these are the basic reading skills to be further developed during high school years, and in fact throughout life.

REFERENCES

1. BENNETT, ARNOLD. *How to Live on 24 Hours a Day*. New York: Doubleday and Company, Inc., 1924.

2. BETTS, EMMETT ALBERT. "Reading as a Thinking Process." *National Elementary Principal*, Vol. XXXV (September, 1955), pp. 88–96.

3. BROWN, JAMES I. *Efficient Reading*. Boston: D. C. Heath and Company, 1952.

4. CAREY, HELEN B. "The Philadelphia Secondary School Reading Program: Its Origin and Evolution, with Special Reference to Its Total School Developmental Aspects." Unpublished doctoral project. New York: Teachers College, Columbia University, 1955.

5. CENTER, STELLA. *The Art of Book Reading*. New York: Charles Scribner's Sons, 1952.

6. CHASE, STUART. *How Language Affects Our Thinking*. New York: Harper and Brothers, 1954.

7. CLEMENS, SAMUEL L., in *Language in Thought and Action* by S. I. Hayakawa. New York: Harcourt, Brace and Company, 1939.

8. CLIFT, DAVID H. (Chairman). *Adult Reading*. The Fifty-fifth Yearbook of the National Society for the Study of Education. Chicago: University of Chicago Press, 1956.

9. GERBER, JOHN C., and HOUP, W. KENNETH. *The Writer's Resource Book*. Chicago: Scott, Foresman and Company, 1953.

10. GILL, NAOMI B. "Depth Reading." *English Journal*, Vol. XLII (September, 1953), pp. 311–15.

11. GLASOW, OGDEN L. "Study-Habits-Teaching Procedures." *Phi Delta Kappan*, Vol. XXXIV (April, 1953), p. 284.

12. GLASER, EDWARD M. *Experiment in the Development of Critical Thinking*.

Teachers College Contributions to Education, No. 843. New York: Bureau of Publications, Teachers College, Columbia University, 1941.

13. GRAY, WILLIAM S. *Increasing the Basic Reading Competencies of Students.* Forty-Seventh Yearbook of the National Society for the Study of Education. Part II: *Reading in the High School and College.* Chicago: University of Chicago Press, 1948.

14. HARDY, THOMAS. "The Three Strangers" in *Tellers of Tales*, W. Somerset Maugham (Editor). New York: Doubleday, Doran and Company, 1939.

15. HEAVEY, REGINA. "High School Students Build Vocabularies." *The Reading Teacher*, Vol. VII (April, 1954), pp. 229–31.

16. HOGAN, THOMAS F. "A Semantics Club in a Junior High School." *School Review*, Vol. LXI (November, 1953), pp. 488–90.

17. HOWELL, WALLACE J. "Work-Study Skills of Adolescents in Grades VII–XIV." *School Review*, Vol. LXI (May, 1953), pp. 277–82.

18. HOWELL, WALLACE J. "Work-Study Skills of Children in Grades IV to VIII." *Elementary School Journal*, Vol. L (March, 1950), pp. 384–89.

19. JOHNSON, WENDELL. "Symbolic Processes in Personality Development," *Etc., A Review of General Semantics*, Vol. IX (Autumn, 1951), pp. 29–34.

20. KAY, SYLVIA C. "Critical Reading: Its Importance and Development." *English Journal*, Vol. XXXV (September, 1946), pp. 380–85.

21. PEI, MAVIO. *The Story of English.* Philadelphia: J. B. Lippincott Company, 1952.

22. SHAW, PHILLIP B. *Effective Reading and Learning.* New York: Thomas Y. Crowell, 1955.

23. SHORES, J. HARLAN. "Reading and Study Skills as Related to Comprehension of Science and History in the Ninth Grade." Unpublished doctoral project. Minneapolis: University of Minnesota, 1940.

24. SIMPSON, ELIZABETH. *Helping High-School Students Read Better.* Chicago: Science Research Associates, 1954.

25. STRANG, RUTH. *Study Type of Reading Exercises* (Revised). New York: Bureau of Publications, Teachers College, Columbia University, 1956.

26. STRANG, RUTH; BURKS, BARBARA; and PULS, HELEN E. *Here and There and Home.* New York: Bureau of Publications, Teachers College, Columbia University, 1938.

27. STRANG, RUTH; McCULLOUGH, CONSTANCE; and TRAXLER, ARTHUR. *Problems in the Improvement of Reading* (Revised and Enlarged). New York: McGraw-Hill Book Company, 1955.

28. TRIGGS, FRANCES ORALIND. *Improve Your Reading; A Manual of Remedial Reading Exercises.* Minneapolis: University of Minnesota Press, 1942.

29. WILBORN, LEE J.; ALEXANDER, NELLE; and BRACKEN, DOROTHY KENDALL. *The Improvement of Reading in Secondary Schools.* Bulletin No. 540. Austin, Texas: Texas Education Agency, March, 1953.

30. WILSON, GRACE ELIZABETH. "The Comparative Value of Different Types of Developmental Reading Programs at Tenth Grade Level." Unpublished doctoral dissertation. Charlottesville: University of Virginia, 1955.

RESPONSIBILITIES OF THE WHOLE
SCHOOL STAFF

IT HAS OFTEN BEEN SAID that "every teacher is a teacher of reading of his subject." An even broader point of view is that improvement in all the communication arts — listening, speaking, writing, as well as reading — is an all-school program.

Everyone Contributes

The *administrator* recognizes fully the importance of helping students read effectively, gives teachers all the help he can through faculty meetings and workshop conferences, and makes every effort to provide a wide range of suitable reading material to meet the needs of all the students.

The *English teacher*, if no reading teacher is employed, takes special responsibility for teaching reading skills common to all subjects as well as the special methods of reading poetry and other kinds of literature. He

157

may teach "special English" classes for retarded readers, who will get credit in English for this concentrated course in reading (12, 20).

Teachers of every subject give instruction in the methods, skills, and vocabulary peculiar to their subject but also reinforce basic skills. They encourage effective communication in talking, writing, and reading in their classes.

The *librarian* maintains a materials center from which teachers and students can get the books they need to work on any unit, project, or problem. She gives instruction to students in how to use the library, selects books suited to students of different reading abilities, and guides individual students in their reading.

The *school nurse* plays an important part in the reading program, too. She may test hearing and vision and see that remediable physical defects are corrected. In her home visits, she may give suggestions to parents about creating the best possible study conditions. She may also learn about parent-child relations that are interfering with the student's learning.

The *counselor* often finds poor reading associated with behavior problems, with failure in school subjects, and with dissatisfaction with school, leading to truancy and school leaving. As a member of curriculum and policy-making committees, the guidance person can suggest changes that will help to prevent reading problems. Guidance problems of many kinds, including the making of educational and vocational plans, often involve reading difficulties, and serious reading problems usually have social and emotional aspects. The well-qualified guidance worker should have some preparation in the field of reading improvement.

The *reading specialist* who serves a school or a district has four very important functions:

1. To help teachers improve the reading instruction in their classes, encouraging them to share successful methods, suggesting other procedures, supplying practice material and books their students need, conducting faculty meetings and voluntary study groups dealing with reading.

2. To work with seriously retarded readers in small groups and individually.

3. To work with administrators and curriculum people in providing experiences the pupils need — books that make sense to them, firsthand experiences in their community, a school atmosphere of working together and learning successfully.

4. To interpret the reading program to the public and gain the citizens' support of it.

Last but not least is the *student*, who should take major responsibility for his own improvement in reading, once he sees clearly goals that are meaningful and important to him.

To begin a program in a situation where the employment of a specialist is not possible, a teacher may:

1. Develop further his own interest and knowledge of reading.
2. Try out methods and materials for teaching reading in his own classes.
3. Talk with others and suggest a survey of what is now being done and what resources are available.
4. Obtain administrative support which eventually would involve the librarian and others informally or in committee work, invite outsiders to participate, bring high school and elementary school teachers together to work on the reading problem.

In the high school developmental reading program all teachers have certain common responsibilities. What are these responsibilities? What are some of the procedures teachers may use in teaching the basic reading skills needed by high school students?

Teachers' Opportunities and Responsibilities

In every class the teacher contributes in two main ways: by what he is and what he does. Relationship comes first. The process of learning is vitally influenced by the relationship between the teacher and the students. The personality of the teacher sets the emotional tone in the classroom. If he is a warm, friendly, patient, understanding person, who likes children and young people, likes his job, he will create a pleasant, friendly, confident feeling among the students. If he is informed about the latest findings on child psychology, he will look below the surface of the student's behavior for the causes of difficulty in learning to read. For example, a sensitive youngster, slow in grasping word recognition skills, may look away from her book. The teacher, irritated with her lack of progress may say, "You need to pay attention more than the others, because you are behind in reading." Being mentioned as a poor reader in front of the class may make this student feel humiliated and resentful. She may give up trying to learn or resort to selective inattention as an expression of resistance toward the teacher. Her reading problem becomes more severe. The teacher calls in the parent who reproaches or punishes the child. This further tears down her self-esteem. She may become more discouraged and begin to daydream, fail in other subjects, be left back. The teacher with a good mental hygiene point of view would understand this child's problem and help her to feel accepted and liked even though she reads poorly.

The teacher will also consider the individual student's home background, physical development, needs and interests, and readiness to read as well as his mental capacity for learning. He will understand the complexity of the reading process — that it involves visual discrimination of likenesses and differences, auditory and speech factors, comprehension of meaning, organization of details into more general meaning, visual-motor coordination in writing what is read. The teacher will be sensitive to the feelings of individuals, such as the shy student who is embarrassed to read aloud and afraid to speak up and tell what he has read silently.

In addition to these personal qualities the teacher has certain things to do — opportunities and responsibilities for better reading:

1. *To provide suitable reading experiences for individuals of widely different reading and learning abilities.* To do this involves first finding out how each student reads; then individualizing instruction on the basis of this knowledge. This in turn implies a wide variety of reading material and activities and projects which make reading desirable and necessary. The teacher may involve the students in a project in which they need to read. All will participate according to their abilities. The better readers will do a greater share of the work that requires advanced reading. The poor readers will do work such as drawing, painting, acting, and construction that will involve some but not much reading. Thus the poorer readers will experience satisfying associations involving reading and become motivated to learn more. As the teacher moves from group to group or from individual to individual, he will watch for opportunities to praise their work concretely and sincerely. If students come from impoverished environments, trips may be planned to enrich their experience — trips to learn more about life and nature, what workers in different fields do and the conditions under which they work. They will visit museums, the aquarium, and art galleries. After the visit, the teacher will ask the group to tell what impressed them most. Having some interesting firsthand experience to relate, the poor reader will speak out. The account of the trip may be typed as dialogue and used as reading material, each student reading the part he originally contributed.

2. *To provide for progression of reading experiences.* The teacher begins where the individual is. He does not give him books above his present reading level or expect him to read in phrases or thought units when he is not able to recognize separate words at sight. But after he has gained fluency on one level, he should not "go to grass" there. He should gradually expand, improve, and develop his basic skills and add new ones to his repertory. There is a nice balance of "timing" — not too slow, not too fast. He does not progress literally step by step, but rather kaleidoscopically from a less expert to a more expert total pattern of basic reading skills.

3. *To make reading an enjoyable experience.* So many high school students think of reading as drudgery. When they read, they become

Seventh grade pupils read to find answers to questions raised in a small group discussion.

Some junior high school classes need instruction in pronunciation, spelling, and word meaning skills.

tense and anxious. They have never learned that reading can be fun. The teacher should help students to select books and articles that are not too difficult, that have meaning and interest to them, that are fun or exciting. Good readers and poor readers alike have found pleasure and profit in reading D. C. Heath's series, *Teen-Age Tales*, for sheer enjoyment and self-understanding.

4. *To help students use what they have read and to get satisfaction from so doing.* As already suggested, reading can be put to immediate use in conversation, in dramatization, in making and doing things, in making group reports, in solving real problems, and in other ways.

5. *To encourage the student's responsibility for improving his own reading.* Teachers in the upper grades and in high school must be concerned with the reading process, not just with the end results — the facts learned, the ideas and appreciations gained. A "good" student — one who can demonstrate his knowledge of the subject — is not always an efficient reader. He may get his high marks the hard way — by staying up late to study or by using his recreation time for doing homework.

It is not enough to have students practice certain techniques of reading. It is more important for them to set goals for themselves and become increasingly "on their own" in reading — aware of the best methods to use for different purposes. If they take responsibility for their own growth in reading, then they will feel that they are masters of the situation. They can also help others to learn how to read better.

Benefits accrue to the teacher, too, from a reading improvement program; he learns and grows from his study of individuals and groups. As the students learn to read more effectively, teaching becomes easier and less frustrating for the teacher.

Understanding the Individual Student

What steps can the teacher take in understanding the individual student? He may turn first to whatever cumulative personnel records are available in the school. These will give him more or less information about home background, previous school achievement in each subject, results of standardized tests, and other information relevant to the pupil's reading development. On a page of a loose-leaf notebook, or better in a manila folder for each child, the teacher may jot down information he thinks will be useful. Unless time is provided during the school day, this study of cumulative records of every student is impossible for the teacher who has five classes of thirty to forty students a day. For the core teacher who has only two groups of reasonable size, getting information from the cumulative record is not such an impossible task.

How well can he see and hear?

Fortunately much can be learned about individual students during the class periods. The teacher's first question is: "Can he see properly?" Some children have very poor vision without realizing it. Reading may be so uncomfortable for them that they avoid it when possible. The teacher can observe obvious signs of eyestrain as the student reads in class — holding the book very close or very far away from his eyes, squinting, having red or encrusted lids, complaining of headache and discomfort in reading. Such students should be referred for an eye examination to a competent ophthalmologist.

Every student should have, as a routine procedure, an eye examination to detect visual difficulties. The school nurse or doctor, the reading teacher, or an eye specialist may be prepared to give a visual screening test (see Appendix, page 358). The improved Snellen Chart Test, the Keystone Test of Visual Efficiency, or the Massachusetts Vision Test may be given by school people; the Orth-Rator should be given only by an eye specialist. School people are not eye specialists; they are visual survey specialists and refer to an eye specialist students who give evidence of eye difficulties on a visual screening test.

Questions that teachers want the eye specialist to answer are:

What is the eye difficulty?

Should the student return to the eye specialist for further examination?

Should his reading activity be restricted?

Have glasses been prescribed? Should they be worn for near work, for distance, or all the time?

Does the student require any special lighting? If so, what kind and how much?

Can he do a normal amount of reading and study?

Should he have a special seat where he can see more easily?

Does he require a special desk, books, large sheets of paper, large black pencils?

Similarly, attention should be given to possible defects of hearing and other physical conditions that might affect learning.

What is the student's mental ability?

After vision has been checked the teacher should try to determine something of the student's mental capacity. Perhaps there are scores from group intelligence tests on permanent record cards. In some schools a senior high school teacher may find a reading readiness score, an intelligence test score given about the third grade, another given at the end of the sixth grade, and maybe another administered at the end of the junior high school period. Several scores would give a general idea of the student's mental ability. Unless there is brain damage and mental deterioration, the highest intelligence score obtained is usually most indicative of the individual's true mental ability. However, great care should be exercised in interpreting intelligence test scores. Any group intelligence test is partly an achievement test; it requires a good deal of reading ability. Group tests like the California Test of Mental Maturity, SRA Primary Mental Abilities, or American Council on Education Psychological Examination for High School Students are more useful than those that give a single IQ because they measure different abilities, quantitative and linguistic. These scores enable the teacher to note students who rank higher in some of these abilities than in others. If, for example, John makes a considerably higher quantitative than verbal score, the teacher may assume that he has more functioning mental ability than he is using in his reading. If his verbal ability is also high, but his reading score is relatively low, the chances are good that he can profit by instruction in reading methods.

If the teacher is fortunate enough to have the results of an individual test such as the Stanford Revision of the Binet, the Wechsler Adult Intelligence Scale, or the Wechsler Intelligence Scale for Children, he will gain still more information about the individual's mental ability. But, to interpret the results of any of these tests, he must insist upon knowing more than the total IQ. He must know the exact name of the test, the date at which it was given, the individual's chronological age at that time, and whether it was given by a well-trained examiner who was able to obtain the individual's interest and cooperation. It is also very important to know the subscores on the Wechsler test. For example, one high school girl, whose vocabulary, ability to see relations, and facility in the use of language indicated superior intelligence, had a total IQ of only 103. An examination of the subscores showed that she was very high in most of the tests, but practically zero in arithmetic and comprehension. The clinical appraisal of her individual test results confirmed the teacher's impression that she was far above average in intelligence. If intelligence test results are to be used at all, they must be interpreted with great care and caution.

With baffling cases it is sometimes possible to obtain a Rorschach test. This test, expertly interpreted, may suggest potential intelligence not revealed by individual or group tests of intelligence. The Rorschach and the Thematic Apperception tests used together are especially valuable in detecting emotional disturbance and indicating the kinds of situations and relationships in which it may be manifested. Other tests used by qualified psychologists to understand an individual's personality better are the Bender-Gestalt Visual-Motor Test and the House-Tree-Person drawings. Reading cases tend to follow a general pattern of inability to put forth effort, to respond spontaneously, and to take initiative. According to these projective techniques, seriously retarded readers tend to be subdued and repressed. The Rorschach may indicate to the reading teacher a need for psychiatric treatment. Or it may indicate personality problems that are less serious than they appear on the surface.

**How does the
student read?**

For information on a student's reading ability the teacher naturally first turns to standardized and informal reading tests (see appendix and Chapter 2). These will give information about the student's reading level, his reading difficulties, and the specific errors he makes.

Reading tests results should also be used in connection with the results of intelligence tests. Quinn (14) suggested methods of using standardized test results to make an individualized kind of evaluation. To do this the teacher makes a Reading Expectancy Chart for each student, setting specific realistic reading goals which he seems to be capable of attaining. This Reading Expectancy Chart is based on the relation between the mental age as determined by an individual test and his initial reading grade. It might look somewhat like this for several students (14):

Stu-dent	Chronological Age			Mental Age		Reading Grade	Reading Expectancy Grade
	Years	Months	IQ	Years	Months		
A.B.	15	7	71	11	1	2.8	4.5
C.D.	15	3	71	10	8	4.1	4.0
E.F.	17	2	75	12	0	3.0	6.0

These expectancy figures should be supplemented by comments on each student, taking into consideration bilingual background, emotional disturbance, irregularities in performance on different parts of the tests at different times, discrepancy between auditory comprehension and reading comprehension, and other factors that might modify the reading expectancy. Evaluation would later be made with reference to the progress that each student had made toward his estimated expectancy. Test results supplement, but do not supplant, the teacher's day-by-day observation.

The practice of having each student in a class take turns reading aloud a paragraph or two from a textbook is certainly not an ideal method of testing reading ability. It is boring or frustrating to able learners and embarrassing to poor readers. Its only justification is as a time saver for the teacher in getting some idea of the difficulties each of his students is having in reading the text or reference books. Mispronunciation and other word recognition difficulties are quickly recognized by both teacher and student. By asking for the main idea of the paragraph and important details related to it and calling for the meaning of key words, the teacher gains important information about the student's comprehension. Some teaching can be combined with this informal testing. The whole class can be given instruction and practice in word recognition skills when encountering unfamiliar words, and in paragraph reading skills in connection with each paragraph. Of course, it would be desirable to do this informal diagnosis and teaching individually, while the class as a whole are working independently. This method has been used successfully, but many teachers feel, quite rightly, that it cannot be used with large classes, with unruly students, or without a wealth of free reading and practice material.

Diagnosis and instruction go hand in hand. As a teacher works with individual students, hears them read aloud, and listens to class discussions and conversations, he learns more and more about how his students read, why they read, what is blocking their progress, and how they feel about reading and about themselves as persons.

Special methods may be used to add to the teacher's understanding of the students' reading interests. Through freely written compositions, records of voluntary reading, and interest inventories (see Chapter 2), teachers learn about the kind and amount of reading each student does. The daily schedule of his twenty-four hour activities shows the place of reading in his total day.

The "Projective Composition" described by Withrow (20) is based on a picture, usually cut out from a magazine, involving some aspect of human relations. The students are asked to make up a story for which the picture is a good illustration. They tell what is happening, and what the people are doing and feeling. This technique has several values. Like the more carefully standardized projective techniques it may reveal the individual's feeling about himself and others. It may give clews as to certain personality traits and the kind of situations in which emotional problems arise. Such inferences, however, must be made cautiously by the teacher. Another value is the use of the stories as reading material for other students. Being in the adolescent's vocabulary and sentence structure, the stories are relatively easy to read. A file of these stories is an excellent addition to the classroom library.

What does the student read?

Students will read if they are stimulated to do so. Book Fairs, in which many popular paper-backed books, selected by teachers with regard to

Three groups reading on sixth, seventh, and eighth grade levels in a seventh grade class. The teacher is working with one group in the rear of the room.

Reading easy, interesting books develops fluency.

their quality, are offered for sale, are patronized to a surprising extent.

If students find other books rewarding, they may gradually outgrow the comics. Teachers have stimulated students to read intensively by letting them choose a field and begin reading in it; then, from time to time, conferring with them individually about the books they have read and suggesting others in the same area. Students have been stimulated to read widely by devices such as *My Reading Design* and skillful publicizing of books by teachers, librarians, and fellow students. They have been most effectively interested in new fields of reading by the hobbies of friends and by certain group activities, such as a play-reading club.

There are a number of excellent reading lists to help teachers, librarians, and the students themselves keep informed about recent literature for young people. Several examples of these lists are:

Basic Book Collection for High Schools, Joint Committee of American Library Association, National Education Association and National Council of Teachers of English. American Library Association.
Basic Book Collection for Junior High Schools. American Library Association.
Carlsen, G. Robert, and Alm, Richard S. *Social Understanding through Literature.* National Council for the Social Studies, 1954.
Haebich, Kathryn A. *Vocations in Fact and Fiction.* American Library Association, 1953.
Heaton, Margaret M., and Lewis, Helen B. *Reading Ladders for Human Relations.* American Council on Education, 1955.
Roos, Jean Carolyn. *Patterns in Reading, An Annotated Book List for Young People.* American Library Association, 1954.
Standard Catalog for High School Libraries. H. W. Wilson Company, 1952. Sixth Edition. (New edition every five years)

There are also a number of magazines such as *The Book List, A Guide to Current Books, Bulletin of Children's Book Center, Elementary English, The English Journal, The Horn Book*, and *Wilson Library Journal* that include references to and reviews of books for children and young people.

At present the sale of comics is enormous. In the United States we spend about 100 million dollars a year for comic books. This is about four times as much as is spent for books by all our public libraries. The comics present a problem because practically everyone reads them. Large numbers of comic readers are found among gifted children as well as among slow learners, among boys as well as girls, among elementary as well as high school students. The comics head the list in popularity of reading material; magazines with lots of pictures usually come next.

The same comic strips are popular in every grade, but interest tends to decrease as the students move into high school. There are pronounced differences between girls and boys as to their favorite comics. For example, the most popular magazine comics for boys deal with sports, crime, and humor — such magazines as *True Sports, Crime Does Not Pay, Donald Duck,* and *Mutt and Jeff.* Girls prefer comics featuring feminine interests such as *Patsy Walker* and *A Date with Judy.*

Comics satisfy the cravings of children and young people for adventure, action, excitement. Comic books have these qualities in a more concentrated form than other books which are popular for the same reasons. Comic books are cheap and even the poorest reader can get some meaning from the pictures alone, even if he does not know the words. Among pre-adolescents, especially, interest in the comics is contagious.

The persistent criticisms of the comics can be grouped under three main heads. The first concerns their poor literary and artistic quality. The second is directed at their tendency to crowd out a more desirable kind of reading. The third relates to their moral effect: their distorted views of reality, absence of standards of right and wrong, and emphasis on violence and crime.

The effect of the comics varies with individuals. The degree of a child's addiction to the comics — the amount of time he spends reading them and the intensity with which he reads them — undoubtedly determines how detrimental their influence may be. The kind of comics the child reads also makes a great deal of difference, since the quality of comics covers as wide a range as that of television programs. Crime comics full of sex and violence are the most common. Despite sporadic efforts to improve the quality of comics in general, there is some indication that increasing numbers of objectionable comics are being published. Actually, the child's needs and emotional receptivity determine to a large extent what he gets out of the comics. Some children merely enjoy the action, adventure, or humor. Others use the comics as an escape from reality. Many more may have their attitudes and values insidiously modified as a result of persistent perusal of the comics.

There is conflicting evidence concerning the relation of comics to delinquency. It is difficult to prove that certain kinds of comics promote crime. Still, continued perusal of comics featuring violence, crime, and brutality might be expected to decrease children's sensitivity to such shocking behavior. One little youngster who had been listening to a murder mystery was asked what it was about; he replied nonchalantly, "Just murder." Evidence on all these points has been admirably summarized in a series of articles by Witty and Sizemore (22).

In a comprehensive appraisal of a student's progress in reading, information on his reading interests and reading habits should be included.

Not only the student's improvement on informal tests and day-by-day exercises, but also the books and articles he has read with comprehension and enjoyment, his attitudes toward reading, and the improvement he has made in other subjects should be considered. In fact, what he reads is the ultimate test of successful reading instruction.

Giving Instruction in Reading While Teaching Any Subject

Instruction in reading can be given informally while teaching any subject. One kind of effective instruction begins with experiences that are meaningful and important to the student. The need for reading grows out of the activity; it is tied in with the student's life and interests.

Discussion of reading

An informal discussion of the reading process and the need for reading can often be introduced as a motivating device. The following discussion took place with three seriously retarded boys of junior high school age in the Teachers College High School and College Reading Center. They had been talking about sports.

Teacher: What does it take to be good in sports? Suppose you wanted to be a good baseball player, what would you have to do?

Tom: Practice.

Teacher: That applies to making furniture, too, doesn't it, David? You need practice to do woodworking well, don't you?

David: You need practice with the tools. You've got to know them. And you have to know how to use them. And you have to practice using them.

Teacher: That's a good point. You have to know how to use the tools as well as to practice using them. Is there anything else you would have to do to be good in sports or in making things?

David: Keep in good shape.

Tom: I'm not in good shape right now. I went to the gym last night to practice basketball. We're going to play a game this Saturday in Columbia University's gym. We were running down the stairs and I fell.

Teacher: It's lucky you didn't hurt yourself!

Tom: Oh, I got black and blue, here and there.

David: Well, you got down first!

Teacher: What else besides practice and "know-how" makes a good player? What about wanting to be a good player? Does that make a difference?

Tom: Yes. My father always says, "If you want to do something, nothing in the world can stop you." If you want to play basketball or football, read, write, or do anything, you can if you want to. Even in religion they can torture you, like in history, but you will not give in.

Teacher: That is a fine point of view, Tom. And it is true: you can do many things if you want to, hard enough. But then, as someone said, "How do you get to want to?" That's a $64,000 question we'll ask some other time. You can think about it. So far you mentioned three things we have to do to be good in sports or shopwork. You have to

        1. want to
        2. know how to, and
        3. practice.

    Would that apply to reading?

Tom: Yes!

Bert: You have to
        1. want to read
        2. know how to read, and
        3. practice reading.

Teacher: That's absolutely right. Now, what are some of the reasons you might want to read? Are there any real reasons why you want to read better, Bert?

Bert: Me? Well, to get along. You get an application for a job. The form asks for your name, where you live, where you were employed last, and all that. You have to know how to read all that.

Teacher: You certainly do. You really have to read to fill out an application and get a job. Are there any other reasons?

Bert: In driving a car. You have to know where you're going.

Tom: You have to take a test before you can drive — how to make a U-turn.

David: Bert was talking about reading the road signs and maps to know where you're going.

Tom: Yes, besides maps, signs on railroad crossings, and all that.

Teacher: Any other reasons for wanting to know how to read that you can think of, David?

David: Well, you have to know how to read to do all sorts of things. Anything practically.

Tom: To do anything in the world, you have to read. Anything except eat.

David: Even to eat — if you go out to eat —

Tom: Oh yes, you have to read the menu —

David: Or prepare the meal.

Teacher: Then you have to read the recipes.

Tom: How about sleep? You don't need to read to sleep.

David: There are whole books on how to sleep. Most people do it wrong. There's a whole book on relaxation.

Teacher: Well, I guess if we need reading to eat and sleep, it's very important. You certainly need reading to be able to do a lot of things you want to do.

Tom: I want to learn to read because I've got a beautiful set of encyclopedias at home, and I want to be able to read them and see what is going on in the world.

Teacher: To see what's going on in the world. That's another good reason and very well stated. We read to get knowledge.

Bert: You need reading for anything you want to do.

Teacher: So it seems. And this has been a very interesting discussion.

The tape recording of this conversation was typed and at the next period it was used as reading material, each boy reading the statements he had made. This procedure helps to change monotonous, word-by-word reading so common in retarded readers.

This is the way one teacher introduced reading into her seventh-grade activities. The period began with a discussion of ways in which we use reading in everyday living. The students mentioned street and car signs, menus, directions, advertisements, movie and television captions, newspapers, magazines, letters, and other common experiences. The teacher summarized by saying, "We read to get facts. We read to form opinions, too. We read headlines in the newspaper to see what we want to read. When do we read aloud?"

Betty: I read poetry aloud sometimes.

Bill: I read aloud the report I made in my club.

Jim: In class, we read our committee reports aloud.

Jean: If you're secretary, you read the minutes aloud.

Teacher: Yes, those are the times people most often read aloud. At what other times do you need to read silently?

Nancy: If you want to join a club, you read to get information about it.

Mike: We have to read our assignments in science carefully.

Teacher: Yes, even if we're not interested at first. "The secret of happiness is not always doing what one likes, but in liking what one has to do." How would you say this in your own words?

This lesson included a discussion of how each new experience helps to build one's vocabulary.

**Relating of reading
to previous experience**

Another approach is to relate the material to be read to the students' life experiences. The same teacher introduced an article on Lou Gehrig with a conversation about baseball:

Teacher: Do you play baseball?
Students (*both boys and girls*): Yes.
Teacher: Which is your favorite team?
Dave: I'm for the Yankees.
Mike: Me, too.
Ted: I'm for the Dodgers every time.
Teacher: This story we're going to read is about a baseball player. His first name begins with *L* and his last name with *G*. Can you guess who he was?

Preliminary word study

If the reading material contains difficult concepts and words, the teacher can clarify them before the students begin to read. Then they will be able to get the meaning of the selection without frustration. Later, if they feel the need for extra drill, it will be meaningful to them. In every classroom there are many incidental opportunities for word study. For example, the word *transportation* comes up. "What does the prefix *trans* mean? Name other words in which it is used — *trans-Atlantic, transcontinental*. The root is from the Latin *porto*, to carry, — What other words contain this root? *Porter*, one who carries; *portfolio*, a case for carrying loose papers." For high school students learning how to divide words into syllables and to pronounce them, to sound the word as a whole unlocks many words which they have in their speaking but not in their reading vocabulary.

Before reading one class discussed several words unfamiliar to them. Sometimes the teacher would give a sentence using the word to show them how they could get the meaning from the context. For example:

Teacher: What does *profusion* mean?
Sally: A great deal.
Teacher: Make a sentence using *profusion*.
Sally: In Florida where I used to live flowers grow in *profusion*.
Teacher: Good; give another one.
Ted: Everyone brought something to eat to the picnic, so they had a *profusion* of food.
Teacher: Good, Ted. I guess you wish you were there.

Then most of the group read the article silently while the teacher helped those who were having difficulty. As needed, they used other word attack skills. After the class had answered the questions on the article they discussed their answers and why one answer was the best. They volunteered to look up in the encyclopedia or other reference books more information on answers that were not satisfactory to them.

Preparation for
independent study

The effective teacher also gives instruction in reading a given assignment. The first step is to get a clear idea of the purpose of the assignment and the main ideas and their relation to the solution of the problem being studied. In this preliminary skimming, difficulties will be uncovered. The teacher may give assistance with these difficulties, either individually or to the group as a whole. Raising questions and finding the answers by reading silently and noting clews to cause-and-effect relations or to character development gives excellent practice in reading for meaning.

Providing Language Arts Experiences

The effective teacher of reading creates an atmosphere in which the students, especially those depressed by repeated failure, anticipate success. This he achieves by supporting the student in reading tasks suitable and vital to him. A purpose, a plan, and guided freedom in carrying it out are ideal conditions for any reading project.

Activities initiated
by the students

Some of these activities arise spontaneously with the students. For example, before school began one group were excitedly discussing a news item about juvenile delinquency. The teacher listened. When the bell rang she asked if they would like to continue the discussion as a panel before the rest of the class. Soon the entire class was interested. Their interest led to the forming of committees to get information about different aspects of the problem. This, of course, necessitated referring to books and articles on their topic. The teacher and librarian helped them to find reading material on different levels of difficulty, so that all members of the group, including the poorest and the best readers, could make a contribution. Finally they worked on presenting the knowledge they had gained to the class in well-organized, attention-holding form. For example, one group presented charts showing the increase in juvenile delinquency and the age groups involved. Another group showed and discussed pictures and articles they had found in newspapers and magazines. Another group, in a panel discussion, suggested their plan for a recreation center in their own community. So effective were their reports that they were asked to give them as an assembly program and later to a parent group. Reading thus embedded in a successful vital activity initiated by the students and guided by the teacher is purposeful and meaningful to the students.

Other activities may be suggested by the teacher and accepted whole-

Students work hard on reading activities
initiated by themselves.

heartedly by the students. Projects of this kind should provide reading experiences sufficiently varied so that all the pupils can participate and make a contribution to the group. Many of these have nothing to do with reading at first, but later involve reading. The following activities focus more directly on reading.

Trips and excursions

Trips may be taken to supply a background of experience for reading as, for example, a trip up the Hudson preparatory to reading Irving's *The Legend of Sleepy Hollow*. Trips will also stimulate reading and writing, for example, a trip to a museum to follow up on individual interests. In one instance, a trip to a housing project was part of a study of family life. Many of the students had part-time jobs. The question arose as to whether they should contribute some of their earnings to their family. This, in turn, involved a study of family budgets and how much a family with a given income could afford to spend for rent. Before the visit, they obtained information about housing from pamphlets, newspapers, and magazines. They read some stories and biographies dealing with family problems. They gave a dramatized reading of scenes from the play, *I Remember Mama*. They raised questions they wanted to answer from the visit. After the trip, in a class discussion, they pooled the information they had obtained. This discussion was transcribed and became a permanent part of the source material for this unit.

Experience reading

Talking, writing, and reading about one's own experiences is effective on any age level, with groups or with individuals. Students like to talk and write about their experiences. They like to read about them because they are written in their own vocabulary and language patterns and are high in interest value. In a group, students may be asked to report orally to the class on "the most exciting or amusing thing that has happened to me," "a movie I have seen," "a tall tale," or "how to make or do some particular thing." These reports may be recorded and transcribed. Sometimes there are senior students in business education who will take stenographic notes on these reports, transcribe them, and return them to the authors for further editing. When bound into small volumes, each on a given topic, these original stories and articles constitute a valuable part of the classroom library.

Sociodrama

The spontaneous role-playing of situations involving problems common to the group may be recorded and transcribed in the same way. Some of these make excellent booklets for dramatized reading. For example, one junior high school class were concerned about being interrupted when they came home to study. Several students volunteered to take the roles of mother, older sister, and the junior high school student who wanted to study. First they described concretely the setting in which the incident was to occur. Then they acted their parts spontaneously:

Student (*getting started on her homework*): I've got a lot to learn before the test tomorrow. Guess I'd better get down to work. (*Starts reading.*)

Mother (*comes in*): Oh, Mary, will you go to the store for me? I need some flour and carrots for supper.

Mary: Oh, I just started studying. Can't Jim go?

Mother: Jim hasn't come home from school yet and I need these things now.

Mary: Oh, all right, but I've just started studying for the exam tomorrow. (*Mary goes to store, returns with the groceries, and begins studying again.*)

Jim (*comes in*): Say, Mary, have you seen my sweater?

Mary: No. And don't bother me! (*Jim goes out.*)

Mother (*comes in*): Mary, I'm sorry, but I don't have enough milk. Will you go to the store for it?

Mary (*begins to get angry, then says*): Well, I'll get it this time. But after this, Mother, I want you to give me the list of *everything* you need so that I can get all the things on my way home from school.

Role-playing is a way of working out certain common problems concretely and of gaining more understanding of oneself and others.

Newspaper reading activities

Students usually enjoy comparing and analyzing the propaganda of headlines dealing with the same topic from newspapers having different viewpoints. They become interested in looking for and bringing to class the headline that seems the most important. They especially like to read news stories with the captions omitted; then write their own captions, and compare them with the original. Some students also like to search for items of interest to read to the class and to post on the bulletin board. One retarded reader attributed an exceptional improvement in reading to this activity.

Reading games and self-checking exercises

Reading games appeal particularly to the junior high school age, though even senior high school students enjoy playing some of them. Some of these games may be purchased (see Appendix, page 348). They are especially valuable in providing practice for individuals deficient in certain specific word recognition, vocabulary, paragraph reading, and other skills.

Reading games should serve some specific purpose, not used just for entertainment. Students may use a given game for practice in some reading skill individually, or in groups of two or more. If a key is provided, they may check their answers, thus requiring a minimum of the teacher's attention.

Some games may be used to give practice in phonics or other word recognition skills. The word wheel is a familiar example of this kind of game. A simple form has consonants written at intervals on the bottom wheel and parts of words on the upper wheel. The player turns the upper wheel until he gets a consonant to complete the word. For example:

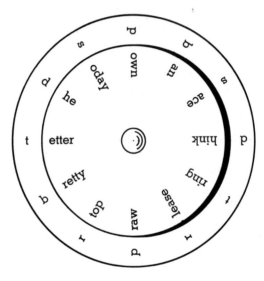

Another form of wheel gives practice in a single sound such as *gr*, which is printed on the upper wheel in front of a slit. On the under wheel other letters are printed which, when moved into place, will form words, such as:

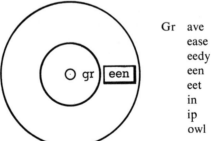

Gr ave
ease
eedy
een
eet
in
ip
owl

Another simple but effective game for practice in initial and final sounds of words consists of a folded slip of thin cardboard on which are written initial sounds. Another piece of cardboard is inserted, having on it a single final sound. The inserted piece is moved down to make a word with each initial sound:

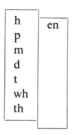

Many vocabulary games have been devised. Various forms of *Word Bingo* may be used. Sets of words of different levels of difficulty may be selected to individualize instruction. Each word is printed in large type on the word card and on separate squares. When a word is called, the player having that word on his card gets it and places it on the appropriate square. Color may be used as a self-checking device. Similarly words may be matched with their definitions as already described (see page 138).

A large colorful picture of a plane, auto, or other object in which the students are interested may be accompanied by words giving its various parts — *wheel, tire, bumper*, etc. The words are placed on the part of the car they describe. Separate small pictures may also be matched with the appropriate word cards. If the pictures are numbered, a scoring key may be made so that the player can check the accuracy of his placement of the words. A science teacher devised a board with a battery and wires connecting a word on one side with a synonym or definition on the other side. When the student touched the correct word, a little bulb at the bottom would light.

Practice in reading words necessary to find one's way around is given by the simple exercise accompanying the map of the streets and places in the neighborhood. A scoring key in an envelope on the back of the map enables the student to check the accuracy of his answers.

A vocabulary game useful in placing words into meaningful categories consists of cards with separate words which can be sorted into piles according to categories, such as words that describe action, coins, feelings, etc. Sentence-building games are high in interest value. They consist of separate words or phrases to be built into sentences. Words to be used in a given sentence may all be printed on paper of the same color. Phrases are better than words for conveying the idea of reading in thought units. Whole sentences may be matched with pictures to give practice in reading sentences.

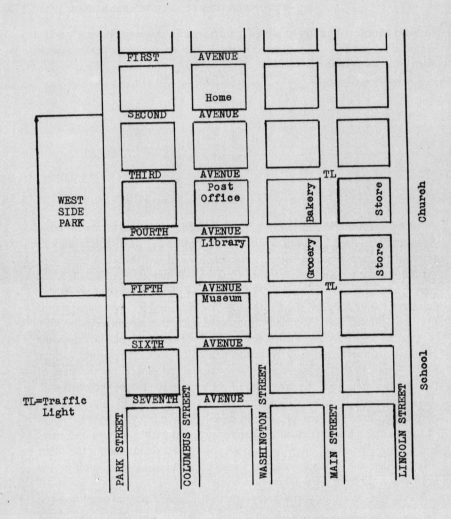

Study the map and fill in the following sentences:

1. The school is on _____ Street.
2. The stores are on _____ Street.
3. The church is on _____ Street.
4. The museum is on _____ Avenue.
5. The grocery is on _____ Street.
6. The post office is on _____ Avenue.
7. The library is on _____ Avenue.
8. The bakery is on _____ Street.
9. The home is on _____ Avenue.
10. The park is called _____ Park.

A practical exercise in reading signs.

Other games use highly interesting pictures as a springboard to give practice in reading sentences. For example, under a photo of a recent football game is printed:

Which is the right headline?
1. Notre Dame back rushes through Navy line
2. Colgate kicks out of danger
3. Army end leaps high to catch pass

A colorful advertisement of a Winchester rifle and a game bird is accompanied by reading exercises such as the following:

1. This picture is from:
   a story about Thanksgiving
   an ad for a certain make of gun
   an article about a country restaurant
2. These guns are used mostly by
   army officers
   criminals
   sportsmen

Similarly, paragraph building games give practice in constructing better paragraphs, with ideas in proper sequence. To make these games, select well-constructed paragraphs and type each sentence on a separate slip of thin cardboard. Put the separate sentences in an envelope, together with a card on which the original paragraph is typed. Students are interested in seeing whether their arrangement of sentences corresponds with the author's. Sometimes they can make a good case for their sequence of sentences. To give further practice in putting ideas in sequence, pictures may be used, first to arrange in order and then to match with descriptive sentences giving the proper sequence of events.

Practice in reading short selections is given by presenting the article or story either in its original or in simplified form and asking questions such as would naturally be answered by the story or article. Some selections that have been highly interesting are:

"We Captured a Python"
"A Car with Wings"
"Fire Walkers"
"Name This Animal"
"High Workers" (accounts of exciting experiences of men who help build skyscrapers) *

* The reading games described in this section were made by the following students in the basic course in the improvement of reading in high school and college at Teachers College, Columbia University: Beatrice A. Premmac, Lillian Wexner, Mildred Wiggins, Deborah Burkland, James Schiavone, Frank T. Wilson, Jr., Joseph Krauss, Alice Howsen, Eula Rathbun.

To introduce and illustrate association and organization of ideas, the teacher shows a picture of the interior of a room. She lets her students look at it for one minute and then asks them: "What did you see in the picture?" The students first mention separate items: *window, stove, stool, trees.*

Teacher: If you have a stove, what else will you need?

Students: *Pan, brush, broom* — to sweep around the stove.

Teacher: When you think of *window*, what else do you remember?

Pupil: *Curtain.*

Teacher: Yes; it's easier to remember things that go together. That's why relating one idea to another and making an outline often helps us remember an assignment.

Individualized spelling drill

Spelling and reading are closely related; few poor readers are good spellers (9). Many students in high school are painfully conscious of their poor spelling and want to improve, and they can. Spelling can be taught systematically with good results, as described by Withrow (20). First, the students are given a spelling test to determine their present spelling level (see Appendix, pages 356–357). Then each day they are given a spelling list of twenty-five words at their present level, taken from the Stanford Spellers (1). Some of these words they will spell correctly; the ones they spell wrong, they will study. The procedure for each misspelled word is to learn the meaning of each word, look carefully at it, divide it into syllables, pronounce it, and test the accuracy of their spelling by writing it. The students make a card file of the words they miss. On one side of the card they write the word correctly spelled, divide it into syllables, and tell the part or parts of speech it may be. On the other side they write a sentence using the word; for example:

```
arbitrary
ar' bi trary
adjective
```

```
My mother made an
arbitrary rule about
the time I must come
home after the party.
```

Then they file the cards alphabetically. They review the words in their file from time to time until they can spell them without errors. Each student goes ahead as fast as he is able. After studying words in this way they feel confident that they know them.

This procedure teaches not only spelling but also grammar, punctuation, and word meaning. It is applicable only for small classes because it requires considerable checking on the part of the teacher. Many students welcome a certain amount of routine procedure, such as this method of teaching spelling involves. They find it upsetting never to know what they are going to do from day to day. The students who have used this method are convinced of its values. One said, "You can't help learning to spell the word correctly." And another made the comment, "Words I always misspelled I now know."

Free reading followed by discussion

Many opportunities should be given for free reading. A homeroom teacher in his fifteen-minute period at the beginning of the day may bring to class a number of articles and books. He reads excerpts from them, parts that were particularly amusing or exciting, and then says, "These will be here on the table all week. You may read them whenever you have a little free time." Students who finish their work before the rest of the class have a good deal of time, which they can use in this way. Then, of course, there are free reading periods for the whole class, followed by informal discussion of the books they have read.

Use of assignments in other subjects as practice material

In giving instruction in one of the basic reading skills, a teacher may cut across subject matter lines. He may encourage the students to apply their newly learned skill in reading to their assignments in other subjects. He may also use the texts in other fields as practice material. This is important to insure the transfer of reading skills from one field to another.

Dramatization

Dramatic reading of stories with a great deal of conversation in them usually has high interest value. It also gives practice in reading with expression (the way the character would say it) and helps to break up word-by-word reading. One class had enough copies of each volume of *Teen-Age Tales* (published by D. C. Heath and Company) to use for dramatic reading. Groups of five or six worked together; each group chose a story, read it silently, assigned parts, and practiced reading it before presenting it to the whole class. For example, one group chose the short story, "The Champ," in *Teen-Age Tales*, Book I. First, they skimmed it to see who were the characters. Then they chose parts — Watson, the

Julius Caesar comes to life when pupils dramatize it.

A record of Robert Frost's poetry read by the author heightens pupils' interest in poetry.

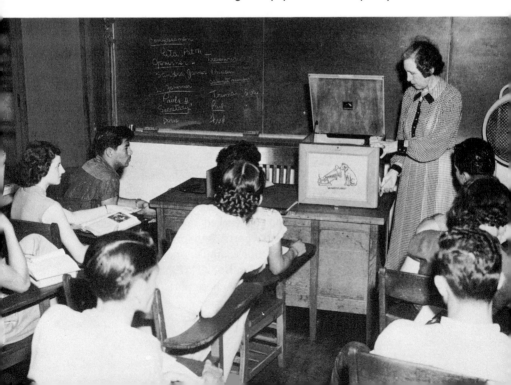

Boss, Herbie, and the narrator. After reading the story silently, with special attention to the understanding of their own parts, they read it aloud. If any member of the group had difficulty with any words or read with poor expression or phrasing, the others would help him. When they felt that they were ready, they gave the dramatized reading before the class. The education of the audience in effective and appreciative listening was also one of the teacher's objectives. After the dramatized reading, the class discussed the story — what kind of people were the characters; how did they get that way; why did they behave as they did?

The dramatized reading of any story or play may be the starting point for a more ambitious project such as an assembly period or a parents' program, or for presentation to another class. The entire class may try out for parts. With this motivation students who ordinarily stumble over words read as smoothly as radio announcers, stutterers overcome their difficulty for the time being, and non-readers become so familiar with a few lines that they can hold the book and "read" for a part. Of course, the class will select the best oral readers for the major roles but the generally poor readers are often chosen for the supporting roles. In rehearsing, many new words such as *stage hand, designer, props,* and other words in the play itself enter naturally into the students' vocabulary. The better readers help the poorer readers find information needed to design the scenery and costumes. A non-reader, with some help, may block in some scene cards ("Act I, Scene iii") and carry them across the stage at the appropriate time. A speech teacher may make a tape recording and point out ways to improve their interpretation and enunciation. Poor readers who had memorized lines in the play from hearing it rehearsed many times might prompt an excellent reader who was momentarily overcome with stage fright. Such a successful experience increases students' concept of themselves as readers. As one group said, "We've done that so well, we must be pretty good readers!" And they tend to live up to this concept of themselves.

Songs and choral reading

An activity some students enjoy very much is the singing of ballads and other songs written during the historical period they are studying. Some of the Shakespearean lyrics that have been set to music may also be sung in class to increase students' interest and appreciation. The words of some popular songs in folk song style such as "The Yellow Rose of Texas" and "Young Abe Lincoln" were mimeographed for retarded readers in a New York City junior high school by the reading teacher, Shirley Levenkron. "Sixteen Tons" appealed especially to the older, rougher boys — the "tough guys" in the group. The following is an amusing selection used by Frances Humphreville (10, p. 59) for choral reading in a class of ninth-grade girls:

Prayer to Saint Catherine

Girls: St. Catherine, St. Catherine, Oh, lend me thine aid
And grant that I never may die an old maid.
1st solo: A husband, St. Catherine!
2nd solo: A good one, St. Catherine!
3rd solo: But anyone, better than no one, St. Catherine!
4th solo: A husband, St. Catherine!
5th solo: Handsome, St. Catherine!
6th solo: Rich, St. Catherine!
7th solo: Young, St. Catherine!
Girls: SOON, St. Catherine!

Films and other auditory-visual aids

Documentary radio and television programs, films, slide films, tape recordings, and phonograph records are being increasingly used to enrich meaning and stimulate interest in reading. One teacher, Martha Allen, while studying at Teachers College, Columbia University, described her use of a series of homemade slide films dealing with topics in eighth-grade social studies. These slides had no subtitles but there was a booklet giving in story form a description of each event depicted on the slide films. The students first read this booklet on a topic; then the next day they were shown the film strip. Then the class made suggestions as to the caption that would best fit each picture. The teacher raised questions such as, "What is the most important thing in this picture? Why was the picture included in the film series? What contribution does it make to the story as a whole?" They next wrote the story on the board to see whether they had included all the important facts — whether someone who had not seen the film strip would be able to tell what it was about simply by reading their story. They also saw whether they had put the events in the story in the proper sequence and in proper relation to one another. Following this group instruction and practice in getting the main ideas in the pictures and relating them in sequence, the class was given a list of source material from which they could get background for the next film strip they were to see. Then the teacher ran through the film quickly so that the students could gather the general idea. Next, as each picture was flashed, they were told to write their own story, focusing attention on the important points in each picture. Then they checked their stories for grammatical correctness and proper use of words. After reviewing and improving what they wrote, they read their stories aloud for the class to discuss constructively. The students enjoyed this procedure which helped them to build vocabulary and concepts in history. They also learned to survey materials as a whole, pick out relevant facts, improve note-taking, and improve their ability to grasp main ideas and cause-and-effect relations. (See Appendix, pages 347–348, for list of films and film strips.)

The tape recorder is useful in many ways: It serves as a stimulus to more effective reporting of ideas gained from reading; it shows a student's progress in learning to read aloud; it records oral reports of experiences which can later be transcribed and used as reading material.

**A repertory of
reading procedures**

Every teacher should have a repertory of procedures on which to draw. These he can adapt to the needs of the individual or the group. Procedures and techniques should never be applied automatically because any one procedure is like one side of a triangle. The "eternal triangle" in the teaching of reading is the teacher — his personality and proficiency; the pupil — his capacity, expectations, interests and needs; and the methods and procedures and materials of instruction. The creative teacher uses his own experience and the experience of the student in the improvement of reading. There is a constant interplay of interpersonal relations through the media of methods and materials. Procedures are always applied in the context of a setting and a relationship. The successful use of the procedure depends a great deal on the personal relation that has been established between student and teacher.

Forming Subgroups within a Class

While many of the activities mentioned are engaged in by the whole class and certain instruction in reading is given to all the pupils, in view of the wide range of individual differences there is often need for diversified instruction in reading. This kind of experience may be given through small groups, formed within an ordinary class. This is one way of providing for individual differences, but it does not make unnecessary the teaching of reading on many levels at the same time.

There are many bases for forming groups. Students may be grouped according to:

1. reading needs or skills on which they need practice
2. their reading level
3. their interest in some subject
4. the contribution they can make to a project or part of a project in which they are interested
5. the beneficial influence certain members will have on one another

In any group, ideally, there should be one or more students who can help the group learn to work together, an able learner who can give some instruction in reading to other members of the group, and a good-humored youngster who helps to create friendly relations.

One advantage of grouping the same students on different bases is that the danger of stigmatizing any child as being in a "low" group is minimized. Jimmie may work with a group of the poorest readers to improve in basic reading skills. But he may also be in a group with the brightest students working on a project in which he, too, is interested and to which he can make his unique contribution. The emphasis in grouping is clearly on flexibility, which prevents the forming of rigid lines between good and poor readers.

Grouping according to reading needs

Students in any class vary in their competency in specific reading skills. They would profit by additional practice and instruction on the skills in which they are weak. In grouping according to reading needs, a few students may work on simple word recognition skills using games devised for this purpose; another group may be learning to get the main idea of the paragraph; an advanced group may be working together on finding character clews in a story. A student-tutor may be helping members of the first group reach their goal; the teacher is free to give instruction in the second group; and the third group is able to work under their own direction with a chairman to coordinate activities. The grouping chart, when the basis of grouping is reading needs, is as follows:

Best Group	Average Group	Poorest Group
Finding character clews with help of student-chairman	Learning to find the main idea of a paragraph with help of teacher	Working on word recognition skills with help of a student-tutor

The success of this grouping depends largely on the agility of the teacher. He needs to give careful directions at the beginning of the period to the two groups he will not work with, and at the end of the period he must make the members of these two groups feel that he has looked at and evaluated, to some extent, what they have done. His materials must also be well organized. Success depends on two other factors, namely, how well the students have learned to work together under student leaders and how well student leaders can handle their groups. In the beginning, teachers often feel as though they were running a three-ring circus when they attempt to form three groups. If so, it is better to begin with two groups until teachers and students have learned to handle the technique of grouping. The various plans using student leaders often work well but teachers must constantly watch to see that those selected for leadership do not become prissy, dictatorial, or arrogant. It is also well to select a student-tutor or student-chairman to help with word recognition skills who is not only capable of leadership but who himself can profit by extra attention to word recognition skills.

**Grouping according to
reading level**

A class may be divided into two or more groups on the basis of their total scores on reading tests. The aim of this kind of grouping is to enable students to master the content of the course with a minimum of frustration and to increase their reading efficiency through practice on reading material suitable for them. If there are several textbooks on the subject, each on a different level of difficulty, the students may form groups on this basis. But each level will also probably be working on different reading skills, thus combining the level grouping with the need grouping. When a student develops his reading skills to a certain point, he may change to another level. If each group prepares an interesting report of their reading for the whole class they will have social motivation for their reading and practice in other communication skills.

Practice materials, such as Simpson's *Better Reading Books* (16), or Johnson's *Reading Improvement Skilltest* (11), for example, can be used in grouping situations to give practice on reading for detail. The grouping chart, when the basis of grouping is reading level, would be as follows:

Best Group	Average Group	Poorest Group
S.R.A. Better Reading,	*S.R.A. Better Reading,*	*S.R.A. Better Reading,*
Book 3	Book 2	Book 1

The teacher can give a brief introduction for each selection to the whole group and build a readiness for the reading. If knowledge of each student's rate of reading is desired the teacher can write the time on the board each fifteen seconds. The student writes the figure he sees on the board as soon as he has finished reading. This gives him a record of the time he took to read the selection.

In general, a good plan is the one in which the teacher introduces a selection to the best readers and then leaves them to work independently for the remainder of the period to improve comprehension, interpretation, or critical reading. While the teacher is with this first group, the average readers may be doing some comprehension exercises on yesterday's selection and some vocabulary study. The poorer readers can profitably engage in word games, which would emphasize vocabulary at their level. Later the teacher may give them instruction in how to read a selection and might ask brief questions that require some comprehension skills.

Most materials which are developed to give practice in a specific reading skill provide comprehension check tests. By taking these tests and keeping a record of his comprehension scores *in relation to his speed*, the student can chart his progress in terms of *speed of comprehension*. One way of doing this is by calculating what someone has called the RI, or Reading Index. The RI is computed by the following simple formula: speed (words per minute) × comprehension (number of questions answered correctly) ÷ 100. If the student computes his RI for one selection, reads several of the *same* type from the *same* material, then computes the RI for a final selection, he may determine the percentage of gain or loss. One teacher uses the chart on the next page to determine each student's progress.

Grouping according to interests

Groups formed according to interest will usually include poor, average, and good readers. This is desirable, if every member of the group is able to make some contribution to the topic chosen. A class frequently forms committees to work on some aspect of a larger problem or to follow up some common interest. Many other topics, some of the "research" type, may be studied in this way. Other groups may be interested in different

PROGRESS SHEET

Name _____   Date _____

Material:

Selection	1	2	3	4	5	6	7	8	9	10
Comprehension Questions										
1										
2										
3										
4										
5										
6										
7										
8										
9										
10										

Summary: RI for Selection 1 (Sp. × Comp. ÷ 100)   =
          RI for Selection 10 (Sp. × Comp. ÷ 100)   =
          Gain (RI for Selection 10 − RI for Selection 1) =
          Percent of gain (Gain ÷ RI for Selection 1)   =

kinds of literature. For example, if a student in English class is interested in poetry, he may join a poetry group. Each member of the group selects poems to read aloud to the group. Members of the group comment on the poem and his reading of it. Even a poor reader may join this group. With the help of the teacher or one of the other students he can select a simple, but not childish, poem, and practice reading it so that he can really give the audience pleasure. If there is a tape recorder available this group may like to make records of a few of the best readings to play to the class as a whole.

Grouping for work on projects

When several projects are suggested, subgroups within a class may each select one. Any project requires a variety of talent for its completion. An original play requires writers, costume designers, painters of scenery, actors, actresses, and stage manager. Often reading is necessary to get authentic information about costumes and scenery. A non-reader may know more about lighting effects and how to produce them than anyone else. Another poor reader may have a part that requires little reading but some skillful acting. For example, in an informal little play written and read dramatically by the students in a small group, a non-reader played the part of the dog. All he had to say was "Woof, woof," but he acted the part so well he "stole the show." In the project form of grouping, each member of the group should be able to make some contribution to the successful completion of the project. Many kinds of projects suggest themselves to students and teachers. One group may select a service project such as reading stories to younger children; another may become interested in making picture dictionaries; other groups may prepare exhibits — a book fair, for example; a class newspaper, such as *Science News*, put out by a general science class; or various kinds of programs for assemblies or parent study groups.

Friendship grouping

Friendship may enter into the last two kinds of grouping mentioned. A student may join a certain interest group or choose a particular project because some of his friends are in that group. And in fact, the success and productivity of any group depends a great deal upon having members who appreciate and respect one another and interact beneficially.

However, when groups are formed primarily on the basis of friendship, certain problems may arise. It is important that each member of the subgroup have an opportunity to contribute to the group according to his ability and to get from the group something to meet his needs. If the individual's needs are greater than the group can meet, he may disrupt the group unless the teacher works with him individually as much as possible. When the difference in reading ability among members of the group is very great, despite the efforts of the teacher and of friends, the student may constantly feel threatened and insecure. The teacher, aware of such a student's need to be of some worth to the group, will frequently refer to something that he does well and will encourage him to use in the group project whatever ability he has. Being with friends, he will be included in their informal conversation and made to feel secure and accepted.

The role of the teacher
with the group

The role of the effective teacher in group work depends on the teacher's knowledge and skill in teaching reading, on creativity, on a genuine fondness for youngsters, and on a sense of humor. These characteristics of the teacher should be coupled with the students' desire to help themselves improve in reading. This initial motivation needs to be further stimulated and maintained at a high level by the teacher.

In one group of senior high school students the teacher's infectious humor created a warm, informal give-and-take. The members of the group were active in asking questions and otherwise seeking information. Following the teacher's example of sometimes admitting being wrong or not knowing the answers to some of their questions, the students felt free to admit their mistakes, without shame or anxiety. They became less tense and responded to the teaching with good humor. Growth in self-confidence was evident. With one boy, the teacher's encouragement led to an excessive aggressiveness and exaggerated idea of his accomplishments. It was necessary to help this boy maintain a reasonable perspective on his achievements and prevent him from increasing the feelings of inferiority of other members of the group. This teacher was remarkably successful in satisfying the needs of each member of the group.

Example of grouping
in a seventh-grade class

In a seventh grade in English, the students were divided into three groups. The best readers were reading a true story about Abraham Lincoln from a seventh-grade reader. The middle group was reading a story from *Teen-Age Tales* on the sixth-grade level, and the lowest group was reading a simplified version of *The Legend of Sleepy Hollow*. They were all reading the stories silently as the first step to dramatizing them for the class as a whole.

In social studies, the same class was working on a unit, "The World's Major Resources." The pupils had first listed questions about the major resources of the United States and then chosen the specific questions they wanted to work on, individually or in small groups. They planned to share the knowledge they had obtained with the class as a whole. Their teacher, over the years, had built up a file of material on different resources. For example, the folder on cotton contained magazine articles, "free" material from commercial companies such as a pamphlet by Johnson and Johnson, reports and pictures made by pupils in previous years, and mimeographed materials prepared by other teachers of the same grade. The teacher moved about from group to group to help pupils locate references on their topic, extract the information they needed, and think of some exciting way to present it to the class. This procedure can be used in any subject, but its success depends largely on having suitable source material available.

Principles underlying
good grouping

Subgrouping within a regular class is not easy. In fact, many teachers shy away from it. They are afraid they will lose control of the class or that the group work will have little educational value for the students. These fears may be realized unless certain conditions are met:

1. The students must be given instruction in how to work together in groups — how to choose a chairman, how to conduct a discussion, how to find references and get information from them, how to appraise their group procedure so that they will continually improve it.

2. The teacher must plan to work with the groups that need his instruction. This necessitates planning with the other groups so that they may work independently.

3. Independent work is impossible without suitable reading materials and other necessary materials of instruction.

4. The class should not be too large and the room should be equipped with movable chairs and tables.

Good group work does not "just happen." It requires instruction in the process of working together, planning of activities that can be carried on with a minimum of teacher supervision, and reading materials to meet varied needs and abilities.

Summary of discussion
of grouping

The skillful teacher, with varied reading materials, can individualize instruction without any system of grouping. There are methods of differentiating the questions asked about a book that all the students are reading; or the teacher can provide all levels of interesting books from which individuals may choose. There are also methods of teaching word meaning and other skills to those who need such instruction. For example, individuals who find the book being read by the class too easy or too difficult for them, may be permitted to leave the group on their own initiative to do independent reading or join a small group working on special skills with the teacher or a student tutor.

If groups are formed, the teacher still has the problem of individualizing instruction within the subgroup and preventing any poor reader in the group from feeling stupid. In successful groups the teacher gives help in reading; he does not just have the students read. The more effectively the teacher can handle different levels of reading ability in one group, the fewer subgroups he will have to form.

Each teacher has to experiment with the kind of grouping he can handle best. Whatever the method used it should be the best one to help the students improve their reading.

Providing Sufficient Variety and Quantity of Materials of Instruction

Any form of individualized or group instruction demands a wide range of appropriate reading material. After the teacher has ascertained the interests, needs, and abilities of his students, he should find books, pamphlets, magazines, and other materials to satisfy these needs and interests on various levels of difficulty.

An illustration of the value of suitable materials of instruction

An incident will show concretely the relation between interest and reading materials. Ted, a ninth-grade boy, was practically obsessed with boats and if an activity had no relation to boats he would withdraw from it. His teacher tried to interest him in other things, though she brought in the subject of boats whenever possible. At the end of six weeks he had made little progress and was convinced that his average reading achievement, which was only second grade, was more indicative of his present functioning mental ability than his intelligence quotient of 126. The special reading teacher agreed to send for him whenever she was doing something in her group that she thought would interest him, and he was called often. At the same time the industrial arts teacher began working with Ted on the construction of a wooden rowboat that could be converted into a sailboat. Ted worked diligently and enthusiastically on this. He dictated the steps in construction so that others would be able to make a similar boat by reading his "Manual of Rowboat Building." This project took three months to finish and his boat was the talk of the school. To compare his streamlined rowboat with boats from

A keen interest in one subject, such as boats or planes, may lead to wide reading.

Making history books meaningful by application to today's affairs.

other countries he went to the library and, with his teacher's help, read to find out how other kinds of boats were constructed and why they were built differently to meet different needs.

Ted's interest spread to other students. Some other boys who formerly had said that they were "just waiting to get out of school" formed a Boating Club. They put on an assembly program showing the books about boats they recommended for reading and some that they had written themselves. They had an art exhibit of boats and sang songs of boatmen and canals.

Ted still centered his activities around boats, but his interest had broadened to include some reading in science, exploration, and sea adventure stories. At the end of the school year Ted was reading at the fifth-grade level. He had a much larger sight vocabulary; he was able to find details, to understand main ideas, and to make comparisons. He had become more aware of his potentialities and how to use his resources. Moreover, he was happier and less withdrawn socially; his circle of friends, based first on a common interest, increased. Thus his growth in reading and his personal development went hand in hand, as indeed they should.

The teachers involved here were understanding and cooperative. They worked together toward common goals. The results with Ted — admittedly an extreme case — show the need and the value of integrating the efforts of one teacher with the efforts of others.

**Ways to obtain suitable
reading material**

How is the teacher to get the necessary reading material? What books and magazines should he order? Where will he get the money to purchase them?

If he has the cooperation of the school or public librarian he is fortunate. Some librarians will practically take over this responsibility. They will study lists of books for retarded readers and select those which they think most suitable for students in the school. (See Appendix, page 351, for bibliographies for retarded readers of high school age reading below sixth-grade level.) They will examine booklets for titles suitable for average and superior readers. As these books are ordered, they will announce them to the teachers who are most likely to use them. From county service centers and from bookmobiles, other books may be obtained.

Subscribing to several magazines is a good investment. *My Weekly Reader* is published on six grade levels; and even the first-grade level, dealing as it does with current events, is often not too childish for non-reading pupils in high school.

A large variety of practice books is an aid to individualized instruction (see Appendix, page 348). These may be used with students in small groups who need practice in a certain reading skill, or they may be used individually by students who have recognized their special difficulties and want to do something about them. These pupils may use a certain kind of exercise — skimming, for example — as presented in several different books.

Some advertising pamphlets on travel, autos, electricity, and other major industries may be obtained without cost. These booklets interest adolescents who will soon be entering the world of work.

Other reading material prepared for adult beginners is appropriate to older adolescents who are reading on a very low level. An excellent annotated bibliography of such material giving the grade level of each reference was prepared by Louis A. D'Amico, Nicholas A. Fattu, and Lloyd S. Standless, Institute of Educational Research of Indiana University, Bloomington, Indiana.

If the school board will not appropriate money to buy books, community organizations and parent-teacher associations can often be interested in this need. The students themselves may raise money through fairs, music festivals, plays, and other creative activities which are in themselves educational.

After the new books have been purchased they may be publicized in various ways: Through exhibits of colorful covers on bulletin boards; through a book fair; through book reviews written by the students and published in mimeographed form in the school newspaper. The teacher or librarian or students may read appealing parts of some of the books as a means of introducing them to the class. These and many other ways will be suggested by ingenious teachers and students.

Concluding Statement

Every teacher has a number of opportunities to help students improve their reading. From the results of any standardized tests that have been given to the students and from informal "teaching tests" and exercises, the teacher can learn much about each student's reading ability. A comparison of students' comprehension, when listening, with their comprehension of comparable material read silently may uncover mental potential for reading or show the need for practice in auditory and visual discrimination. On the basis of this knowledge the teacher can provide instruction and practice which the entire class needs. He does all he can to individualize instruction within his class. To do this successfully, he must have a variety of reading materials covering a range of difficulty as wide as the range of reading ability represented in his class. Equally important

*Every teacher should teach the reading skills needed
in her particular subject.*

Groups of two or more read to prepare reports of
interest to the class.

is a repertory of reading methods and procedures, games, and practice exercises that he can adapt, combine, and use as needed for individuals and groups. He must also have up his sleeve, in case the pupils do not think of them, suggestions for projects and activities in which all the pupils can participate and which involve reading for their successful completion. Each teacher will invent, adapt, and experiment with various procedures and develop further those which prove most successful.

For students so retarded in reading that they cannot profit by the regular class work, but yet have potentialities for improvement, special instruction can be provided in a section of the regular English class for which they get credit. If the reading deficiency is still more serious they may be helped through small special reading groups or individual case work.

The relation of work with individuals to work with groups is a complementary one. The self-confidence a student gains from success in individual sessions frequently permeates other areas of his experience in school and even at home. Often the reading teacher selects materials for work in special reading groups which enable the student to gain recognition from his classmates. This is more important to an adolescent than an adult's approval. Reading experiences of both these kinds may have important therapeutic effects.

REFERENCES

1. ALMACK, JOHN C., and STAFFELBACH, ELMER. *The Stanford Spellers.* New York: Laidlaw Brothers, 1939.

2. BLUME, CLARENCE E. (Chairman); GRAY, WILLIAM S.; and TRUMP, J. LLOYD. *Attacking Reading Problems in Secondary Schools.* Lincoln, Nebraska: North Central Association, 1944.

3. BOND, GUY L., and BOND, EVA. *Developmental Reading in High School,* New York: The Macmillan Company, 1941.

4. Bulletin of the National Association of Secondary-School Principals. *Improving Reading Instruction in the Secondary School,* Vol. XXXIV, No. 168. Washington, D.C.: National Association of Secondary-School Principals, 1950.

5. CARRUTH, IRBY B.; SPEARS, HAROLD; and DOUGLAS, MARY P. "Directions in School Library Service Today." *American Library Association Bulletin.* Vol. XLVIII, No. 2, February, 1954.

6. DURRELL, DONALD D. *Improvement of Reading Instruction,* Chapters VI, VII. Yonkers, New York: World Book Company, 1956.

7. FRANK, JOSETTS, *Comics, Radio, Movies — and Children.* New York 16, New York: Public Affairs Committee, Inc., 1949.

8. GRAY, WILLIAM S., and LARRICK, NANCY (Editors). *Better Reading for Our Times.* International Reading Association Conference Proceedings, Vol. I. New York: Scholastic Magazines, 1956.

9. HORN, ERNEST. *What Research Says about Spelling.* Washington, D.C.: National Education Association, 1955.
10. HUMPHREVILLE, FRANCES T. "A Teachers' Handbook for Teaching Retarded Readers in High School." Unpublished doctoral project. New York: Teachers College, Columbia University, 1952.
11. JOHNSON, ELEANOR M. *Reading Improvement Skilltext.* Columbus, Ohio: Charles E. Merrill Company, 1947.
12. PHELPS, MARGARET E. "The Evolution of a Reading Program in a Special English Class." Unpublished doctoral project. New York: Teachers College, Columbia University, 1955.
13. PORT ARTHUR PUBLIC SCHOOLS. *Development of Reading-Study Skills in Secondary Schools.* Port Arthur, Texas, 1950.
14. QUINN, THOMAS J. "A Reading Program for a Group of 14–17-Year-Old CRMS Pupils in a New York City School." Unpublished doctoral project. New York: Teachers College, Columbia University, 1955.
15. RUSSELL, DAVID, *et al. Reading Aids through the Grades.* New York: Bureau of Publications, Teachers College, Columbia University, 1951.
16. SIMPSON, ELIZABETH. *S.R.A. Better Reading, Book 1, Book 2, Book 3.* Chicago: Science Research Associates, 1951.
17. STRANG, RUTH. *Exploration in Reading Patterns.* Chicago: University of Chicago Press, 1942.
18. STRANG, RUTH; McCULLOUGH, CONSTANCE; and TRAXLER, ARTHUR E. *Problems in the Improvement of Reading* (Revised and Enlarged). New York: McGraw-Hill Book Company, 1955.
19. TULSA PUBLIC SCHOOLS. *Promoting Growth in Reading.* Tulsa, Oklahoma, 1948.
20. WITHROW, DOROTHY. "The Philadelphia Secondary School Reading Program: Small Remedial Reading Classes and Individual Cases." Unpublished doctoral project. New York: Teachers College, Columbia University, 1955.
21. WITTY, PAUL, and BRICKER, HARRY. *Your Child and Radio, TV, Comics and Movies.* Chicago: Science Research Associates, 1952.
22. WITTY, PAUL A., and SIZEMORE, ROBERT A. "Reading the Comics: A Summary of Studies and an Evaluation." *Elementary English*, Vol. XXXI (December, 1954), pp. 501–506; Vol. XXXII (January, 1955), pp. 43–49; Vol. XXXII (February, 1955), pp. 109–114.

HOW TO TEACH READING IN THE
CONTENT FIELDS

SUCCESS IN EVERY SUBJECT, not just in English, social studies, and science, depends more or less on reading. Practice in reading in every subject, to some extent, makes the student a better reader.

Students read for various purposes: To learn more about the world of nature and the world of man, as in science or social studies; to gain proficiency in certain skills, as in music and foreign languages; to learn how to carry out experiments and to make things, as in science laboratories and shops; to enjoy recreational aspects of the subject, as in reading popular articles and stories. Reading in each subject should be part of the total developmental reading program.

There are three special aspects of the teaching of reading in every subject:

1. The general attitude or approach to the kinds of reading required in the subject.

2. The technical or special vocabulary of the subject.

3. Certain specific reading skills needed in the subject, as, for example, the reading of maps in social studies and the reading of directions in shop or science laboratory.

The teacher needs to take the following steps to improve students' reading in any subject:

1. Find out how each student is reading the textbooks and references required in the subject and help him with his specific reading problems.

2. Give the entire class practice and instruction in the reading skills they all need to improve.

3. Divide the class into subgroups according to special reading needs. For example, (a) a group that needs to work on vocabulary, (b) a group that needs practice in seeing relations and sequences of ideas, (c) a group that is lacking in ability to get the thought of a passage, paragraph by paragraph, and needs to study how paragraphs are constructed (see pages 187–193 on grouping).

Many of the procedures already described may be adapted for use in any subject class. In this chapter we shall briefly mention some of the special reading problems of different subjects and give illustrations of procedures used by teachers in these subjects.

Reading in English Classes

Most people think the English teacher should take major responsibility for the improvement of reading in high school. It is better, however, for the English teacher to share responsibility in a program in which every member of the staff contributes to reading improvement. As has already been stated, one kind of reading program does feature the small, special English-remedial class, but, specialized reading instruction should not be set apart from the rest of the school program. Too often reading teachers give instruction in reading skills without using the content of the school curriculum or even of the required English courses. It is sounder to blend the teaching of English with the teaching of reading. Two extremes should be avoided: Neglect of instruction in reading in English classes; and sole responsibility for the improvement of reading delegated to the English teacher.

Finding out how students read

In most school systems reading tests are given to entering high school students. If the school does not have a psychologist to administer and interpret tests, the Cooperative Reading Test (18) may be given by the English Department early in the fall. This test is available in four forms and on two levels — C_1 for junior and senior high schools and C_2 for upper high school grades and college. Each test contains two parts, vocabulary and reading, and yields scores for vocabulary, speed of comprehension, and level of comprehension, as well as a total score. The total working time for the test is forty minutes. This test is especially suitable for English classes because it includes more items on literary appreciation than most standardized reading tests. If the students' test results are to be compared with the test norms — the average scores of students in other schools — the test must be given according to directions. The test manual and scoring key give detailed directions for administering and scoring the test.

Too frequently the results of these tests are never given to the subject teachers who could make the most use of them. Every teacher should at least have the total score and the subtest scores for each of the students in his classes. If the students' names are arranged in order from the highest score to the lowest score in the class, the teacher can see at a glance which students are capable of doing a great deal of independent reading and which need instruction and practice in basic reading skills. Scores for each subtest will give him even more information on specific weaknesses of each student, such as vocabulary or comprehension. This list of scores will also show at a glance the general distribution of reading ability and suggest a basis for grouping students within the class.

Further study of each student's answers to the test exercises will yield more information about the kinds of errors he made. In addition, an interview with him shortly after he has taken the test might uncover reasons why he made certain errors — carelessness in marking the exercises, lack of knowledge of key words, a tendency to jump to conclusions or to generalize from insufficient data, emotional associations that interfered with correct interpretation, or many other possible explanations. Going over each student's test paper with him in a personal conference while the other students are reading independently is a rewarding experience for both teacher and student.

On the basis of this initial understanding of the reading ability of each student, the teacher is better able to plan instruction in reading and to provide appropriate reading materials.

Sectioning English classes

Sectioning English classes according to students' reading ability is one way to make the teaching of literature a little easier. The usual way of doing this is by using a standardized reading test (such as the Diagnostic Reading Tests: Survey Section, or the Reading Comprehension: Cooperative English Test, C_1) administered in the ninth or tenth grades to give an initial idea of students' reading levels. Although these sections would be far from homogeneous, more appropriate reading material and methods of instruction could be provided than if the range of reading ability were wide.

According to this plan all sections would become acquainted with the literature considered appropriate for the grade. Variations, however, would be made in methods of teaching. The poor readers would gain most of their appreciation of the literature from dramatizations and films and from hearing parts of the stories or plays read by the teacher, by students who had practiced until they could read them well, or by professional readers on records. For example, one class dramatized key scenes from *Silas Marner*, such as the scene in which Silas Marner discovers that his gold has been stolen. One of the best readers in the class read the narrative part, after he had practiced reading it aloud, while a poor reader, with considerable dramatic skill acted out in pantomime the part of the poor distraught man. Another class in which two of Shakespeare's plays were required reading first read the story of the plays in *Lamb's Tales from Shakespeare*, either in the original or in a form simplified by the teacher, and then listened to records of certain scenes recorded by superb actors. (A list of "Recordings for Teaching Literature and Language in the High School" has been prepared by Arno Jewett (42).) The able learners in the same grade would be given instruction in higher levels of appreciation and would read and discuss related works of literature. Many of the reading procedures already described in Chapter IV are used in these special English classes.

All sections would give attention to all the language arts — listening, writing, speaking, reading — as a unified process. For example, reading a novel or short story might naturally lead to conversation about it or to writing a review to acquaint others with it. Some analysis of sentence structure and the part played by different parts of speech might be necessary for a comprehension of difficult passages, and key words in the passage would have to be spelled correctly in written compositions.

The amount and kind of emphasis given to instruction in reading skills would vary with the students' ability. The lowest section would probably need considerable instruction in word recognition skills, in sentence and paragraph reading. The best readers would probably need instruction in judicious selection of significant parts of the passage, in critical reading and interpretation.

Within a class, students in St. Louis work individually and in small groups on what they need to learn.

Teaching special
English classes

There are advantages in the small special English class scheduled for seriously retarded readers who have potentialities for improvement. The stigma of "remedial" is not attached to these classes. The students are not taken out of other regular classes for instruction in reading. They get credit for English, become acquainted with the content of the books required in regular English classes, and may go on to next year's English class, if they have improved sufficiently in reading. The smaller size of class and a teacher who understands students and their reading problems create conditions conducive to learning. For all but the most seriously retarded readers the trend seems, quite rightly, to be in the direction of these small English classes instead of remedial reading classes required in addition to the student's regular program.

Students in the special English classes are usually selected on the combined basis of reading score checked by intelligence test score, teachers' recommendations, and the student's own recognition of his need. A few of these students in junior or senior high school may be non-readers; they should be given extra instruction individually or in groups of four or five. More will be able to read books of only third- or fourth-grade difficulty. The rest will probably have trouble in reading most kinds of material beyond fifth- or sixth-grade level of difficulty. Since these retarded readers need more guidance and individualized instruction than the average student, they are usually placed in smaller classes of twenty or less. This type of special English class has been admirably described in detail and evaluated by Phelps (63) and by Withrow (88).

The reading instruction given in the special English classes will vary with the needs of the group and with the responsibility that other teachers are taking for reading. Probably most of the students in this group will need help on general study habits, such as budgeting sufficient time for study in a well-balanced schedule, taking effective notes, and learning to concentrate and prepare for and take the kind of examinations different teachers give. Some will also profit from instruction in word recognition skills, in how to read and write paragraphs, in how to adjust their reading methods for different purposes, and in how to quickly appraise a book to determine the best method of reading it.

In developing these reading and study skills the teacher will use various methods. Before beginning to read a novel, a play, or poetry, he may reinforce his instruction and the class discussion by showing a film such as the Coronet films (see Appendix, page 347) on how to read these kinds of literature. He may use various exercises in practice books (see Appendix, pages 348–350) to increase proficiency in a particular skill and to give objective evidence of mastery. Most frequently he will teach any of the reading skills as the students, individually or in small groups, feel the need for them.

All of these communication skills fit into a total pattern of meaningful reading. Let us assume that the entire class should obtain some appreciation of Charles Dickens's *A Tale of Two Cities.* A film might be used first to arouse interest and to give background. The Coronet film on the life and times of Charles Dickens or a radio script of the play, as presented by Maurice Evans, might be obtained. Copies of the simplified version of the book (20) with pictures taken from the motion picture film should be available for members of the class who would find the original too frustrating.

Before beginning to read the book unfamiliar words from the book may be studied in context, using various word recognition skills; students may make some of the key words into games or picture dictionaries. The study of some typical paragraphs would also make the initial reading easier and consequently more enjoyable. When the class begins to read the book, the teacher should spend time in helping students to find character clews and to relate their understanding of persons and events to their own lives.

Various projects might grow out of their reading of the book. Some students might try to visualize certain of the vividly described scenes and draw or paint a mural of them for the classroom. Other students may work together in writing scenes or a radio script to dramatize the entire story. All might write a review which they think would interest the next class in the story. The best of these reviews would be saved and read to motivate next year's class. One class became greatly interested in making a newspaper, supposed to have been printed during the French Revolution. They included events in the story written as news items.

These and other activities offer many opportunities to improve students' communication skills. In their writing, they would have to give attention to correct spelling and language uses. In their discussion of the characters and why they behaved as they did, some preliminary instruction in speaking could be given. These are just a few ways in which instruction in reading and other communication skills may grow out of common class experiences (63, 88).

There would also be opportunity in such a unit for individual work — more practice in word recognition and basic comprehension skills if needed, voluntary reading of other books by or about Dickens or about the French Revolution, the making of reading games or film strips, or other experiences of special interest or value to individuals.

If other teachers are giving little instruction in the reading of their subject, the teacher of the special English class may spend some of his period in helping students to read books in other subjects. It is better, though, if the teachers of each department work out materials and methods for developing reading skills needed for success in their own subjects.

One period each week, usually on Friday, is profitably devoted to free reading and discussion of the books chosen. To be most successful, three conditions must be met: books appropriate in interest and reading difficulty must be available; the teacher or librarian must know the interests and reading ability of each student in order to guide his choice of reading; and the student must get satisfaction in his reading and use it in discussion, conversation, or just as a good way of spending leisure time. As a student listens to others' expression of enjoyment in a wide variety of reading material, he will expand his interests. Instead of reading one author or one kind of book exclusively, he will become interested in a wider range of books and articles. He may adventure into biography, travel, historical novels, popular science, plays, or poetry.

Individualizing instruction

In a small high school, where there is only one class in English at each grade level, there may still be a wide range of reading ability. Then it is necessary to do whatever grouping and individualizing of instruction is possible within the class. Some ways of individualizing instruction have already been described (see Chapter 4).

Instruction should be individualized in any class or special reading group; there is no truly homogeneous group. Some of the ways of getting to know individual students and provide the experiences they need may be summarized as follows:

1. Flexible, varied subgrouping within a class.

2. Giving different assignments and asking different questions on the same reading selection. For example, in reading a short story, the less able learners may do well just to get the main idea of the story. Others will be able to trace the sequence of events in the plot. More able learners will find clews to character development and relate motives suggested by the author to the behavior of the characters. The gifted will be able to do even more subtle aspects of interpretation and engage in creative activities growing out of the reading.

3. Giving individual instruction particularly needed by an individual, while the class as a whole is reading independently or working in small groups. Giving practice exercises to be done alone or arranging for games to be played in pairs or small groups.

4. Guiding individuals as an intrinsic part of teaching. For example,

one teacher called on a very poor reader who was foreign born to give the correct pronunciation of certain places in his native country, about which the class was reading. Being considered an authority in this respect increased his self-esteem. As a result of his increased self-confidence, he was able to put forth more effort in learning to read. In another class, the teacher, instead of saying "wrong," when a pupil said a museum was a place where fish are kept, asked him where he got that idea. The pupil said, "Well, I went to a museum and I saw the skeleton of a whale there." "Yes," said the teacher, "you do find the skeletons of fish sometimes in museums, but the place where live fish are kept is called an aquarium." By staying with the student, the teacher helped him to relate word meaning to his experience and thus make his understanding of the words more precise and adequate.

5. Providing a wide range of reading material and guiding individuals in their choices of reading matter.

6. Encouraging projects that enable all members of the class to participate according to their ability. In writing and giving a dramatized reading of a play, for example, the poorest readers may take minor parts. Even though they have only a few lines to read, they enjoy being in the play with the others and will practice so they can read their parts well.

7. Stimulating all individuals in the group to describe concretely and tell others about the methods they have found most effective for reading literature of different kinds.

8. Encouraging students to keep a simple progress report of their reading — the new words they have learned, the books they have read, the skills in which they have improved. "Nothing succeeds like observed success."

Effective individualization of instruction in reading depends on:

1. Knowing how each student reads and if and why he is having difficulty.

2. Giving him the experiences he needs to improve.

3. Helping him to get satisfaction and enjoyment from the content of the books and articles he reads and from evidences of his progress.

**Approaching different
kinds of literature**

Some of the instruction in English classes will be for the purpose of showing pupils how to read different kinds of literature, each of which needs to be approached in a somewhat different way. The way in which a piece of literature is introduced makes a difference. Students need to know whether a particular selection is intended to be serious or humorous, to be purely enjoyable or to serve as a spur to action. The short story is a dramatic episode that can be grasped in one sitting. A novel, on the other hand, requires the reader to keep the various strands of plot and character development in mind while reading the entire story. Reading a play requires visualizing the stage and interpreting the characters largely by what they say. Poetry necessitates reading beyond the lines to catch the meaning implied by a few "winged words." Essays require a knowledge of type and purpose.

The novel. Initial instruction in how to read a novel may be introduced by asking students to share their previous experience in reading novels. The following discussion questions help to guide students in understanding some of the characteristics of the novel.

1. Someone has said that every person, from his own life experiences, could write a novel. If you were to write a novel, what characters would you include? What events would you describe? What understanding do you have of how these persons were able to change the course of events and how they were changed *by* the events?

2. How is the action in a novel different from the quick action of radio and TV? What is the advantage of the slower development of ideas and characters which occurs in the novel? Have you sometimes been disappointed in a movie or play based on a novel you had read? Did you like your own imagination of the persons and places better on the whole? Or, did the play or movie make your reading of the novel still more vivid?

3. Which shows better cause and effect relations — the novel or radio and TV? Why?

4. How do you choose the novels you read? What makes you decide to read a particular novel? (40, p. 3)

After some discussion of this kind, the group will profit by raising questions about how to read a novel and then seeing the short Coronet Instructional Film on the subject. Following the film the discussion might include questions such as:

1. All the characters in a great novel have some good and some poor qualities. The most exciting part of reading a novel is to get clues of character development. What did the characters in Silas Marner think of each other? How did they affect one another? How did their thought affect and explain their actions?

2. After you read a novel, how do you decide whether it is good or poor? Has your imagination been stimulated? Is the story true to life as you know it? Or, does it give a distorted, unrealistic view of life? Has it made clearer your own experience? Has it helped you to look at persons and situations in your own life in a different way? (40, p. 3)

Drama. Plays require more reading between the lines than novels. There are no detailed descriptions of scenery, only a few stage directions.

There are no descriptions of the personality of the characters; this must be inferred by the reader from the character's words and actions. The reader of plays must use his imagination and picture the play as it might be produced on the stage. The following are some discussion questions and projects that might be used in helping students to learn to read plays:

1. What kind of character clues can you get from the dialogue? Give examples from plays you have read. How are individual characters revealed? What do they think? How do they feel? Why do they act as they do?

2. Have you ever read a play before you have seen it? Were you pleased or disappointed with the stage performance? Why?

3. What are some of the differences between reading a play and reading a novel? Which gives more exercise to the imagination?

4. What are some of the advantages of looking at television plays or listening to radio plays over the reading of plays? What are some of the advantages of reading plays over seeing them on the stage?

5. Why are some plays that were written long ago of interest to us today?

6. It has been said, "A plot is a sequence of events working out a conflict." Can you illustrate this from some play you have read?

7. What are some of the kinds of body movement that convey ideas or emotion, such as a turn of the head, lifting of the eyebrows, etc.?

8. How will this film [*How to Read Plays*, Coronet Instructional Films] help you in the reading of a play?

9. What has been your attitude toward reading plays? What difficulties have you met? How do you usually read a play?

10. Why do different actors give different interpretations to the same character?

11. Which do you think to be most important in a play: the setting, the characters, or the action (what happens to the characters)? (40, p. 2)

Poetry. Poetry requires still more imagination and reading between the lines and beyond the lines; it leaves much unsaid. The reader translates verses into poetry. Students are helped in their interpretation of poetry by knowing something about the poet, by trying to share with him the experiences and feelings he is presenting, and by understanding how he uses comparison and contrast, rhythm, and sound of words to create the impression he wishes to convey. The following are discussion questions and projects useful in guiding students' reading of poetry:

1. Which of the poems quoted in the film [*How to Read Poetry*, Coronet Instructional Films] did you like best? Why?

2. At the beginning of the film, one boy is enjoying poetry more than the others. Why did it mean more to him?

3. How did Poe's personality affect his poetry?

4. How does knowing something about a poet help us understand his poetry?

5. What did Thoreau mean when he said of Walden Pond, "I am its stony shore, and the breeze that passes o'er"? Is there any place that you have ever felt a part of?

6. The film says that poets "share their experience" with us. What does this phrase mean to you? Do they do more than share their experience?

7. What are some of the poetic devices mentioned in the film?

8. Which poem do you think made the most striking use of rhythm?

9. How did Southey in the poem beginning, "How does the water come down from Lodore," * achieve the effects of the motion of a mountain stream in the poem?

10. From hearing *High Flight* how would you describe the feelings of the poet toward flying? What did you like most about the poem? By what poetic devices did the poet achieve an effect of freedom and exhilaration? Do you think you would have known without being told that *High Flight* was written by a young man? How?

11. Do you enjoy reading poetry aloud more than silently? Why is this so?

12. Do you think we find out something about ourselves from reading poetry? Have you ever discovered that a poet has said something that you have felt but have not been able to put into words? (40, p. 4)

Essays. Essays are of many different types and require preliminary consideration of the author's mood, intent, and purpose in writing the essay. Knowing this will guide the reader in his method of approaching each type of essay. In reading one of Burke's historical essays, he will have a mind set to follow the logical sequence presented. In reading an informal essay, he will relax and be prepared to share the author's casual thoughts and feelings. If the essay is a humorous one, the reader will anticipate being amused.

Using films and recordings. If films on how to read different kinds of literature are available, they will reinforce and make more vivid the teacher's instruction. The showing of the film should be preceded by a sharing of previous experience and followed by discussion and immediate application. For example, the film *How to Read Novels* (see Appendix, page 347) was shown to a ninth-grade class just before they read their first novel — Cooper's *The Deerslayer.* The teacher reported later that she had never before had such good comprehension and appreciation of the first novel read in her class. Other films may be used to enrich the students' background for reading a particular piece of literature, as, for example, the Coronet film showing the Scottish scenery which was the setting for Scott's *The Lady of the Lake.* Some of the unusual words used in this poem were also pictured in the film. Recordings of selections from great literature read by speech experts, famous actors or actresses,

---

* "The Cataract of Lodore" in *Poems by Robert Southey,* edited by Maurice H. Fitzgerald, p. 348. London: Oxford University Press, 1909.

Round table reading of poetry to develop skills of interpretation and appreciation.

or by the writers themselves add emotional meaning to the students' own reading of the selection.

Vocabulary difficulties

There are also special vocabulary difficulties connected with the teaching of literature. Figures of speech require special study. With what is the person or thing compared? "Shall I compare thee to a summer's day?" What are some of the characteristics of a summer's day? With which of these might the poet be comparing the lovely girl about whom he is writing? Sometimes the comparison is not openly stated. "She was ready to fly" might not mean she had boarded an airplane. It might mean she was so harassed or disturbed that she had only one thought — to get away from it all. In reading figures of speech it is necessary to imagine how the person to whom the figure of speech is applied might feel and to think of the characteristics of the thing to which he is compared. Sometimes, too, it is helpful to think of the usual meaning of the comparison.

Sometimes dialect in literature causes difficulty. The dialect may be a short form of words you already know. Or it may be peculiar to a region and have to be learned like a foreign language.

Unless the student knows the history of certain literary allusions, he will miss the meaning of the passage. For example, "He's a Jonah" would not be understood by a person who did not know the Bible story of Jonah and the whale. When selections from the Bible, mythology, and other frequently quoted literary sources are included in the English course of study, they have double value — the value inherent in the selections themselves and their future usefulness in helping the reader to interpret allusions in other books.

Examples of procedures

Systematic study of spelling and vocabulary. English teachers are sometimes confronted with classes that are deficient in the most fundamental spelling, reading, and writing skills. In such situations the English teacher may be the only person in the school who can teach this remedial work. Consequently, he devotes time not only to individualized instruction, but also to practice with the whole class, if the problem is common to all. Such basic instruction in spelling and vocabulary was given in one exceedingly heterogeneous class, where the students represented a wide range of background, mental ability, reading ability, and personalities. First the whole group took a simple spelling test to determine their present spelling level. Then they all worked as a friendly group on their individual levels.

This group used a variety of approaches to word knowledge. In addition to the constant attention given to words in context in the stories or articles they were reading, they worked on

1. their spelling files, correlated with grammar, syllabication, and word meaning (see Chapter 1)

2. vocabulary study of descriptive words derived from pictures, synonym lists, and words encountered in their reading

3. Bingo games using words, plots of stories, and characters.

The instruction was definite and the practice systematic. They clearly saw evidence of progress in their individual spelling files and vocabulary cards showing words they had mastered and in the 100% written on tests in which they had made no errors. As a result, these students felt a sense of confidence in their ability to learn and a mastery that many of them had never before experienced. The same group became familiar with what prefixes do to words by exercises such as the following:

Prefixes which mean "the opposite" or "not" are *im–, un–, dis–, il–, in–, mis–,* and *ir–.* Change the meanings of the following words by adding one of the above prefixes:

regular	continue	probable
legal	prove	understand
agree	legible	active
capable	happy	logical
possible		

Words may be changed to mean "a person" or "one who" by adding the suffixes *–er, –or, –ist,* or *–ian.* Change the following words so that they will mean "a person" or "one who" does a certain thing:

sail	build	manage	library
science	magic	music	senate
act	buy	piano	humor
speak	electric	history	profess

Variety in word study. Word study on a higher level was introduced in a class of able learners who were performing far below their mental potentialities. "Words, words, words!" How to interpret them, how to use them, how to become interested in them — this can be taught in various ways by English teachers. On a reserved space on the blackboard, one teacher wrote quotations such as the Chinese proverb, "A thousand-mile journey starts off with a single step." The students expressed these sayings in their own words, often writing several paragraphs to explain and illustrate the meaning.

Another teacher stimulated a high school class of superior students to describe a piece of music, an experience such as watching people in a subway or on the street, or some aspect of nature such as the light of the late afternoon sun in the woods or on the distant rows of city houses. One student said about this teacher who in many unusual ways encouraged creative expression:

> It probably was mere showmanship, but he got my interest thru his use of a portable victrola. He played the "Poet and Peasant Overture" over and over until our class had filled a blackboard space with words we connected with the music. I have never liked the overture since, but that was the day words first became fascinating (66, p. 551).

Teaching interpretation and appreciation. There is a still higher level of creative reading and appreciation. Instead of merely getting a thrill from the bare plot and action of a story, students may learn to appreciate an author's skill and to experience the emotion he has aroused through his writing. They may learn to recognize hidden meanings and subtle character clews and gain an understanding of "why we behave like human beings."

This higher level of appreciation is not acquired easily or suddenly. A gradation of materials is necessary — first stories where the main interest is in action, adventure, suspense; then stories in which character development plays an important part. From these, the pupils may move to stories of mood and social problems.

Gainsberg (30) gave the following suggestions for teaching students to become more proficient in creative reading of literature:

1. Introduce them to one type of clew at a time, and help them to make appropriate inferences from it.

2. Organize clews into groups — for example, character description.

> Almost every story offers clues of appearance that give hints of character ("shrewd and sharp eyes, but a mouth that curled upward at the corners," "eyes that gleamed coldly under shaggy eyebrows"). There are things *said* to the character, about him, by him. There are his actions. Major actions are easily recognizable, but there are also subtle actions ("his lips tightened," "his chin rose," "he glanced down"). There are ways in which others respond to him (with fear or distrust, or tenderness) (30, p. 24).

3. Develop the following types of appreciational skills:

> a. Making inferences about the feelings and motives of the characters; anticipating what they will do next, and interpreting the meaning of figurative language.
>
> b. Recognizing clues from which inferences may be drawn: conversation by, to, and about a character; his actions, gross and subtle; few but suggestive details; emotional words and connotative expressions; figurative language, especially irony and exaggeration; forebodings;

unusual language style (choppy sentences or telescoping of events to show haste); sentence inversion for word emphasis (30, p. 25).

Each of these clews, one by one, should be brought to the attention of the students. They will first look for them, as a class exercise, in the stories or plays they are reading. The teacher raises questions that rouse curiosity and eagerness to find the answers. Clews given by the author as to the mood of the story and the feelings and motives of the characters often need to be pointed out to students at first. Later the students will recognize these clews themselves as they read selections silently.

> The teacher who learns this technique will find her class more excited and more enthusiastic about such reading than ever before. The taste of *complete* understanding and of mental responses never made before is a thrilling experience to them. The added understandings are well worth the time they take (30, p. 25).

Children and young people have many personal reasons for reading a selection. They will appreciate it more if they are helped to see its relation to their past experience. If the selection is illustrated, the pictures should be used to guide its interpretation; the creative reading of pictures should be encouraged. Any unusual words or key words necessary for the appreciation of the story may be clarified by means of pictures or shared experiences.

There is no substitute for the teacher's genuine enthusiasm for literature; his own enjoyment of it is contagious. But he does not force his preferences upon his students. He shares his knowledge with them and lets them make their own choices. These choices may be quite different for different classes and for different individuals. The emotional responses of students to a story (73) should be studied as they are reading, instead of relying on their final judgment of the story.

Students also need instruction in following the sequence of events, in grasping the author's pattern or structure, in distinguishing between fact and opinion, between real and make-believe. Asking the student to predict outcomes is one way of checking his interpretation, the soundness of the inferences he derives from various kinds of clews, and his ability to read between the lines. Some time should also be spent in interpreting figures of speech and creating mental pictures of scenes and characters suggested by the words. Reading of this kind develops imagination, which is in danger of being impaired by much viewing of television and motion pictures.

Creative reading often leads to other forms of creative expression such as drawing illustrations for the story, making a radio script of it, writing and giving a play or puppet show, telling the story to an audience, adding another chapter or modifying the last chapter.

Creative reading contributes to child and adolescent development in many ways. The sheer enjoyment derived from such reading should not be minimized. Too often students view reading as drudgery. Literature broadens horizons, stimulates the imagination, gives understanding of oneself and others and the world in which we live. It may contribute also to the solving of personal problems.

Using simplified reading material. For students who cannot attain these higher levels of appreciation, other reading material and methods of instruction should be provided. One ninth-grade class that was "all in a fog" attempting to read the prescribed course of study began by reading short accounts of their own exciting or amusing adventures, which they first gave orally and later had transcribed. Another teacher provided copies of simplified modern stories (76) for high school students who were reading around fifth- and sixth-grade level. Small groups planned dramatized readings of their favorite stories. They all read the story silently, chose parts, and practiced reading their parts aloud. When they had learned to read them well, the better readers helping the poorer readers, each group presented their dramatized reading to the whole class. These stories proved so popular that the superior readers wanted to read them, too. Thus any embarrassment on the part of the poor readers from having books different from the rest of the class was avoided. Every English teacher should try to secure for his classroom books covering a wide range of interests and reading difficulty. (See Appendix, pages 350–354.) From this collection students, with the guidance of the teacher, can individually choose the books most appropriate for them.

During free reading periods, when the students are preparing dramatized readings or are independently reading books that they can comprehend without too great difficulty, the teacher can have conferences with individual students. These are important for several purposes: establishing a personal relationship; learning more about the student's interests, reading difficulties, and habits; giving specific instruction; and suggesting practice needed and books that would contribute more to the students' personal development.

As in every class, the English teacher can help students improve their reading through class experiences, through subgroups within the large class, through differentiated assignments, and through appropriate methods.

Reading in the Social Studies

The aim of social studies is to see how the present came from the past and how it may guide us in making a better future. To accomplish this aim, many reading skills are necessary. Perhaps in no other subject is comprehension such a complicated and involved process. Students need instruction and practice in understanding the language and seeing cause-and-effect relations in their basic textbook. In reading historical documents, newspapers, and magazines they need to acquire skill in distinguishing fact from opinion and in judging the authenticity of sources. In reading autobiographies, historical novels, and travel books, they should have some historical background to appreciate the persons and places and times portrayed. The reading of maps, too, is a specialized aspect of reading in the social studies. It involves acquaintance with different kinds of maps and the kind of information that may be obtained from each kind. It is also necessary to note the scale to which the map is drawn, to know the significance of symbols used, and to understand latitude and longitude. To apply the knowledge gained from the map to the particular problem on which they are working likewise requires special skill.

Reading skills necessary

Shepherd (70) listed the following skills which he found to be needed:

1. ability to read for a purpose
2. skill in using parts of a book
3. skill in locating and using various sources of information
4. ability to understand and use correctly the key words and concepts essential to the social studies
5. ability to gain accurate information from maps, graphs, charts, diagrams, and pictures and to relate it to other sources of information
6. ability to note the main ideas
7. ability to identify supporting details
8. ability to organize the ideas gained from reading, to recognize relationships and sequences of events
9. ability to read critically — to interpret the reading passage, to make appraisals of it, and to draw conclusions from it
10. ability to recognize propaganda
11. ability to apply what is read to certain current problems of the individual and of society
12. desire to read widely, both for pleasure and for information (70, p. 102)

Of these reading skills, several deserve special emphasis: Reading to recognize relations between and sequences of events, critical reading, and understanding of the key words and concepts in the social studies. Organizing and relating facts gained from reading is an aid to understanding and remembering. Without this ability to make significant groupings, the myriad ideas and details are meaningless. One student expressed his appreciation of the instruction in organizing the facts read by saying, "Yes, grouping them as we did makes them easier to remember. Also, the discussion we had about each one helps."

Use of informal tests

As in teaching reading in other subjects, the first step is to find out what students get out of the textbooks they are expected to read. With a relatively small expenditure of time, the teacher may construct, administer, and study the results of an informal test in his subject. He will select a passage from a book the students will be using and construct two kinds of questions: A free response to a general question such as "What did the author say?" and objective-type exercises to test the students' comprehension of the main ideas, significant details, key words, inferences, and generalizations. The free response will show better than any other testing device how the student organizes ideas as he reads and whether he can grasp and communicate in writing the author's pattern of thought. On the next page is an example of a teacher-constructed test exercise based on the social studies text (46) the class was using.

If all the students have the text, the selection need not be mimeographed; they can just be asked to turn to the proper page and begin reading when the signal is given. The teacher notes on the blackboard the seconds in five-second intervals as they pass so that each student as soon as he finishes reading the passage may see how long he has taken.

To relieve the teacher of scoring this test — which is a teaching more than a testing device — and also to give students instruction in how to read this kind of social studies text, the students may exchange papers and correct and discuss the answers in class. Several may read the answers to the first question and determine a rating from 1 to 10 based on criteria which they will set up. Among the points they will include as a basis for scoring are:

Inclusion of all the main ideas.

Relation or sequence of ideas shown.

Significant supporting details given.

Ideas reported accurately.

Conclusions or generalizations correctly stated.

According to such criteria, a response that consisted of a few scattered details, some of them inaccurate, would be rated *1*, while a well-organized pattern of the author's thought including accurately all the main ideas and some of the supporting details, would be rated *10*. In discussing the reasons for their ratings, students will gain appreciation of what constitutes effective comprehension of social studies material. By asking those who achieved a high quality of comprehension to describe their methods, other students will be helped to improve their reading procedures. Students often learn more easily from directions given by fellow students than from instruction given in the teacher's words.

Practice in Reading History

Name ___Mary Johnson___ Grade _10_ Age _15_

Date _May 16, 1956_ Section _10 B_ Boy _____ Girl _✓_

Directions:

When the signal to begin is given, read the following pages from a history book in the way in which you usually read similar historical material. As soon as you have finished reading, look at the board and write on the blank, Time, the figure you see on the board, which is the number of seconds you have spent in reading the selection up to that moment.

Turn to the next page and answer all the questions on the following pages.

REMEMBER, ONCE YOU TURN THE PAGE TO WRITE THE ANSWERS YOU ARE NOT TO TURN BACK TO READ OVER ANY PART OF THE SELECTION.

The title of the selection is:

New Classes Form in Towns of Western Europe

In the Middle Ages the cities of Europe were not large compared to modern cities or even compared to medieval China. The typical inland town of England, Germany, or France had but a few thousand inhabitants. It was enclosed by a stone wall or a stockade built on a rampart of closely packed earth. After dark the city gates were locked and closely guarded. When they were flung open at daybreak, many citizens left the cities to labor on their near-by farms. During the Age of Knights farming still occupied so many townsmen that even in London, the largest city of England, the law court ceased to meet at harvest time.

Within the walls, rows of wooden houses over-
hung crooked streets. Pigs wandering loose found
good feeding in the garbage and waste, which piled
up in the streets until some town official made a
fuss and had it carted away to be dumped into the
river. Under these conditions the water was so
dangerous that the rich rarely drank it, and the
poor bought beer or wine, if they possibly could.
Drunkenness and dirt were the twin evils of
medieval towns.

Taverns were only one of the attractions which
drew men and women to the towns from the countryside.
Crowds at play or work gave a never-ending variety
to town life. The cries of men hawking meat, honey,
or onions mingled with the shouts of old and young
watching a cock-fight or a football game on the vil-
lage green. Before the stone church which towered
above the thatched roofs a holy festival might draw
the respectful attention of the people.

The heart of the town was the market place,
for without a market the town would die. Though
some townsmen had farms outside the walls, most of
them depended on food brought from near-by manors.
Every town took care to insure its food supply,
and frowned on dealers who tried to buy grain in
order to haul it off to a town where the price was
higher.

The narrow streets leading to the market place
were lined with shops where the country people came
to buy and where the townsmen bought from each other.
Shoemakers, ironsmiths, hatters, glovers, and tailors
did their work in full view of the passers-by, ready
to stop work and sell to customers. The shop was
usually the ground floor of the craftsman's house.
Opening on the street was a glassless window, closed
up at night by a wooden shutter which was swung back
on its hinges in the morning to form a counter.

Though the transaction of business seemed open
and aboveboard, the purchaser did well to be wary.
Bakers, whose business was taking the housewife's
dough and baking it into bread, sometimes had a tiny
trap door in their counter. While the baker kneaded
the dough on the counter, a small boy might be steal-
ing parts of it through the trap door. If the baker
was caught, he would be fined for his trick by his

guild. But such a trick was only one of many that
some tradespeople practiced on their customers.

Every craftsman and shopkeeper had to join and
be subject to some guild. At first only the merchants ruled all the economic life of the town but,
as the town grew, separate guilds distinct from
the merchant guild were organized for each craft.
These craft guilds embraced all the men engaged in
one special line -- the leather workers in one guild,
the carpenters in another, the smiths in a third,
and so on. Each craft guild maintained a monopoly
in its field and thus was able to regulate the
quality of the products made by its members. For
example, the weavers' guild specified the proper
width for cloth and forbade the dishonest trick of
stretching it. Most of the guilds prohibited night
work because it lowered standards of workmanship.
The members also attempted to prevent any one master
from getting so much of the business that the others
would be at his mercy. The ability of the guilds
to maintain standards and regulate working conditions
gave the workers a feeling of independence and of
pride in their craft.

Boys and young men learning a trade knew that
the craft guild regulated their training. Instead
of vocational schools, such as we have, they had
the apprentice system. When they were six to ten
years old, boys were placed under some master in
the guild, to live with him, clean his tools, prepare materials for him, sit beside him, and so learn
how the work was done. Most boys were apprenticed
to their own fathers, for both fathers and sons took
pride in a family's reputation for skill. But if a
son of a butcher, for example, had a strong bent
toward carpentry, his family would make a contract
of apprenticeship with some master in the carpenters'
guild. In such a contract, the master promised to
feed the apprentice well, to teach him the craft,
and to teach him also to live honestly and as a good
Christian.

At about eighteen, after serving as apprentice
for the number of years required by his guild, and
after giving some proof of his skill to the committee of examiners from the guild, the youth became a
journey-man. He could then move about and select
the master with whom he wished to work. Unmarried
journeymen were likely to board with the master, but
they were paid wages, for they had learned enough to
make their services of real value.

When a journeyman married and set up housekeeping in a home of his own, he naturally wanted to have his own shop, usually in some part of his dwelling, and to take as apprentices his own sons at least. Generally, the guilds required that before a man became a master he had to do a special piece of work, the masterpiece, as proof of his skill. On this point some guilds adopted a selfish, narrow policy. They required from everyone except their own sons a masterpiece which was extremely difficult. The guild masters could thus make their craft a monopoly of their families. Craftsmen aided themselves in many ways through their guilds. Often the craft guilds were represented in the town government, and the townsmen were organized by guilds into military companies for the defense of the city. Guilds built special chapels for their members, maintained private burial grounds, and collected funds to be used for accident, health, and old age insurance. They guided the medieval craftsman from his youth to his grave, overseeing his education as an apprentice, regulating his labor as a master, caring for him in sickness and misfortune, and holding services for his soul when he died.

The larger the town, the more different kinds of craftsmen and craft guilds it was likely to contain. In a small town, a craftsman skilled in leatherwork might have to tan his own leather and to make a number of articles such as gloves, harness, and shoes. Otherwise he would not have enough employment to make a living. In the large towns, workers could specialize, one tanning the leather, another making the shoes, and so on. Such a division of labor enabled craftsmen to increase their skill and the amount they could produce. Nevertheless, division of labor was practical only where there were enough customers to keep each craftsman employed at his specialty.

A still further specialization among the craftsmen was possible when merchants widened the market for their wares by finding customers in distant cities. This happened increasingly during the Later Middle Ages (1300 A.D. to 1500 A.D.). Many craftsmen then ceased to buy and sell for themselves through the windows of their shops. Instead they were employed by the merchants who shipped the wares. Under an arrangement known as the "putting-out system" the merchant-employer bought the raw

material -- wool, for example -- and "put-it-out"
to one group of craftsmen to be spun, then to
another to be woven, and then to another to be
dyed. The craftsmen were then dependent on the
merchants for employment, and became wage earners
having nothing to sell but their skill.

Craftsmen who worked as wage earners for merchant-
employers helped create the wealth of the few large
cities in medieval Europe. The Italian city of
Florence, with a population of about a hundred thous-
and in 1300 A.D., was one of the biggest cities in
Europe. Cities stayed small, for plagues kept down
the size of medieval towns. When the population of
Florence rose to one hundred and twenty thousand,
two-thirds of its citizens were swept away by the
terrible Black Death of 1347 A.D. to 1348 A.D., the
most death-dealing of medieval plagues. Yet Florence
recovered its prosperity and remained rich and beautiful. No pigs roamed the streets, and its handsome
squares were faced by the stone palaces of wealthy
merchants. Behind the grated windows of these palaces, merchants thumbed the ledgers containing records of wool imported from England, put out to
Florentine craftsmen to be manufactured, and then
shipped to Constantinople, Syria, or even back to
England.

Another source of wealth in Florence was banking.
In large towns there were many men willing to deposit
money with a respected merchant in the confidence
that they could get it back, perhaps with interest,
when and where they wanted it. The merchants who
accepted such deposits, and became bankers, had all
the more money to invest in their own commercial
enterprises. They could also make loans and arrange
payments for other people.

Time *560*

As soon as you finish reading the selection, put after the

word Time the figure you see on the board. That figure

tells how many seconds you have spent in reading the selec-

tion.

Answer the following questions without looking again
at the article:

Part I

A. What did the author say about life in towns in the Middle Ages?

They were not large and there was only a few thousand inhabitants. The houses were wooden and built over narrow winding streets. Pigs went around and garbage was over the streets until someone complained and it was taken and put into the river. Couldn't drink water 'cause it was unhethy and so drank wine and beer. Great drunkenness. People from country came into town quite often. Towns attracted them. People sold there wares on the street. They had guilds to help the workers. Young boys were apprenticed.

B. It is important for you to get the main ideas from your
   reading of history. Below are three questions asking for
   main ideas in the selection you have just read. Write
   the answers to these questions clearly and briefly.

   1. In what ways was life in a medieval town different
      from town life today?

Well, they don't have garbage all over the streets. Most everyone isn't a drunk and they don't have there working places in the street.

---

* The responses are reproduced just as one tenth-grade student wrote them.

2. Why were the craft guilds important?

Because they helped to organize working conditions.

3. How did the growth of foreign trade affect craftsmen?

X *   *It helped them.*

C. It is important for you to draw conclusions and make applications of what you have read. Below are four questions of
this kind for you to answer.

1. From your reading of the article, what new social classes
do you think grew up in the Later Middle Ages?

X

2. Do you think most Europeans in the Middle Ages traveled
widely, living in many different places?

No.

3. Do you think most young boys in the Middle Ages were able
to choose their life work from among many kinds of work
they might do?

X   *Yes.*

4. What use can you make of the information you gained from
reading the article?

You can appreaciate what we have in our world of today.

Part II

A. It is important to select and remember the important details
in the history you read. Below are statements of details in

---

* X = incorrect or incomplete response.

the selection you have read. If a statement is true, put a
T on the line before the statement. If a statement is not
true (false) put an F on the line before the statement.

_T_ 1. The typical inland town of medieval England, Germany
        or France had only a few thousand inhabitants.

_T_ 2. The medieval craftsman often made his product and
        sold it in the same shop.

_F_ 3. The Middle Ages were between 347 and 1200 A.D.

_T_ 4. All the workers in one special kind of work in a
        medieval town would belong to the same guild.

X   _T_ 5. The most important duty of the guild was to look after
                the workers' welfare.

_T_ 6. In a small town a craftsman skilled in leatherwork
        might have to tan his own leather and make a number
        of articles such as gloves, harness, and shoes.

_F_ 7. The "putting-out" system made the craftsman more
        independent than he had been before.

X   _T_ 8. The Black Death in 1347 and 1348 A.D. destroyed the
                power of Florence, Italy, as a trading city.

B. It is important to know the exact meaning of the words you
    read. Below are sentences with a word underlined in each.
    Under each sentence are four choices. Put a check in front
    of the best meaning for the underlined word as it is used in
    this passage.

1. "Each craftsman and shopkeeper had to join and be subject
    to some guild."

    ___ a warm bed covering.

    ___ a society for a charitable purpose.

    ___ a social club to which certain classes belonged.

    _✓_ an association for mutual aid and regulation of a
        trade or pursuit.

2. "In such a contract, the master promised to feed the
   <u>apprentice</u> well."

   ✓ boy who learns a trade by working for an experienced
   workman.

   ___ visiting member of the guild.

   ___ low-ranking sailor on ships going between Florence
   and England.

   ___ slave who had to work long hours and received no pay
   or education in return for his labor.

3. "Each craft guild maintained a <u>monopoly</u> in its field."

   ___ best method of production

   ___ airplane having but one wing on each side.

   ✓ exclusive right or control of a business.

   ___ company that possesses the sole right of the production of some article.

4. "In the large towns, workers could <u>specialize</u>, . . ."

   ___ branch out into many kinds of work.

   ✓ concentrate on a particular kind of work.

   ___ enter whatever guild they pleased.

   ___ find work outside their guilds.

5. "Cities stayed small, for <u>plagues</u> kept down the size of
   medieval cities."

   ___ flat, thin pieces of metal or earthenware upon which
   a picture or design is placed.

   ___ high walls around a city.

   ✓ deadly diseases causing sickness and death of many
   people.

   ___ things causing misery.

6. "When they were six to ten years old, boys were placed
   under some <u>master</u> in the guild."

   ___ owner of slaves.

   ___ man who rules or commands others.

_____ man who is learning a trade.

✓ skilled workman of top rank.

7. "An unmarried <u>journeyman</u> was likely to board with the master."

_____ a traveler in many countries.

_____ a worker who had finished service as an apprentice.

✓ a man beginning to learn a trade, who worked with a master without pay.

_____ a man without a wife.

Part III[*]

1. What method or process did you use in reading this account of life in the Middle Ages?

2. What did you do to get the main idea?

Just thought it over and tried to remember.

3. What did you do to get the details?

Tried to remember them by associating them with something.

4. What did you do when you met a word you did not know?

Tried to figure it out from what or how it was used.

5. Do you like to read books of this kind?

Sometimes.

---

[*] Used for class discussion of methods used by readers who showed the best and fastest comprehension.

One day a week at the beginning of the term may well be devoted to this kind of practice in reading — taking the test on the passage selected, scoring and discussing the answers, and sharing their most efficient methods. For several weeks, one section of the daily assignment may be used as an informal test. In this way, students will begin to read their social studies homework much more effectively.

Examples of a similar test on a senior history textbook may be found in the Appendix to Eleanor Peterson's research study (62).

Examples of procedures

Reading newspapers. In accord with the purpose of understanding today's situations, we should expect current events to play an important part in social studies instruction. Many teachers include a unit on "How to Read the Newspaper." In this unit students learn what to expect from different parts of a newspaper — unbiased facts from news stories, main ideas from the headlines, personal opinions from the editorial page.

But as they continue their study, they see that personal opinion may enter into all the news. Certain events may be given a position of importance on the front page of one newspaper and relegated to an insignificant position in another paper. As they study and compare headlines of different papers, they see how the choice of "color" words and slanted statements influences the opinions and attitudes of the reader. They may underline and discuss such words and their effect. For example, one newspaper in reporting the World Health Organization's report on alcoholism wrote this headline: "First Foreshadowing of Alcoholic Addiction — the Blackout." Another newspaper introduced the same report with the headline: "'Happy Glow' to Blackout." These two headlines arouse diverse associations. The first associates alcoholic beverages with *addiction*, usually thought of as *drug addiction*, something to be intensely feared. The second headline associates drunkenness with happiness and a feeling of well-being. The associations formed help to determine how a person perceives a situation, and one's perception of the situation largely determines his behavior. Students can learn to be on their guard against statements designed to distort the facts and influence their judgment by

Reporting only one side of the question.
Appealing to emotion and prejudice.
Using "glittering generalities."
Using names of prominent persons to give prestige.
Implying that "everybody's doing it."
Mixing facts with questionable statements.
Neglecting to give the source of the information.

In analyzing editorials for the soundness of their thinking, effective readers learn to withhold judgment until they have an adequate basis for forming an opinion. They examine all sides of the question. They look at their own reasoning to see if it has been influenced by stereotyped thinking, wishful thinking, singling out one characteristic from others that might just as well have been emphasized. They also learn to avoid premature generalizations and those not based on facts.

Using a documentary approach. In the development of critical reading, Spencer Brown (9) described a documentary technique to encourage students to base their statements on accurate information. Students, on invitation, visited the homes and neighborhoods of varied races, nationalities, and backgrounds represented in the school. They discussed the special contribution that each group could make, being careful to present objective evidence for every statement or generalization they made. They then used the facts which they had verified in writing a play entitled "America Is Only You and Me." Instead of firsthand experience Lillian Hinds, Supervisor of Reading in Euclid, Ohio, used films on the subject. She prepared the following guide for teachers introducing a unit on the Sahara and the Nile:

For class discussion
Teacher: If you were making a film of life on the desert what would you need to know about the desert and the people who live there? What is a desert?

Questions to promote discussion if necessary. . . .
What does the land look like? How much rain is there? How much water? Where? What kind of trees? What grows there? What is winter like? What kind of animals? What kind of house would you live in? Why? What kind of furniture? What kind of fuel used? What kind of cooking facilities? What would you wear? What would you eat? Where would you get your food? How would you get your food? How would your father earn a living?

Name some deserts. _____
Where are they? _____
Are there any deserts in our own country? Today we are going to find answers to questions about the Sahara Desert and about the people who live there; and about the fertile area along the Nile River called the Nile Delta.
Who are some of the people who you think lived or live in these areas? What did they invent that helps you know what month of the year it is? What did they develop that has to do with communication? (What is communication?)

After this preliminary discussion in which the teacher lists questions on the board she says. . . . Look for further answers to the questions we have asked in the films we are about to see. See whether or not you are correct in the ideas you now hold about the Sahara and the Nile.

Films: "How Desert People Live," State Department of Education
"Desert Nomads," State Department of Education

Other desert pictures were also shown with the opaque projector. Many books on Egypt were available for the directed study period. Some of these, such as O'Donnell's *If I Were Going* (pages 325–328, published by Row, Peterson and Company), were on the second- or third-grade levels. Many teachers have found that the documentary approach arouses interest, adds authenticity to the information obtained from books, and leads to a critical attitude toward the printed page (89, p. 6).

Appraising the author. If students are to read critically, they also need to know whether the author is qualified to write on the subject. This skill can be taught. Wide reading in the social studies is sure to confront the student with the contrasting points of view of two or more authors. In one class, the teacher recorded verbatim the following questions raised by one of the students:

> Bill notes two divergent viewpoints: "Say, there's two points of view here. Dave's reference says the League was not strong enough and Doris' reference says the League refused. That indicates, Doris' reference that is, that the League could but didn't. Now which are we to believe? There are two authors and both say something different. Which is right?" (70, p. 71).

One type of assignment suggested in the Nyack Public Schools, New York (59), is, "Who would be better qualified to write a book about the American Civil War — Bruce Catton or Albert Schweitzer?" The students would read about the educational experience and background of these two men in *Current Biography* or some other source to find out the answer to this question. Similarly in reading a news story, they would try to find out the answers to such questions as, "Who is reporting the news story?" "Does he have background for interpreting this kind of news?" "Did he write the account on the spot or from some distant place?"

Students also need instruction and practice, not only in examining the author's qualifications in the field, but also in appraising the information he offers as evidence and the inferences and conclusions he draws from the facts presented.

Clarifying concepts and word meanings. To think critically, students must clarify concepts that are inherent in the subject matter. Shepherd gave this example:

> Many times new reading materials contain concepts that are new to the pupils, and basic to the understanding of the subject matter. Very often a new concept can be vitalized for the pupil through his experiences. The

concept of *constitution* was clarified for the pupils through referring to a use of the word in their experience, the Student Council Constitution. From the discussion of the Student Council Constitution Dick was able to define the word *constitution*. He said: "It is a written paper telling us how our government is set up, with regulations as to powers of our government. And also it would list qualifications for members of the government before they hold office" (70, p. 44).

Shepherd gave further illustrations of how the study of word meanings can be integrated with the teaching of social studies:

Many new vocabulary meanings in the social studies can be clarified for the pupil through some aspect of his experience. Joe illustrated from his personal experience a ready understanding of the word *union* as it applies to labor organization: ". . . I have to pay two dollars and a half every month in union dues because I clerk in the grocery store."

The use of context [is important] in determining the correct meanings of the new vocabulary. It is widely realized that the dictionary is not always at hand, and sometimes it does not seem appropriate to break a train of thought to find the word in the dictionary. Therefore, skill in deducing the meaning of an unknown word from the context is a valuable reading technique. The pupils developed the meaning of the term *social reform* from the context. Loretta read the contextual material illustrating the meaning of the term. When asked how the contextual material gives the meaning of the term she replied: "Well, it's about things that affect people." Richard added: "Yes, they include laws relating to working, schools, debts, taxation, monopolies, and voting. They're things that affect all people — not just the worker." The lesson also illustrated the use of context clues to select from several dictionary definitions of a word the meaning that was related to the social studies material. This was shown in the development of the meaning of the word *status*. For instance, after Jim read the three meanings of *status* from the dictionary, he said: "I think the first definition is the one. It says *condition* and the paragraph is about the conditions of the workers." Loretta then used the word in the proper social studies context: "Ah, then Big Business changed the status of the workers" (70, pp. 52–53).

The question always arises: Of all the social studies concepts, which are most important to teach? Vocabulary studies (16, 62, 84) in this field, supplemented by the teacher's own judgment, are useful in helping him determine which are the key words, worthy of intensive study.

Having a purpose for reading. To provide an immediate specific purpose that serves as an incentive to read, Shepherd suggested the following procedure:

In preparing for effective reading of the material in their textbook concerning the topic, "The Constitutional Convention of 1787 and the Formation of the Constitution," the pupils imagined problems that would beset the

Convention. Purpose was developed through helping the pupils become acquainted with the type of information they would find in the new reading material. As a result of their questions, the pupils looked through the reading material and noted the reading aids to check the accuracy of their list of convention problems. Many of the pupil-predicted problems were found in the textbook. Albert's predicted problem was: "If the central government was to be made more powerful, then the states would be less powerful. That would be a problem, I think, to get the states to accept giving more power to the central government." As he looked through the reading material, Albert noted: "On page 105 there is a topic 'State selfishness versus the general welfare.' I bet that would be about the states giving up some of their power to the central government" (70, pp. 42–43).

Purpose also is aroused by relating the reading to real life problems. Reading is vitalized when it can be applied to current problems.

Instruction and materials must emphasize and meet the interests, concerns, and problems of pupils on present-day issues. In this way reading becomes really functional. The problem of this class was to determine ways for improving labor-management relations. This was a problem recommended by the pupils for study. It is, indeed, a current problem. The teacher observed the spirited interest of the pupils during the discussion as evidence of the functional value of their reading. Many of the pupils would work in industry. Their concern and interest was evidenced by such comments as Eddie's, who as a member of the labor group, said: "You say that labor should be loyal to the company. But you've got to run a business that we can be loyal to." . . . The entire class discussion was an application of the facts derived from reading. The discussion ended with listing eight suggestions for better labor-management relations. One suggestion that evolved from the discussion was that labor should accept the fact that industry, in order to be financially healthy, must make a profit (70, p. 79).

Locating information. The skills used in locating information, taught in the elementary grades, need further development in high school. Many students could increase their reading and study effectiveness by:

using the following parts of their textbook: foreword, map index, table of contents, index, illustrations, and study aids. Effective reading and study habits are increased if the pupils know how to use the aids in the textbook. These act as guides in the reading of the subject matter. Throughout the lesson these parts of the textbook were located and discussed. Examples of pupil comments were: Dolores' "I think the *Foreword to the Student* is interesting. . . . It tells of one of the best ways to learn history and then lists helps in the book that will help us to learn it"; Betty's "There is a list of maps in the beginning that'll make it easier for us to find the maps because it gives the page each map is found on"; and Ralph's (speaking of the index) "Well, if you want to find out about any of these places or people or events, all you have to do is to look in the index, find the page given, and then look it up" (70, p. 47).

Motivating reading through projects. Projects may be introduced in social studies that enlist a wide range of abilities and interests. For example, a teacher, Emily Spinelli, doing advanced study at Teachers College, described a newspaper project undertaken by her eighth grade. The class had been reading about the Civil War and decided to put out a newspaper presumably published during that period. They first examined their favorite newspaper and decided on the general organization of their paper, which was to include a news section, a feature section, and an editorial page. The class as a whole did preliminary work on each of these three sections. Then each student looked for some particularly newsworthy events occurring on or near the date they had chosen for their edition. From then on they began writing news items, feature articles, and editorials and letters to the editor. They worked in small committees or individually, reading their stories to others, checking on the historical authenticity of them, improving their headlines, and finally producing the paper. This project afforded meaningful opportunities for developing and practicing different reading skills and purposeful writing and listening. In working on their newspaper, students became more aware of the practical value and importance of effective reading skills.

In ninth-grade civics classes, a project on the radio often encourages wide reading. The students bring in magazines, newspapers, Sunday supplements, and the radio pages from their daily newspapers. They select articles, mount clippings, index, and file them under headings. A radio issue of the magazine *Modern Literature*, though difficult, may be read by some of the students. They may then summarize their findings in imaginary radio programs for which they practice oral reading and speaking.

Another example of highly motivated reading in a social studies program in the eighth grade was described by St. Clair Holman, while a graduate student at Teachers College. The content for the course was divided into three units:

1. The builders of America — the political leaders, inventors, scientists, businessmen, builders of railroads, writers, artists, athletes, and others who took part in the building of America.

2. Social life in America — how people lived, their food, jobs, homes, stores, schools, churches, newspapers, games, and other recreation.

3. Relations with other nations — Canada, Mexico, other Latin American nations, European and Asiatic neighbors.

Before beginning each unit the entire class discussed the projects or activities. From time to time the group was assisted by the reports of five committees. A planning committee suggested individual and group

Finding facts for projects
in social studies.

activities. A library committee, working closely with librarian and teacher, made, displayed, and distributed, lists of books on the unit that members of the group could read and enjoy. A picture committee arranged room displays of books, pictures, and maps from magazines, newspapers, and current events papers and also worked with the teacher in providing slide films, movies, and other visual aids. A current events committee reported to the class outstanding current events connected with American history, put selected clippings on bulletin boards, and filed those of permanent interest and value for future classes. A vocabulary building committee made and kept a dictionary of new words, giving an illustration, the pronunciation, the definition, and a sentence using the word. This committee also made flash cards of new words showing how they were divided into syllables and other word games.

At the close of each unit, individuals and small groups presented their findings to the class. They worked hard in presenting their report in a dramatic form that would interest all members of the class. Each report was followed by a discussion period and a short test of its content given by the committee that prepared it.

Differentiating assignments. When the entire class is working on the same topic, the students may be guided in their reading by questions requiring different levels of ability. Slow-learning students may find the answers to concrete factual questions; more able students can answer questions requiring more ability to generalize and make inferences; superior students may be stimulated to do "research" on certain questions. Shepherd pointed out:

> A well-planned assignment is closely related to the problem-solving approach to reading. Such an assignment makes possible the success of all the pupils with their varied reading levels, and provides them with a specific purpose for reading. The entire discussion of one lesson culminated in three topics that were to guide the pupils' reading. Alvin, Gloria, and Douglas summarized the topics just before the class began to read. The teacher observed that the pupils seemed well prepared and ready to find the information needed in the assignment. They were prompt in beginning to read and sustained their reading interest for the entire class period (70, p. 45).

Encouraging wide reading. Much of the value in the study of reading comes from personal interest in the people and the times in which they lived. To develop this kind of appreciation, detail on human relations is necessary. Such detail can be obtained only by reading more widely, beyond the textbook crammed with bare facts. One history teacher (31) reported that at the outset of each history unit (Colonial and Revolutionary, Nationalism, Sectionalism, etc.) he distributed reading lists of novels, plays, and biographies on the period, many of them paper-back books. Copies were available for inspection. The students examined these, asked questions, read blurbs, and placed orders with the teacher. The books were mailed to the teacher directly from the publisher and he distributed them to the students. Each student prepared a brief written report on books he had read. The major emphasis, however, was placed on the oral report, for which the teacher prepared a guide. The teacher also prepared specific questions for each unit. Students who needed still more guidance were given specific questions for each book. For titles of such books see:

Robert G. Carlsen and Richard S. Alm, *Social Understanding through Litera-ture*. National Council for the Social Studies, 1954. Washington, D. C.

Random House, *Landmark Series*. New York, N.Y.

Row, Peterson and Company, *Basic Social Education Series*. Twenty-nine titles, e.g., *Youth Under Dictators, Fight against Germs, From Barter to Money, Newspaper and American Life*. Evanston, Ill.

Row, Peterson and Company, *Human Interest Biographies of Leading Men and Women in American History Series*. Twenty-four titles: I. Early Settlers, Early Explorers; II. Leaders in the American Revolution; III. Leaders in Western Expansion; and IV. Leaders Since 1860. Evans-ton, Ill.

For those who turn to comics:

Simon and Schuster, *A Golden Story Book Series*. Ten titles. Rockefeller Center, N.Y., 1949.

Examples of books that foster tolerant attitudes and cooperative behavior:

Eleanor Estes, *The Hundred Dresses*. New York: Harcourt, Brace and Company, 1944.

Gregor Felsen, *Struggle Is Our Brother*. New York: E. P. Dutton and Company, 1943.

Florence Crannell Means, *Shuttered Windows*. Boston: Houghton Mifflin Company, 1938.

This approach resulted in individual students reading eight or ten books each year. "Most of the students seemed to enjoy this approach. Few neglected to do the reading. All reacted quite positively to the books they read" (31, p. 565).

Students' appraisal of procedures. To a greater degree than at present, students should become aware of the reading methods they are using and of the teaching methods that seem to be most effective for them. As a guide to future teaching of reading in the social studies, Shepherd asked the class to appraise the experiences they had had during the past semester. In answer to the question: "Which of the reading skills listed below were you able to improve in this course?" pupils mentioned most frequently the following specific skills:

Mechanics of Reading: Do I adjust my rate of reading to the purpose of the reading and to the difficulty of the material? Do I read by thought phrases rather than a word at a time? Do I avoid pronouncing the words while reading?

Directed Reading: Am I able to skim an article quickly for useful material? Do I "size up" the reading task before beginning it? Am I able to register agreement or disagreement with what is read? Do I look for something definite when reading? Do I make a preliminary survey of a book, chapter, or selection before reading? Have I learned to interpret my reading in light of facts I already know? Have I learned to recognize propaganda? Can I apply the facts from my reading to real-life situations?

Word Meaning: Do I try to discover meanings of new words from their context? Do I attempt to find meanings through the prefix, suffix, or root? Do I look up their meanings in the dictionary?

Understanding: Am I able to see relationships of one topic to another? Can I outline a section or a chapter? Have I learned to relate similar ideas from other books or sources? Can I select the central idea of each paragraph, section, or chapter? Can I distinguish important points from minor details?

Location of Information: Do I make use of the index of a book? Do I make use of the table of contents in front of a book? Am I able to use the library file cards? Do I consult the *Readers' Guide* to periodicals? Do I know how to use the encyclopedias, dictionaries, and other reference books? Do I know how to read and use charts, graphs, tables, and maps? (70, p. 86).

Application to other subjects. Although the social studies teacher's focus is on social studies content, most of the reading skills he teaches are applicable in modified form to other subjects. Thus the teacher has the opportunity not only to improve the learning of social studies through reading, but also to improve students' reading in general through the teaching of social studies material. In many ways both reading and social studies content contribute to good citizenship.

Reading in the Core Curriculum

The core curriculum or "block," whether it is a combination of English and social studies or general education or "social living" or "life adjustment," offers special opportunity for the teaching of reading. This is because the teacher, through his longer contacts with his students, has a good chance to observe and understand them and can find time for needed instruction in reading. This is a logical period in which to give informal reading tests, to give instruction and practice in paragraph reading and writing, and to build up a file of practice material to meet individual needs.

The teacher can also plan projects to increase interest in reading and to give practice in improving basic reading skills. Many high school students

need practice and instruction in sensing sequences, deepening their understanding of words, expressing their ideas in sentences, drawing conclusions
and making generalizations. From pictures, rich in detail, students can
obtain vivid impressions of people and events. They can later read the
stories or accounts they dictate or write about a picture or a series of
pictures. One non-reader gained status in the group when he was able to
make an interesting report in class based on pictures in *A Visual History
of the United States* by Harold Faulkner (illustrated by the Graphic Arts
Institute, published by Henry Schuman, New York, 1953). *Let's Take a
Trip to the Skyscraper* by Sarah R. Riedman (published by Abelard-
Schuman, New York) written on the fourth- or fifth-grade level of difficulty, is so well organized that it is excellent for teaching the retarded
reader skills of skimming and outlining. Books such as *Cotton Farm Boy*
and *Texas Ranch Boy* by Merritt Mauzey (published by Henry Schuman)
are excellent to develop, through pictures, attitudes, and understanding
of the life of a cotton farmer.

When a teacher has a large block of time with a group of students,
conditions are favorable for recognizing and correcting reading difficulties,
and building self-esteem and appreciations.

Reading in Science

In the teaching of science and mathematics, as in other subjects, two
ends may be served by teaching reading as an intrinsic part of the class
period: Students will learn more effectively in these fields and they will
develop reading skills generally useful to them, especially skill in seeing
cause-and-effect relations and making inferences and generalizations.

The approach to reading in the fields of science and mathematics puts
more emphasis on slow, thoughtful reading than on skimming or speeded
reading. In fact, persons who have read exclusively in these fields tend to
read more slowly than the average. This is because they have had so
much practice in precise, analytical reading and have neglected other
kinds of reading that develop fluency and speed. Reading in science and
mathematics is problem-solving reading. It should be highly motivated
reading.

Reading in science involves reading directions. Unless these directions
are accurately read, the experiment fails. Reading in science also involves
applications of laws and principles. This too requires thoughtful, de-
liberative reading. Often each word must be weighed so as to get its full
significance.

Formulas, charts, and diagrams require special study. Every detail
must be noted; mistaking an *o* for a *c* in a chemical formula may make an
entirely different product. Failing to see relations in diagrams and charts

makes it impossible to get the meaning they are intended to convey. Photographs of eye movements frequently show a record of the eyes moving back and forth in one place in the process of puzzling out the formula or diagram.

Informal tests to find how students read, such as have been described on page 222, may be used in science. Examples of these tests are given in *Problems in the Improvement of Reading* (75, p. 258). The teacher should select passages from the text or reference book he is expecting the students to read.

**Teaching reading in the
regular science period**

As in social studies, teaching reading of different kinds of science material should be an intrinsic part of science instruction. Ways of teaching reading skills *as a part of* the regular science lesson were illustrated by Carter (15) in a description of an elementary science class:

In an elementary science class, it is the *aim* of the teacher to show causal factors affecting rainfall. The materials available are texts in elementary science, glass tubing, mercury, thermometers, Bunsen burner, a large dripping pan and other equipment generally found in an elementary science laboratory. The *procedures* employed by the teacher in using these materials to accomplish the specific goal may be briefly summarized as follows:

1. Ask the students to determine from the rainfall maps in their texts the amount of precipitation on the western slopes of the Rocky Mountains.

2. Determine the amount of rainfall on the eastern slopes.

3. Stimulate interest in determining why the marked difference between the amount of precipitation on the western and the eastern slopes of the mountains.

4. Attack the following minor problems in solving this major problem.

a. Why are the prevailing winds moisture-laden?

b. What are the causes of ocean currents?

c. Why do winds blow?

d. Why are the prevailing winds from the west?

e. Why does condensation take place?

5. Guide the students in a solution of these problems by the following means:

a. Constant referral of the students to the various parts of their texts such as index, table of contents and the various maps, charts, and illustrations made available by the author. Encourage students to ask questions and read for answers.

b. Construction of a barometer and the illustration of its use.

c. Demonstration of ocean currents by making use of water in a large dripping pan covered sparsely with sawdust and with one corner placed over Bunsen burner.

d. Demonstration of condensation on drinking glass filled with ice water.

e. Development of such terms as high and low pressure areas, air mass, altitude condensation, convection, dew points, evaporation, Fahrenheit, front, isobars, isotherms, barometric pressure, water vapor, relative humidity, temperature, and velocity.

f. Demonstration of how to gather *facts* and how to use these facts in establishing *inferences*. Encourage students to substantiate their inferences by careful reading of their texts and supplementary references. A critical evaluation of all inferences should be stressed.

In the activities previously outlined, it is evident that mental content and ability to read can be developed simultaneously. The young student has been encouraged to add words to his vocabulary and to use his text and supplementary materials as he has participated in problem solving. He has read to learn and he has learned to read (15, p. 568).

Three reading skills
essential to the study
of science

To gain scientific knowledge from science books and articles the student should know the meaning of key words, be able to get the author's thought in a fairly long unit such as a chapter, and use the problem-solving approach in his reading. He will appreciate the teacher who helps him to acquire these necessary skills; teachers should feel responsible for developing them (15).

Learning technical and other key words. Technical words are of special importance in both science and mathematics. Some of these words, such as *humidity*, are used in everyday situations; students can share their experiences with these words as the teacher writes them on the board. Some words are the names of substances and processes with which students have firsthand experience in the laboratory. Some are ordinary words used in a special way; many words in mathematics are of this kind. Whenever possible, refer the word back to the object or action it represents; enrich it with firsthand experience.

Some teachers encourage their classes to compile "Words of Science" charts, or "Words of Mathematics" charts. As one student said, "If we feel it is important for us to know, then it is added to our chart." Whenever a new word is met, the students look at it carefully, noting the beginning, middle, and ending, and any distinguishing features. They discuss its meaning and use it correctly in sentences. If a student has special difficulty with the word the teacher may write it large and have him trace the word with his finger as he pronounces it, syllable by syllable. Students are encouraged to make their own science dictionaries in small, loose-leaf notebooks and add two or three new words to their vocabulary each day.

Getting the author's thought. To master a chapter a study type of reading must be used. The formula, Survey Q3R, so effective in any study type of reading, should also be used in the reading of science. *Survey* stands for the preliminary process of recalling what one already knows about the topic, considering one's purpose in reading it and how it relates to something important in his life. *Q* refers to questions which may be answered in the chapter. These questions may be obtained from a rapid skimming and by changing headings to questions, as, for example, the heading *Humidity* into *What Is Humidity?* Each question may be written on a small card and used to test one's knowledge of each question. The first *R* refers to careful reading to get the answers to the questions; the second *R* to reviewing to be sure one has obtained the necessary information; and the third *R* to reciting the knowledge gained in the form in which it will be used — in giving a report, in class discussion, in an examination, in conversation at home, or in other ways. The Coronet film *How Effective Is Your Reading?* (19) describes the reading method a high school boy uses in a science assignment. First he looks at the title of the chapter and relates it to his own life and what he already knows about the subject. Then he skims, looking at headings, italicized words and phrases, topic sentences. Now he knows in general what the chapter is about and is able to jot down questions to which he wants to find the answers. Then he is ready to *R*ead. He varies his rate as he reads, slowing up when he comes to a section that answers one of his questions, pausing to study the diagram that helps explain the text. After his first reading he *R*eviews to see whether he has gained the information he needs. Finally he *R*ecites in the form in which he will probably use the ideas. When he has finished he has mastered the subject and has derived satisfaction from the process.

Using the problem-solving approach. As a guide to reading for the purpose of problem solving and to develop this skill in mathematics and science, Carter (15) suggested that the student ask himself these questions:

A. What is to be found?

B. What facts are known?

C. What are the steps to go through for a solution? The best way to see the steps is to rewrite the problem, omitting all numbers, so as to get the meaning. The numbers are not important as far as the steps of the interpretation are concerned. Another set of numbers would do just as well. Read the problem as one would a story — for its meaning.

Some other questions are:

D. Can the student make a picture of the problem or summarize the procedure he should follow in solving the problem?

E. Can he show the actual procedure — the figures he has used?

F. Is the answer reasonable? How can it be proved? (15, p. 569)

**Reading difficulty
of science texts**

Since 1950, G. G. Mallinson and others (53, 54, 55) have been studying readability and reporting the difficulty of textbooks in elementary science, high school physics, chemistry, biology, general science, and junior high science. These studies on science textbooks may be summarized as follows:

1. Reading levels of many are too advanced for students for whom they are written.

2. There are wide differences between levels of reading difficulty of the easiest and the most difficult science texts.

3. In some texts whose average level of reading difficulty seems satisfactory, there are passages that would be difficult for even some college students.

4. Many texts contain words — other than technical key words — that could be replaced with easier synonyms.

Another investigation examined the difficulty of eleven physical science and seven earth science textbooks, taking into consideration the number of words in sentences in the sampling, the number of personal references, and the number of polysyllabic words. Conclusions relative to this study are:

1. Levels of reading difficulty within textbooks vary greatly. For example, the easiest passage of one text was Grade VI while the most difficult was college level.

2. The average levels of difficulty of textbooks in both physical science and earth science vary greatly. The easiest was Grade VII while the most difficult was Grade X.

3. Earlier passages in texts do not seem to be consistently lower in level of reading difficulty than later passages. Hence, no provision is made for growth of reading (54, p. 616).

The need for improving the readability of science texts is obvious. Fortunately some of the science books for lower grades do not have the appearance of being for little children. Consequently, adolescent retarded readers will accept them and gain some basic concepts in science and some fluency in reading science material from them.

Suggested procedures

Many procedures may be used in science classes to increase students' interest in reading science. They like to test the scientific accuracy of advertisements which they read in magazines or hear and see over the radio and television. They enjoy informal discussions and programs.

Brown (7) suggested a number of informal science activities involving reading for junior high school classes:

1. Having a "Clearing House Program" — free discussion of questions students have asked.

2. Organize a "How and Why Club" — encourage students to read to find answers to their questions rather than to "just read."

3. Have a "Science in the News Program" — reports of reading from newspapers and magazines.

4. Encourage brief written reports including the student's own comments, following a free reading period; these reports may be given in the "Science in the News" program.

5. Conduct science seminars, formed on the basis of students' reading interests, which provide more intensive study and discussion. These seminars may be scheduled during study or club periods or after school.

6. Form a club, "The Experimenters," in which students plan additional demonstrations and group experimentation to enliven text and reference readings.

7. Encourage recreational reading from library sources. There is need for collaboration between science teacher and librarian in providing materials, in pointing out differences in reading science and non-science books, in organizing a group of reading critics, and in clipping into library books students' brief written commentaries, giving their opinions and their recommendations.

Some science classes publish a magazine which is eagerly read by the entire school. Such a project not only extends the science vocabulary and knowledge of the writers and readers of the magazine, but also gives the magazine staff valuable social experience in working together.

To help retarded readers gain an appreciation of the practical importance of reading, skill in reading to follow directions, basic concepts in science, and status in the group, it is useful to have books that describe simple experiments they can perform and simple machines they can make. *Let's Find Out* by Herman and Nina Schneider (William R. Scott, New York) describes in simple language experiments youngsters can perform for the group. *Now Try This* by the same authors and publishers describes machines and suggests making toy machines that will win the interest and admiration of other junior high school pupils.

Leisure reading in science

There is a wide range of leisure reading in popular magazines in the field of science, from astronomy to keeping a zoo, from science fiction to technical articles to practical physics. This wide range of material may

Reading in science must be more than half right.

be represented in the class library of the science teacher or loaned for a period or longer by the school or public library. In a free reading period, students may be guided, but not restricted, in their choice of books. After they have read the books or articles they have selected they should discuss both the quality and the content. In science fiction, for example, students can learn to distinguish between good, bad, and mediocre examples. As a result of their discussion and reading, some of them will add their comments to the book review file; others may make "reading ladders" beginning with absurd unscientific science fiction found in some newsstands and going up to the creative speculations of modern authors. Some books of this type currently popular with boys are:

Carl L Biemiller, *Starboy*. New York: Henry Holt and Company, 1956.

Arthur C. Clarke, *Going into Space*. New York: Harper and Brothers, 1954.

Lee Correy, *Rocket Man*. New York: Henry Holt and Company, 1955.

Albro T. Gaul, *The Complete Book of Space Travel*. New York: World Publishing Company, 1956.

Robert A. Heinlein, *Rocket Ship Galileo*. Junior Literary Guild. New York: Charles Scribner's Sons, 1947.

Robert A. Heinlein, *Space Cadet*. New York: Charles Scribner's Sons, 1948.

Robert A. Heinlein, *Tunnel in the Sky*. New York: Charles Scribner's Sons, 1955.

André Norton, *Space Police*. New York: World Publishing Company, 1956.

Donald A. Wollheim, *The Secret of the Martian Moons*. Philadelphia: John C. Winston Company, 1955.

Teachers need to remind students of the distinction between "research reading" and reading for fun and to teach them the best techniques for each kind of reading with questions they have formulated in mind. One class in "research reading" worked in groups on the solution to specific questions and problems and presented the results of their study to the class in oral reports, radio plays, dramatized interviews, puppet shows, and a homemade movie. In another class the students worked alone or in pairs on science problems they had chosen. They spent a period discussing what they already knew about the problem and what they wanted to know. It took several periods more to locate, with the help of teacher and librarian, sources of information on the subject. They learned how to locate and examine books and magazines in the school and public libraries and wrote to persons who might have information. Some of the pictures and articles they found were put on the bulletin board. From a wealth of books and pamphlets they found information on their problems and read diligently. In their reading they found many new words and learned to look up their meaning in glossaries and dictionaries. The words that kept recurring they put into a class dictionary of their own. Students low in reading ability were getting information from books of third- and fourth-grade level of difficulty. Some of these, like the *Golden Nature Guide Series* (Simon and Schuster, New York), the *Morrow Science Series* (William Morrow and Company, New York), and the *First Book Series* (Franklin Watts Company, New York), contain accurate information in a fascinating form. Others read science books written for fourth-, fifth-, and sixth-grade pupils, such as those listed below:

> Roy Chapman Andrews, *All about Dinosaurs.* New York: Random House, 1953.
> Wilfred Bronson, *Wonder World of Ants.* New York: Harcourt, Brace and Company, 1937.
> Jack Coggins and Fletcher Pratt, *By Space Ship to the Moon.* New York: Random House, 1952.
> M. B. Cormack, *The First Book of Stones.* New York: Franklin Watts, 1951. This is one of a series of books that might be used.
> Herman Schneider, *Everyday Weather and How It Works.* New York: McGraw-Hill Book Company, 1951.
> Herman and Nina Schneider, *Let's Look Under the City.* Chicago: Scott, Foresman and Company, 1950.
> Addison Webb, *Song of the Seasons* New York: William Morrow and Company, 1950.
> Anne Terry White, *All about the Stars.* New York: Random House, 1948.
> Herbert Zim, *Snakes.* New York: William Morrow and Company, 1949.

Having books on different levels of difficulty made it easy for the students to present their reports to the class in such an interesting manner that they won genuine approval. Students of superior reading ability were given the problem of extracting from supplementary sources facts other members of the class had not read and presenting them in an appealing way.

Some suggested materials for leisure reading in science include the following:

Newspaper and other clippings on bulletin board displays and in files.

Magazines — nature, current science, and aviation, *Life, National Geographic, Popular Science, Popular Mechanics.*

Free publications distributed by General Electric, Bell Telephone Company, American Forestry Products, etc.

Hobby and science instrument catalogues.

Radio and television announcements of science programs.

Reading current science books and articles and listening to sound radio and accurate television programs helps to develop lifelong interests in science.

Reading in Mathematics

Many people do not realize how much success in mathematics depends on reading ability. Of course, a special kind of reading is required, but common reading skills and a basic vocabulary are also needed.

Problems of reading in mathematics

There are several reading problems in mathematics. First, the proper approach to mathematics materials must be understood. There is the difficulty of "density" — facts or problems briefly and concisely stated in the most condensed form. Details are important — for example, where the decimal point is placed. They require concentration if one is to get the exact meaning. There is also the problem of grasping essential information and recognizing the specific question or questions to be answered. The problem must be read carefully to understand the significance of each symbol, word, or phrase. Skimming is not appropriate. "By reading once, twice, or even three times the student must be able to picture the problem and to separate the facts given from the facts required. From geometric proposition he must be able to pick out the data and the aim" (27, p. 602).

Next, a minimum technical vocabulary must be mastered. Highly technical words are often introduced too early, too quickly, and without relating the new concepts to experiences and ideas already meaningful to the students. The new concepts are also too infrequently used to be thoroughly learned. If a student reads with the intent to apply or use what he learns later, he will be more likely to understand and remember the new technical words. Moreover, many of the words have special meaning when used in an arithmetic problem — *sum, product, divisor, denominator, multiplier* and other expressions like *goes into*. Besides the technical vocabulary there are symbols such as $-$, $+$, $=$, and $\times$, and abbreviations such as *qt., ft., bu.,* and *doz.* To add to the difficulty many hard words used in problems are not necessary to the understanding of the mathematical ideas in the problem; they are irrelevant.

Mathematics also requires special kinds of reading — equations, formulas, tables, graphs. It is most effective for students to try to read material of this kind and, from this experience, derive generalizations and principles themselves.

Reading of problems in mathematics

Different kinds of thinking require different kinds of reading. In reading mathematics, going back over the line of print (regressive movements) is not undesirable. Arithmetic problems involve relationships that require clear thinking. One must read them carefully so as to understand the significance of each word and phrase. They are usually briefly stated and require concentration if one is to get the exact meaning. An adequate approach to the reading of problems in arithmetic might include five steps:

1. Reading carefully to learn what the problem is about and what is given; this may involve forming a mental picture of the problem situation.

2. Finding out what information is asked for.

3. Deciding which facts are needed for the solution of the problem; this requires logical thinking.

4. Choosing the methods of computation needed.

5. Testing the reasonableness and accuracy of one's answers.

To gain information about the students' ability to read problems in mathematics, the teacher may present a number of problems to be read, but not solved. Problems such as the following * may be used as reading exercises. For each problem students should write the answers to each of the five questions:

What kind of problem is it?

What is asked for?

What information pertinent to the solution is given?

What computations are necessary, and in what order?

How can I test whether the answer is correct?

1. Mary earned $8.00 last week baby-sitting for her aunt. If she banked $\frac{3}{4}$ of her earnings, how much did she have left?

2. Jimmy bought two model airplane kits. One was $1.75 and the other was $.98. How much will he receive in change if he gives the shopkeeper a $5 bill?

3. On four arithmetic tests Mary had marks of 87, 93, 89, and 100. What is her average mark?

4. How much will 18 inches of ribbon cost at 24 cents per yard?

5. Jimmy's mother gave him $2.00 and sent him to the store for a loaf of bread, a pound of butter, $\frac{1}{2}$ dozen eggs, and 1 quart of milk. The storekeeper charged him $1.84. How much change did he receive?

6. If I have 79 cents and divide that amount equally among three children, how much will each receive? How much will be left over?

7. Eight men are working on a new house. It will take them 10 days to finish it. How much sooner can the house be completed if two additional men are put on the job?

* Used as a reading exercise by Dr. Marion Carrol, Child Study Center, State University of New York, College for Teachers, Buffalo, New York.

Browsing in books and reading to plan is part of shopwork.

Translating words into mathematical symbols.

The same general type of practice in reading may be given in algebra classes. The following problem is typical of ninth-grade algebra:

Two automobiles start at the same time from towns 330 miles apart and travel toward each other. If one averages 30 miles an hour and the other averages 25 miles an hour, in how many hours will they meet? One teacher, Douglas J. Erath, when a graduate student at Teachers College, described his method of teaching the reading of the above problem.

The first impulse of many students upon reading a verbal problem is to get panicky. Where does one start? One way to allay this fear is to point out that very few mathematical problems can be solved by one quick reading. All we can hope to gain the first time we read the problem is the general idea. The subsequent readings must be more deliberate. During the second reading we can select all the active forces which appear in the problem and list them on the right side of our paper. If the nature of the problem alters any of these forces we must list the altered form also.

From the first reading we learn:

    rate of speed of first auto

    rate of speed of second auto

    distance traveled.

On our third reading we must supply the numerical and symbolic description for each of these factors. We must also determine what our unknown is to be. If the unknown is not immediately apparent, it will unfold as the result of the process of elimination as we fill in the data for all our factors. This leads us to:

    30 m.p.h. = rate of speed of first auto

    25 m.p.h. = rate of speed of second auto

    x = number of hours traveled

    330 miles = distance separating automobiles.

We now have the elements but lack perception of the entire problem. Let us read again (fourth reading) with an aim of gaining this understanding and setting up an equality. This is the crux of the problem. The teacher may help by asking such questions as, "Have you ever seen a similar problem?" or "What are all the plausible relationships you can think of?" Insight must arise at this point. In this problem it is the recall of the formula that distance is equal to the rate multiplied by the time. It is wise at this insightful moment to estimate the probable answer in order to confirm our understanding and to serve as a safeguard against a mechanically defective solution.

Solution	Check
$30x + 25x = 330$	$30(6) + 25(6) = 330$
$55x = 330$	$180 + 150 = 330$
$x = 6$	$330 = 330$

One more cautious reading must be made in which each detail of the preceding steps is carefully checked. It is here that the "careless" mistake is found. The mathematical "check" only verifies the mechanical manipulation of the preceding information. The verbal check verifies the correct interpretation of the information.

The steps in this procedure of reading a mathematics problem are:
first, reading to get the general idea
second, reading to find the factors in the problem
third, reading to supply the numerical and symbolic detail
fourth, reading to see the problem as a whole and to use insights related to it.

A high school teacher, Matilda S. Cohen, taught her students to read an algebra problem in phrases. First they read the problem through once silently. Then one member of the class read it aloud, one phrase at a time, while others volunteered to translate the phrase into algebraic terms. The following problem illustrates the method:

Twice a certain number increased by 5 equals 18 diminished by the unknown number. Find the number. The last sentence tells the class what the unknown is, so they begin by writing:

Let x equal the number.

Reader:	*Secretary writes on board:*
twice a certain number	$2x$
increased by 5	$2x + 5$
equals 18	$2x + 5 = 18$
diminished by the number	$2x + 5 = 18 - x$

In this way the students get the whole meaning of the problem, and realize how it must be read to form an equation.

Reading problems first as a group experience is effective in teaching reading methods. If students understand and become aware of the method, they will apply it to their reading of other problems. For some classes, practice exercises in reading problems will be necessary in addition to the group reading.

Reading of a Foreign Language

"I'm interested in what should be included in a reading program in Spanish in the senior high school," said a teacher who thought of the teaching of reading of a foreign language as parallel to the teaching of reading English and as part of the total school reading program. Teachers can apply many general reading principles and procedures to the teaching of foreign languages. In this field, as in the reading of other subjects, there are certain basic problems — motivation, need, progression of experience, and satisfaction in the reading process.

In learning to read a second language, as in reading one's native language, one must make a direct association between the printed word and its meaning without hearing the word spoken. For efficient reading of a foreign language, the reader should get the idea directly from the printed image of the word, without the intervening process of translation. If any vocalization is necessary, it should be done in the foreign language. This direct comprehension of the language of the writer insures the best communication between author and reader.

To develop direct reading habits, the teacher should help students build vocabulary by the use of pictures, context clews, synonyms or antonyms, and definitions in the language. From the beginning the student should learn to think in the foreign language. To do this successfully he should at first read material that is easy and familiar. Before the student begins to read, the teacher should ask questions that stimulate him to anticipate and read directly for meaning. Direct and immediate comprehension of the author's thought is the goal of reading in a foreign language.

Special reading problems
in each foreign language

The teacher should analyze the special reading problems that his foreign language presents. For example, Spanish has certain structural characteristics, such as the word order, that have a bearing on the reading of the language. Vocabulary, idioms, the structure of phrases, and other unique features of the language should also be recognized. To compare a foreign language with English is more likely to cause confusion than to clarify.

Reading abilities and ways
they can be improved

The building of a reading vocabulary in a foreign language presents many of the same problems as in English. Students need to acquire a basic vocabulary of the most common words. This can be done better by use of meaningful sentences than by formal drill. However, word recognition drills, the building of word families, and other interesting exercises should be used as needed in the reading of very simple material. As the students gain proficiency they can pay special attention to new words as they are introduced in interesting context. Making their own dictionaries in which each word is defined, illustrated, and used in one or two sentences helps students fix these words permanently in mind, with meaningful associations.

A favorite word exercise is one in which the teacher says: "Write all the Spanish words that you can which will tell what you like on this fine, sunny morning." The students start: "*Me gusta. . . .*" When at a loss for the word to convey a particular feeling they use the dictionary. While they are doing this, the teacher watches to see whether the student knows how to use the guide words at the top of the page, and whether he merely copies the first word given or rechecks to be sure he has found the meaning he is seeking.

Group practice in phrase reading may be given by the use of flash cards or a far-point projector. Individual practice may be given by a simple device in which a series of phrases are exposed one at a time through an aperture in a card that covers the list as a whole. A machine called a near-point projector which flashes words and phrases at reading distance may also be used for this purpose. Another type of exercise employs incomplete paragraphs with missing phrases or words indicated by a dash. The students fill in these gaps to complete the meaning of the sentence. Familiar phrases, such as "once upon a time," "at home," "in the morning," should be used at first. More difficult phrases may be gradually introduced.

Learning to draw conclusions and predict outcomes is just as important in reading a foreign language as it is in reading one's native language. However, aiding students to read creatively in a foreign language presents difficulties for several reasons. One reason is that many students have not learned to do this in their native language. Another reason is that much of their attention is occupied by the mechanics of comprehending the literal meaning of the passage. Asking thought-provoking questions as the students read will help to develop this ability. For example, the teacher may ask, "What do you think will happen next?" "What would you expect Marie to reply?" "If the young man did this, what do you think the consequences would be?" "What conclusion do you draw from this series of events? How is one related to the other?"

In giving an assignment the teacher should encourage students to set their own goals and clarify their purpose in reading a particular passage. He should also help them to choose the most appropriate methods and techniques for reading it. As a basis for doing this the teacher studies the methods he himself would use and the methods that the most successful students in his classes have used in reading different kinds of material.

With the book closed, students may be asked to discuss why a certain word was used in the passage read, who made a certain remark, or what words help to create the mood of the story.

To develop interest in reading widely or extensively at an advanced level, the teacher or students may introduce certain controversial issues or problems. Carboni (13) gave the following illustration: The teacher capitalized on the students' interest in the famous statue of Christ of the Andes, which had been pictured in the text and in film strips and movies on Latin America. She told the story in Spanish of the conflict that arose between Argentina and Chile as to which country the statue should face. One nation said that it should face its boundary, but the other retorted that Christ had never turned His back on them before. Because of the bitterness of the quarrel, it seemed unlikely that the statue would ever

A newspaper project stimulates reading and writing.
Here students are preparing an Italian newspaper.

Dramatization is an effective way to use reading in any language.

be erected. All seemed hopeless until one of the two countries suddenly decided that it would prefer having the statue face the other country. Why? Students read the Spanish text to find out. They discovered that this nation agreed to have the back of the statue in its direction because the other nation could not be trusted, and the statue facing it would be able to watch eternally!

Reading materials and
audio-visual aids

Books should be graded according to level of difficulty. The beginning vocabulary should be limited to words of few syllables, with special emphasis on verbs and nouns. The sentences should be short and simple. Every effort should be made to provide interesting material, so that the reading will be rewarding.

To facilitate reference reading, some Spanish classes cut apart old copies of the *Inter-American Magazine* and other magazines and filed the articles of permanent interest and value. Some of these articles consisted mostly of pictures with a few easy sentences of explanation. Others were of different degrees of reading difficulty. The process of building up the file gave the students excellent practice in reading; it involved reading each article, evaluating it, and deciding on its acceptability for further use. The completed file supplied excellent free reading material for other classes.

Projector slides and film strips, as well as motion pictures, help to build a background of experience which not only enriches the meaning of the foreign words but acquaints students with other cultures. For beginners, films such as those prepared for rural people in Latin American countries, in which the teaching of the language is combined with practical suggestions for health and community betterment, would be of much interest and value. Disney films — *Planning for Good Eating, Cleanliness Brings Health*, and other simple, amusing pictures — with Spanish sound tracks have been produced by the Institute of International American Affairs. More advanced students could take responsibility for writing descriptive captions and commentaries for film strips prepared by the class, or commercial strips which have inadequate explanations. The creative teacher will develop many other methods and materials for accomplishing the objectives of foreign language courses.

Problems and projects

Further study is needed of the teaching of reading of foreign languages. Teachers may contribute valuable understandings through "action research" on such problems as:

1. Apply principles and methods of teaching beginning reading in English to the teaching of reading in a second language.

2. Determine the difference between beginning reading in one's native language and learning to read a foreign language.

3. Study the vocabulary difficulty and actual readability of books now available in your class by giving informal tests (see page 222) on passages from the books you are expecting the students to read. Recommend other materials of instruction.

4. Describe one of your most successful procedures in teaching the reading of a foreign language, and share this description with other language teachers either orally or in a mimeographed or printed bulletin.

5. Read available articles, such as the following, to gain suggestions for solving problems in the reading of a foreign language:

H. Purvis, "A Reading Course in French," *Modern Languages* (London) Vol. 33 (September, 1952), pp. 90–95.

Elaine M. Townsend, "The Construction and Use of Readers for Aymara Indians," *Fundamental Adult Education*, Vol. 4 (October, 1952), pp. 21–25.

John T. Waterman, "Reading Patterns in German and English," *German Quarterly*, Vol. 26 (November, 1953), pp. 225–27.

Reading in Business Education

As in other subjects, reading difficulty accounts for the failure of some students in business education courses. Most beginners in typing start by reading a single letter, then a word, a simple phrase, and finally longer phrases, clauses, and sentences. If they learn to read and comprehend the thought of the selection, they will type more accurately and at a faster rate. Reading ideas instead of words widens the student's span of recognition and increases his reading rate.

**Reasons for in-
effective reading**

Among the reasons for ineffective reading in business courses is the teacher's lack of recognition of the reading problem and how to deal with it. Very little has been written on how to teach the reading skills needed in business education. Teachers of business courses, like many other teachers, feel the pressure to "cover" a certain amount of subject matter. As in other subjects, the texts used are above the reading level of a large number of students in the department, and the texts have a heavy technical vocabulary, much of which is introduced in the first few chapters. Many students do not realize that part of their difficulty with the subject stems from their lack of reading proficiency.

Detecting reading difficulties

Teachers of business education subjects should first of all identify the students in their classes whose reading difficulties are interfering with their success in the subject. There are a number of ways of doing this. Study of the students' cumulative records and their scores on standardized reading tests indicates students who may have difficulty in reading in business education. Students who are poor readers in general are likely to be poor readers in shorthand and other subjects. Low scores on intelligence tests also may alert the teacher to potential reading problems. The influence of intelligence on proficiency in commercial subjects may vary with different kinds of tasks. One might expect the least influence of intelligence on straight copying in typewriting, since this requires little or no thought; and the most influence on the typing of tabulations and rough drafts, since reading comprehension is basic to transcribing manuscripts difficult to decipher and interpret.

Observation of students in class and analysis of their errors may reveal those who are having reading difficulty. Students' introspective reports and spontaneous comments often identify reading inability as a cause of failure in one or more business education subjects. An informal test based on passages from books which the students will be expected to read will indicate specific difficulties common to the group or peculiar to individuals.

Correcting reading difficulties

The most obvious line of attack is through improvement of spelling and the technical vocabulary. The spelling test (see page 356) and the drill on words misspelled are described elsewhere (see page 217). There are daily opportunities for building a useful vocabulary. For example, in bookkeeping, a list of all the important technical words should be compiled. These words should be memorized and understood as they are used in the text, in business experience, and in everyday life. Lawrence (48) prepared a list of single words and phrases which should be understood by teachers of business and students in business courses. Some of the single words that occurred with highest frequency in seventy-eight issues of *Time* magazine and the *Saturday Evening Post* were, in order of frequency:

produce	invest	reserve
stock	business	industry
security	federal	company
net	market	bank

index	common	dividend
rate	manufacture	purchase
profit	earn	issue
public	commerce	export
commission	retail	compete
exchange	chairman	finance
insure	prefer	asset
economic	report	interstate
union	income	broke
sale	capacity	goods
consume	organize	executive
corporate	condition	statement
capital	manage	bargain
work	act	percentage
bond	share	install
employ	receive	balance
operate	pay	machine

The original study gives a much longer list of words and phrases and compares them with frequency of mention in the Thorndike-Lorge list.

The following are some specified devices described by Mrs. Gladys D. Mosee, graduate student at Teachers College, for building the vocabulary needed by students in her advanced stenography:

1. Make their own spelling book. Under each letter the students listed the correct spellings of words beginning with that letter which they had misspelled. They divided each word into syllables, and under each word they pasted or drew a picture illustrating it.

2. Write new words in large print on cards; put the cards on the board sill; let the students take several minutes to look at all the words to associate them with concrete experiences. Then remove the cards from the sill and see how many of the words the students can write correctly. Use words recently learned in the business letters they compose, and in class discussion and conversation. In all vocabulary exercises the teacher should have in mind the technical words in his subject that are most important for students to learn. Vocabulary studies (36, 38, 67) help him to select the most important words for special study.

3. Write on the board definitions of five new words from the dictation for the day. Let students find the word that fits each of the definitions given. "Today's Most Frequently Misspelled Word" is the heading for a small chart giving the definition and correct spelling of the one word most commonly misspelled in each day's dictation. Another chart gives comparative definitions of pairs of bothersome words, such as *complimentary* and *complementary*.

In addition to these devices Mrs. Mosee planned to adapt certain procedures and principles that have been used in the teaching of reading. To forestall initial failure and build initial confidence in taking dictation, she kept the first selections within the range of the students' present vocabulary and chose selections of high interest — appealing news stories and humorous articles. To help each student evaluate his work, she kept an individual folder containing a record of his progress in charts, figures, and descriptions, to give him a knowledge of the results he was achieving. These folders also served as a springboard for personal interviews.

To enlarge students' vocabularies along lines of practical usefulness, she gradually introduced other material from the fields of medicine, law, insurance, etc. The class often suggested the kind of material they wanted to transcribe. To develop word meanings, she helped students associate unfamiliar words with concrete experiences, relate them to certain events, and use them in class discussion and conversation. In a "Vocabulary Question Box" students put questions about vocabulary problems, such as "What is the difference between *accept* and *except?*" "What are some rules about dividing words into syllables that really work — at least most of the time?" Some of the most troublesome words may be dictated by the teacher or a student on a tape recorder and played back as often as necessary for members of the class to transcribe either in longhand or shorthand, until they have mastered them. Younger students like the element of chance in the exercise of picking one of the week's troublesome words out of a hat, and running the risk of having a penalty imposed by the class for giving an incorrect definition of it. A small amount of time spent daily in lively study of the vocabulary which occurs frequently in dictation is well worth while.

To increase students' facility in getting the thought of paragraphs as they type, the teacher may have students type a few paragraphs according to specific directions. After they have completed the exercise and handed in their papers, the teacher may ask them to type a paragraph telling in their own words what they have just typed or to answer specific questions on the material. By these methods the teacher learns whether the student has read as he typed and how much information he has gained from the passage.

The teacher of any business education subject should discuss with the class the approach to each new assignment. Many students do not know the best way to go to work on a given type of assignment — the preview, the questions to ask, the ideas to remember, the form in which they may be used. After going through the first steps in the study process the teacher may select a difficult part and give instruction and practice in how to read it. He may demonstrate how to use the illustrations, study guides, headings, italicized words, enumeration of items, summary questions, and other aids to effective reading given in the book. The teacher should also allow time for immediate application and use of the facts and processes learned through the reading.

By including in bookkeeping tests opportunity for the student to demonstrate his ability to solve bookkeeping problems and actually carry out procedures, the teacher can distinguish between the student's competency in bookkeeping methods and his ability to pass a verbal test requiring considerable reading proficiency. Many students, after having learned a particular procedure, will be able to describe it clearly in their own words. If their oral description of the process is typed, the poor readers will be able to read it much more fluently than they read the usual printed instructions in a textbook.

By helping students to build technical and general vocabulary, by demonstrating suitable approaches to each kind of reading, by teaching skill in getting the meaning of difficult passages and putting the ideas gained to immediate use, the business teacher contributes to the overall school reading program.

Efforts of one faculty

The faculty of one business education department (11), after a study of their reading problems, encouraged improvement in reading among their students in the following ways:

1. The best possible books in business education are used.
2. An effort is made to see that the books and other materials are really read by the students. This is accomplished by:
   a. Checking on comprehension
   b. If an indication of a reading problem exists, students are referred to the school reading clinic.
3. Students are encouraged to read every type of material related to the subject matter field. They are encouraged to discuss these materials with their instructors after class and to form reading clubs for discussion and evaluation of the readings.
4. The Department is determined to make the reading material of business education courses as interesting and vital as possible by strong verbal introductions and good use of motivation techniques (11, p. 70).

Problems and projects

In this field also there is need for "action research" on the part of teachers. They may work individually or in groups on such studies as the following:

1. From their own experience and from the vocabulary studies that have been made in this field, they may make a list of the most important words for business education students to know.
2. From cumulative records available, they may study their own students — the relation of their marks in other subjects, reading test

scores, intelligence test scores, and socio-economic status to success in their course.

3. They may try out the methods suggested here and adapt them to their own classes; then evaluate the results they have obtained from the use of these methods.

Reading in Music Education

There are many unanswered questions concerning reading in the field of music. Here are several that teachers have asked:

"Have any studies been made of eye movement patterns while reading music, or of methods of reading music notation, which correspond to studies of reading printed words in books?"

"When starting a developmental reading program in a music class (vocal music), how effective is choral reading — reading in unison?"

"Have studies been conducted on the contribution of music to reading? Is there a place for music in the remedial reading program or clinic?"

The first question relates to the reading of music; the second, to reading as a prerequisite for singing; the third, to the place of music in a reading program.

Learning to read music

It would be enlightening to photograph the eye movements of a skillful musician reading at sight. How many notes does he recognize in one fixation of the eyes? Does he make regressive movements? If so, what causes them? Does the pattern of eye movements vary with the kind of music he is reading? It is probable that eye movements in scanning the musical score are similar to those of ordinary reading except that in reading music there is more uniformity among individuals in the number of fixations.

Reading music is first of all a visual task: the printed notes must be perceived and comprehended correctly. The methods by which beginners are taught to read music closely parallel the methods by which beginners have been taught to read print. Just as formerly, the beginning reader was taught first single letters and sounds and then encouraged to put them together to form words, so the beginning music student was taught one note at a time until he could put eight notes together to make a scale. After the introduction of the word, phrase, and sentence method in reading, larger units were also introduced to readers of music so that today music students are more likely to read in groups or patterns of notes. In music, the grouping of notes corresponds to phrase reading in English. Just as present-day reading methods produce more rapid read-

Reading music is like reading English in many ways.

New words are easily learned in favorite songs.

ers, so, also, do these methods produce more proficient sight readers of music.

Other general reading methods may be applied to the reading of music. Firsthand experiences with rhythm come before reading of music, just as other kinds of firsthand experience are prerequisite to reading stories. Interest, motivation, and enthusiasm are as important here as in other learning (60). From the beginning, melodies are now substituted for drills. Some music teachers recommend that children learn rhythm patterns, even identifying these patterns of notes at first with words (12). The principle of progression in difficulty also applies to the reading of music.

Reading about music

Why might students want to read about music and musicians? If they have had the experience of singing, or playing a musical instrument, or listening to and looking at certain musical programs, they may want to learn more about composers and their times, and about when and how their favorite musical selections were composed. Broadcasts of music festivals in America and other countries may arouse interest in reading, as well as in further listening. Students who have done some reading about music are in a better position to appreciate music on visits to radio stations and in attendance at concerts, musical comedies, and operas.

A class dictionary of musical terms or a cumulative music vocabulary chart calls students' attention to key words to be learned. The younger students enjoy matching or quiz games — matching words with their definitions; grouping related words such as orchestra families, words that tell how a piece should be played, words that describe different kinds of dance music.

Stories about music and musicians are written on different levels of reading difficulty (1, 32, 49, 83). This makes it possible for poor readers as well as gifted students to select readable books and to make interesting reports to the class. The more mature readers in high school should begin to read reviews and music news in newspapers and magazines.

The place of music in the reading program

Music can make an important contribution to the total reading program. Singing may aid in the correct pronunciation of words. In singing the vowels are given special attention since the vowel sounds are naturally stressed. Students obtain extra practice and emphasis on syllabication as they fit words and syllables to the notes. To convey the meaning of the song, the singer must also pronounce the words distinctly.

One reading teacher borrowed a song book from the music teacher when he discovered a musical interest in Carol, one of his reading cases. Since Carol had special difficulty with syllabication, he began using the song book to show how words were divided into syllables. Through various experiences — singing with the teacher, making up tunes to fit rhymes, and making rhymes to fit tunes — Carol was helped to learn to read when other methods had failed. Her first successful reading centered around reading from song books. Once confidence had been established, Carol moved on to other kinds of reading, using her newly gained skill in syllabication in the recognition of unfamiliar words in all her reading.

Students who enjoy singing may learn the words of many songs; this is purposeful reading for them and increases their vocabulary. In action songs, words are associated with bodily movement, thus bringing into play the kinesthetic reinforcement of learning. Songs associated with a historical period deepen students' understanding of and feeling for the times and the people. Choral speaking requires correct interpretation, pronunciation, and phrasing of a passage which the entire class enjoys.

Interest in particular musical instruments and musicians may lead to specialized reading activities. The history of musical instruments (1), from the time when primitive man first made crude musical sounds to the complicated story of the manufacture of modern musical instruments, is fascinating reading. Biographical information about present-day musicians may be compiled by students whose interests run along this line. Gifted students interested in music could be referred to books such as the following:

> Jacques Barzun, *Pleasures of Music*, A Reader's Choice of Great Writing about Music and Musicians from Cellini to Bernard Shaw. New York: Viking Press, 1951.
>
> Wallace Brockway, *Men of Music;* Their Lives, Times, and Achievements. New York: Simon and Schuster, 1950.
>
> David Ewen, *A Journey to Greatness.* The Life and Music of George Gershwin. New York: Henry Holt and Company, 1956.
>
> Harry W. Schwartz, *The Story of Musical Instruments from Shepherd's Pipe to Symphony.* New York: Doubleday, Doran and Company, 1938.

One teacher encouraged four of her students to make scrapbooks of clippings about their favorite performers from newspapers and musical magazines. One student clipped all the articles he could find on the orchestra; another collected those relative to the piano; the third and fourth worked together on collecting information about bands. The work of these four students, begun on an individual basis, served in the end as stimulus for a creative unit on modern-day music. The scrapbooks they made were soon being read by all the class.

Problems and projects

The more advanced students interested in music as well as teachers may make special studies such as the following:

1. Observe the eye movements of a skilled musician when he reads music by sight. By looking at his eyes over the top of his music sheet, it is possible to get some idea of how his eyes move as he reads the music. The number of pauses per line of music, the length of pauses, and any backward movements, or regressions, may be noted.

2. Apply the methods of reading in phrases or thought units to music. Divide a selection into phrases or patterns and try to read each as a unit.

3. Explore reading material in the field of music by having a free reading period in the library in which each student selects a book about music and reports on it in a subsequent class discussion. Ideally the librarian should prepare for this period by bringing out books about music and musicians on different levels of difficulty. She would introduce these books by telling something especially interesting about each one, and then guiding students in their choice of the book they want to read and can read.

Reading in Home Economics

Reading in home economics is highly practical; it is the kind of reading people often have to do in life situations. The reading experiences encountered in school may be applied immediately at home. Among the practical applications of reading which students learn in home economics are the reading and comprehension of recipes, bills, and invoices; the reading of gas, water, and electric meters; the reading of thermometers and indicators on various home gadgets; the comprehension of labels and other descriptions of the contents of foods and the quality of goods; and the reading of charts and graphs showing trends in prices. In addition, home economics students should be given instruction and practice in reading advertisements, appraising their accuracy, and analyzing their appeals. They should be encouraged during school years to read newspaper and magazine articles on child care and homemaking. If they begin reading this type of article in school, they will be more likely to continue these interests after they leave school.

Kinds of reading required
in home economics

Home economics gives practice in reading directions. The student's reading of recipes, directions on dress patterns, or suggestions as to how to make and do things, is immediately tested by her ability to follow the directions. This is the most effective kind of reading test. The student cannot pass it by parroting the words of the text without real comprehension of their meaning. Instead, she must have an accurate comprehension of every significant sentence. Errors result in a sad-looking cake or a dress that does not fit. By providing this practice in the reading of directions, home economics contributes to the student's appreciation of reading as a means to an end — reading for some practical, personal purpose.

Wide reading in home economics, as in other subjects, can increase the student's technical and general vocabulary. Articles on every aspect of home economics, found in newspapers and magazines, should be brought in by the students and placed under appropriate headings on the bulletin board or in folders. The student bringing in the article may be responsible for underlining the new technical words in it and adding them to the class dictionary. Each day the teacher may put on the board several new words and their definitions. Even though no class time is spent in studying these words, it has been found that students gain some vocabulary knowledge in this way. Most effective is the study of the words simultaneously with the learning of a certain process, or the use of ingredients or materials.

The home economics teacher also has a fine opportunity to teach critical reading. Advertisements offer practice in discriminating between facts and distortions of facts. One class collected samples of various ways in which advertisers camouflage the facts about their products. These are some of the "tricks of the trade" which they detected:

Presenting only a partial picture — withholding facts that would give a different impression.

Associating the product with prestige value, such as expensive flowers, aristocratic homes, people of importance, sports, etc.

Associating the product with other social values, such as attracting the opposite sex and being popular in general.

Generalizing from insufficient data.

To encourage permanent reading interests in the field of home economics, teachers should encourage students to select, evaluate, and read magazine and newspaper articles. Many of these give excellent, up-to-date information on homemaking and child care — including both physical and psychological aspects. The best way to develop discriminating adult readers is to give students instruction and practice in the art of functional reading while they are still in school.

Examples of procedures

The home economics teacher can adapt many of the methods and practice exercises used in the teaching of reading in other fields. If a class has been having difficulty in reading recipes, she may give them special practice. For example, in a lesson on making hot cross buns, the following recipe was given:

1 cup scalded milk	$\frac{1}{4}$ teaspoon salt
1 pkg. active dry or	$\frac{1}{2}$ teaspoon cinnamon
1 cake compressed yeast	or nutmeg
$\frac{1}{4}$ cup lukewarm water	4 cups sifted flour
$\frac{1}{2}$ cup butter, margarine	$\frac{1}{2}$ cup currants or
$\frac{1}{2}$ cup sugar	raisins

Mix fat, sugar, salt, spices in a bowl. Stir in hot milk and cool to lukewarm. Mix in the yeast, and then 2 cups flour. Add currants and rest of flour. Let stand in a warm spot until it has risen double in size.

Knead dough on a lightly floured board until springy. Shape pieces of dough into buns about 2 inches in diameter. Place on greased cookie sheets. Let rise until double in size.

Cut crosses into tops of buns with a sharp knife. Brush tops gently with mixture of egg yolk and water. Bake in a 375°F. or moderate oven 15 or 20 minutes or until light brown.

Make a frosting of $1\frac{1}{3}$ cups confectioners' sugar mixed with 2 tablespoons water.

With a spoon put the frosting into the cross indentations on cool buns. This recipe should make 18 to 20.

Before the students read the recipe, the teacher should give them firsthand experience with the unfamiliar words which it contains. She may show them a picture of hot cross buns and bring out the following ingredients for all to see: active dry yeast, a cake of compressed yeast, margarine, cinnamon, nutmeg, currants, raisins. Students may be asked to name the different kinds of spices which they know, and to compare dry with compressed yeast, cinnamon with nutmeg, raisins with currants. These words should be printed on the board as they talk about them, and also on cards placed in front of the respective substances. They should be read from the labels on boxes and cans. They may also be copied into class or individual dictionaries for later review.

Each unfamiliar process should be demonstrated by the teacher or a student or acted out in pantomime: Kneading dough, flouring a board, greasing a cookie sheet, putting frosting in indentations, shaping pieces of dough about 2 inches in diameter.

Before going to work, and after reading the recipe, the group should write and then discuss briefly the answers to such questions as these:

What ingredients are to be mixed together first?
How can you tell when milk is lukewarm?
What makes the dough rise to double its size?

Number in order the following steps as they should be taken:
Knead dough until springy.
Brush tops of buns with mixture of egg yolk and water.
Add hot milk to fat, sugar, salt, spices.
Make frosting.
Let dough rise until double in size.
Put frosting into cross indentations.
Mix fat, sugar, salt, spices in a bowl.
Shape dough into buns.
Cut crosses on buns.
Add yeast and half the flour.
Add currants and rest of flour.
Let buns rise until double in size.
Bake in moderate oven (375°F.).
Let buns cool.
Heat milk until bubbles appear around edge.
Cool to lukewarm.
(Correct order is: 15, 7, 3, 16, 10, 11, 5, 1, 8, 12, 9, 2, 13, 14, 4, 6.)

This exercise will give students practice in reading and will also serve as a guide for practical work. Such instruction, however, is best given in the previous period. Youngsters coming into the home economics room are eager to cook or to make things. They have had enough of studying from books. Consequently they are likely to be impatient with the reading instruction unless they feel that it will help them get to work faster and more efficiently.

A common problem is the wide range of reading ability represented in most classes. Some students do not need practice in reading directions; they can assist by printing labels, setting up exhibits, giving demonstrations, making the class dictionary, and helping other students with their reading difficulties. Retarded readers may learn the process from the oral instruction and demonstrations. After having had this firsthand experience, they may write how they did it, thus making their own book of recipes written in their own words.

Problems and projects

Teachers of home economics may make a real contribution to the teaching of reading in their field by making special studies such as:

1. Study recipes in cookbooks and magazines and directions for other homemaking activities from the standpoint of vocabulary and sentence structure. Since the students will have to read this printed material later, the teacher should prepare mimeographed practice exercises on reading recipes and following dressmaking directions.

2. Build up a file of articles on homemaking and child care and classify

Lack of reading comprehension spoils the broth.

Reading a recipe should be taught before cooking begins.

them according to topic and reading difficulty. Clippings that students bring in, if of permanent value, can be classified by a committee and added to the file each year.

Reading in Industrial Arts and School Shops

The reading problems in auto mechanics, electric wiring, plumbing, and other shopwork are somewhat similar to those in home economics, beauty culture, and the like. The student must be able to read the names of tools and materials and he must know the "terms of the trade." He must master the reading of directions — the true test of his reading is in a practical situation.

A sound instructional sequence is:

1. demonstration of the tools, materials, and processes
2. vocabulary study
3. practice and instruction in reading the specific directions needed for today's work
4. testing comprehension by carrying out directions

If the reading level of the class is very low, the students may, as a group, dictate the steps in the process they have learned. These directions, when typed and duplicated, serve as a manual for future reference.

Study of vocabulary

In demonstrating the tools, materials, and processes, the teacher should teach the words associated with them. For example, in the print shop, students must learn the meaning of *em, ream, pica*, and other technical words essential to understanding the field and the culture of the society in which printing is done. Methods of vocabulary study already described may be used. It is helpful for teachers to know which are the basic words in these fields. Studies of the vocabulary used in industrial arts and vocational education (78, 87) give this information.

Reading materials in shopwork

Much of the reading students do in shop classes is the reading of directions, which requires a slow, study-reading approach. Formerly, most directions were written by technicians whose style and vocabulary were above the average high school shop student. Today, however, attention is being given to the readability of materials used by shop people. A simple device for measuring the readability of material is the Reading-Ease Calculator (64). The rough estimate of reading difficulty obtained by using this device is based on length of sentence and difficulty of vocabulary, as indicated by words of more than one syllable. It was developed by one of our largest manufacturing companies when a member of the staff discovered that instructions, directions, company pamphlets, and the like were too difficult for practical use.

Much may be done in school shops, as well as in industry, toward simplifying directions for workers. Many job specifications and directions, as well as textbooks, are unnecessarily difficult in vocabulary and sentence structure; they could be made more readable (62). This would be an efficiency measure for employers, as well as a means of reducing frustration among workers who are poor readers.

There also is need for simply written pamphlets about vocations relating to shopwork in which the boys are interested. The majority of pamphlets and books about vocations are difficult to read and deal with professions or other vocations too skilled for many students to enter. Readable pamphlets on unskilled and semiskilled work are needed. The following short list might encourage shop teachers to compile their own lists with the aid of interested students:

> Superintendent of Documents, Washington 25, D.C.
> > "The Worker's Story"
> > "Hand Tools"
> > "Job Guide for Young Workers"
> > "Duty, Honor, Country"
> > "You Can Make It: Woodworking and Furniture Repair"
> > "Industrial Safety Charts"
> Bristol-Myers Company, 45 Rockefeller Plaza, New York 20, New York
> > "Guide for Good Grooming Program"
> > "Teaching Dental Care"
> General Motors, Detroit, Michigan
> > "ABC of Hand Tools"
> General Electric, Schenectady, New York
> > Comic book type material on the atom, electricity, etc.
> National Association of Manufacturers, 14 West 49th Street,
> New York 20, New York
> > "Your Future Is What You Make It"
> > "Preparing for Industrial Work"
> > Charts

Leisure reading

Since our schools should prepare young people for the leisure of life as well as for the work of life, students taking shop courses should, somewhere in their program, be given the experience of reading for enjoyment. Leisure reading should be emphasized in their English classes especially. Recognizing the lack of interest in recreational reading on the part of eleventh-grade boys in a technical course, one teacher introduced a three weeks' reading project in her class. She selected stories high in interest, such as *Pigs Is Pigs* by Ellis Parker Butler; *The Lady or the Tiger* by Frank R. Stockton; *The Tell-Tale Heart* by Edgar Allan Poe; and stories of suspense and mystery from the *Reader's Digest* and *Coronet*. These stories appealed to this group. Since they had foreign backgrounds and needed to hear good English spoken and since they enjoyed reading aloud, the teacher let small groups of five or six select a story they wanted to read. In each group there was at least one good reader who could help the poor readers pronounce difficult words and understand the meaning of the selection. After reading the story aloud, the small group planned to present it to the whole class as a book review, dramatization, series of pictures, or in other interesting ways. Some of the stories were supplemented by radio and movie versions. Although no outside reading was assigned, the boys wanted to read more such stories, and began to read outside of class. This group of initially reluctant readers participated practically 100 per cent in this reading activity.

As in all types of curricula, sheer enjoyment is certainly one legitimate objective of reading. Students must experience enjoyment if they are to take advantage later on of this inexpensive use of leisure time. This kind of enjoyment frees the individual from the tyranny of commercial entertainment, and opens unlimited avenues of contact with all kinds of people, places, and times. Moreover, enjoyable leisure reading in different fields, by developing general vocabulary and fluency, increases the student's efficiency in the kind of reading demanded in the work-a-day world.

Problems and projects

Shop teachers need to study these problems further:

1. On their own experience, supplemented by published vocabulary studies, make a list of words most important to teach in the subject.

2. Show how the meanings of each of these words may be most effectively taught through demonstration, showing the object, using pictures or diagrams, and other means.

3. Collect interesting books or articles on different levels of difficulty about workers in the fields for which the various shops give preparation.

Reading in Physical and Health Education

In physical education, and still more in health education, some reading is necessary. Practice thus obtained adds to the student's total reading proficiency.

Physical education

In physical education students sometimes need to read with accurate comprehension the rules for basketball and other games. Those who are physically unable to participate actively in sports may become team photographers, sports writers for the school or local paper, or authorities on major league scores. In one school students returning after a serious illness rested on cots in the open patio, which they called "the sun deck," where they could read and relax. For boys, sports stories are high in interest, though it does not always follow that those who like to engage in sports will enjoy reading about them.

Health education

In health education classes, introducing methods of improving reading about health may increase the interest of both teacher and students. This was true of a high school health education class, which was large and heterogeneous, including many slow-learning students. It met once a week. The teacher was bored with the health education guide sheets. So were the students.

At this point a reading project on personality was introduced. First the students selected the topics on which they wanted to work and elected seven chairmen for these interest groups. While the class as a whole was taking a general health knowledge test, the teacher met with the chairmen to help them improve their leadership of the small groups. For five weeks these groups worked in the library, gathering and organizing facts and planning how to present their ideas about their topic. Students who were not capable of doing independent study in the library met for instruction in the classroom with the teacher. Finally, each group reported to the whole class in dramatic form the results of their study.

The teacher, who had previously preferred to teach only the bright students, was thrilled by the achievement of the slow-learning students. Her success with them encouraged her to continue work along these lines. As she worked with them she became more and more aware of their reading problems, and, with the help of the reading teacher, more and more competent in solving them.

From the first grade of elementary school, health education offers special opportunities to teach reading. Its subject matter deals with familiar personal experiences; it lends itself to dramatization, both written and spontaneous; it uses a variety of supplementary material from newspapers and magazines, and from commercial pamphlets and advertisements, some of which, such as those published by General Mills, are colorful and richly illustrated. Moreover, health information can be put to immediate use in solving real personal and community health problems. Although a small part of the reading in health education is primarily for enjoyment, its main purpose is to impart information about how to keep well and happy, and thus to make our world better in one fundamental respect.

Problems and projects

In health education there is a real need to study problems of reading. The teacher, working either with individuals or with groups, may:

1. Give a simple vocabulary test of common health words to her class, letting them write their own definition of each. She will probably be amazed at the many misconceptions.

2. Select books (5) related to each of the "developmental tasks of adolescents" for recommended reading.

3. Build interest in reading health articles and columns in newspapers and magazines and in listening critically and judiciously to radio and television programs relating to health.

Improvement of Reading through Student Activities

Clubs of various kinds require reading to carry on their activities. Athletic and social clubs require the least reading; science and departmental clubs require somewhat more; and poetry appreciation, dramatic, and other reading clubs necessitate a large amount. Success in speech and dramatic clubs depends upon efficient reading. To read aloud effectively, the person must understand word meanings, phrase correctly, emphasize important words, and make smooth transitions between related ideas.

Clubs also give practice in certain kinds of writing which are required in adult life — writing social and business letters, minutes of meetings, reports of committees, news stories about club activities. From the standpoint of proficiency, these reading and writing tasks have the quality of urgency; they call for the application and use of communication skills.

Concluding Statement

The question is frequently raised as to whether a teacher of any subject other than English needs to be concerned with his students' reading. It seems clear that teachers of every subject will do more effective work if they will devote some time to the teaching of reading in their respective fields. Each can adapt procedures developed by creative teachers in his own field and by reading teachers who have worked with small groups and individual cases. However, reading instruction alone will not insure general scholastic improvement. Students may learn to read better, but still not know how to communicate the ideas they have gained. Listen-

Social development and reading development join hands.

Language arts are involved in singing and in other life activities.

ing, speaking, and writing — in short, the communication arts — have a place in every subject.

Teaching reading is not an extra duty; it is an intrinsic part of every teacher's job — the job of teaching students *how* to learn as well as *what* to learn. What does this view of teaching involve? First, at the beginning of the term, the teacher should find out how well each student in his class can comprehend the books he is expected to read. The teacher learns this best by informal methods, such as by diagnosing difficulties while listening to a student's oral reading and by using "teaching tests." These serve as a springboard to instruction and practice in better methods of reading the subject.

The teacher also uses incidental opportunities to teach reading skills. In every class opportunities arise to learn how to recognize unfamiliar words, to use various techniques to get word meaning and enrich key concepts, to relate ideas in a historical or a fictional sequence, to adapt rate and method of reading to the material and purpose. The teacher makes students aware of the method and encourages the use of it until it is mastered.

In this task of teaching how to read his subject, the teacher is seriously handicapped if he does not have a range of reading material in his field as wide as the reading interests and abilities of his students. With materials, knowledge, and sound teaching methods every teacher can help students to develop the necessary reading skills and to enjoy reading.

REFERENCES

1. BAUER, MARION, and PEYSER, E. *How Music Grew; from Prehistoric Times to the Present.* New York: G. P. Putnam's Sons, 1940.
2. BLACKSTONE, E. G., and SMITH, SOFRONA L. *Improvement of Instruction in Typewriting* (Second Edition). New York: Prentice-Hall, Inc., 1949.
3. BLANC, SAM S. "Vitalizing the Classroom — Slides, Film Strips, and Films." *School Science and Mathematics*, Vol. LIII (April, 1953), pp. 255–58.
4. BOND, GUY L., and BOND, EVA. *Developmental Reading in High School.* New York: The Macmillan Company, 1941.
5. BROOKS, ALICE R. "Integrating Books and Reading with Adolescent Tasks." *School Review*, Vol. LVIII (April, 1950), pp. 211–19.
6. BROOKS, CLEANTH, and WARREN, ROBERT PENN. *Understanding Poetry.* New York: Henry Holt and Company, 1952.
7. BROWN, CLYDE M. "Reading in Science as a Means of Improving the Junior High School Program." *Science Teacher*, Vol. XXI (November, 1954), pp. 281–83.
8. BROWN, KARL F. "Developing Reading Skills through Literature and Social Studies." *High School Journal* (University of North Carolina), Vol. XXXVI (October, 1952), pp. 12–16.

9. BROWN, SPENCER. *They See for Themselves.* New York: Harper and Brothers, 1945.

10. BROWNELL, WILLIAM A. "When Is Arithmetic Meaningful?" *Journal of Educational Research,* Vol. XXXVIII (March, 1945), pp. 481–98.

11. BUDISH, B. E. "Business Education Instructor Also Teaches Reading." *Journal of Business Education,* Vol. XXX (November, 1954), pp. 68–70.

12. CANTWELL, D. C. "Use of Mnemonics in Music Reading." *Music Educator's Journal,* Vol. XXXVIII (November, 1951), p. 52.

13. CARBONI, JANE A. "A Plan for the Improvement of Reading in the Spanish Department as a Part of a Developmental Reading Program in Sewanhaka High School." Unpublished doctoral project. New York: Teachers College, Columbia University, 1949.

14. CARPENTER, HELEN McCRACKEN (Editor) with the advisory assistance of Dorothy McClue, Ole Sand, and Alice W. Spieske. *Skills in Social Studies.* The Twenty-Fourth Yearbook of the National Council for Social Studies. Washington 5, D.C.: National Council for the Social Studies, 1954.

15. CARTER, HOMER L. J. "Reading, A Contributing and Concomitant Factor in the Study of Science." *School, Science, and Mathematics,* Vol. LIV (October, 1954), pp. 567–70.

16. COLE, LUELLA. *The Teacher's Handbook of Technical Vocabulary.* Bloomington, Illinois: Public School Publishing Company, 1940.

17. CONANT, MARGARET M. *The Construction of a Diagnostic Reading Test for Senior High School Students and College Freshmen.* Teachers College Contributions to Education, No. 861. New York: Bureau of Publications, Teachers College, Columbia University, 1942.

18. Cooperative English Test C_1. Princeton, New Jersey: Educational Testing Service.

19. Coronet Instructional Films, Chicago, Illinois.

20. DICKENS, CHARLES. *A Tale of Two Cities.* Adapted by Elizabeth Toomey; edited by William Kottmeyer. St. Louis: Webster Publishing Company, 1947.

21. EAGLE, EDWIN. "The Relationship of Certain Reading Abilities to Success in Mathematics." *Mathematics Teacher,* Vol. XLI (April, 1948), pp. 175–79.

22. *The English Language Arts.* Prepared by the Commission on the English Curriculum of the National Council of Teachers of English. New York: Appleton-Century-Crofts, 1952.

23. EOFF, S. H., and BULL, W. E. "Semantic Approach to the Teaching of Foreign Languages." *Modern Language Journal,* Vol. XXXII (January, 1948), pp. 3–13.

24. ERNST, K. D. "Place of Reading in the Elementary Music Program." *Music Educator's Journal,* Vol. XXXIX (January, 1952), pp. 26–28.

25. FEHR, HOWARD F. "General Ways to Identify Students with Scientific and Mathematical Potential." *Mathematics Teacher,* Vol. XLVI (April, 1953), pp. 230–34.

26. *Five Steps to Reading Success in Science, Social Studies, and Mathematics.* 525 West 120th Street, New York: Metropolitan School Study Council, 1954.

27. FLEMING, ROBERT E. "Mathematics and Its English." *School Science and Mathematics,* Vol. LIII (October, 1953), pp. 601–602.

28. FORSHEIT, SAMUEL. "Conversation through Reading." *French Review,* Vol. XXVI (February, 1953), pp. 299–303.

29. FREDRICK, F. "All Music Reading Is Sight Reading." *Etude,* Vol. LXIX (November, 1951), pp. 14+.

30. GAINSBERG, JOSEPH C. "Critical Reading Is Creative Reading and Needs Creative Teaching." *The Reading Teacher,* Vol. VI (March, 1953), pp. 19–25.

31. GALL, MORRIS. "The History Teacher as a Reading and Literature Teacher." *Education,* Vol. LXXIII (May, 1953), pp. 561–65.

32. GRAHAM, ALBERTA P. *Strike Up the Band.* New York: Thomas Nelson and Sons, 1949.

33. GRAY, WILLIAM S. (Editor). *Improving Reading in All Curriculum Areas.* Supplementary Educational Monographs, No. 76. Chicago: University of Chicago Press, November, 1952.

34. GRAY, WILLIAM S. (Editor). *Improving Reading in Content Fields.* Supplementary Educational Monographs, No. 62. Chicago: University of Chicago Press, 1947.

35. GRAY, WILLIAM S. (Editor). *Promoting Growth toward Maturity in Interpreting What Is Read.* Chicago: University of Chicago Press, 1951.

36. HICKS, C. B. "Shorthand and Business Vocabulary Understanding." *UBEA Forum,* Vol. V (October, 1950), pp. 13–16.

37. HOOK, J. N. *The Teaching of High School English.* New York: The Ronald Press, 1950.

38. HORN, ERNEST, and PETERSON, THELMA. *The Basic Vocabulary of Business Letters.* New York: Gregg Publishing Company, 1943.

39. HOUSE, FOREST WAYNE. "Are You Solving the Reading Problem in Bookkeeping?" *Business Educational World,* Vol. XXXIII (February, 1953), pp. 291–92.

40. *How to Read Novels, How to Read Plays, How to Read Poetry.* Coronet Guides. Chicago: Coronet Instructional Films.

41. HUMPHREVILLE, FRANCES T. "Learning about Pupils through Their Written Comments on Selected Stories." *School Review,* Vol. LX (December, 1952), pp. 541–44.

42. JEWETT, ARNO. *Recordings for Teaching Literature and Language in the High School.* U.S. Office of Education Bulletin, No. 19. Washington, D.C.: Government Printing Office. 1952.

43. KANZELL, MAXWELL. *How to Read Music.* New York: Carl Fischer, 1944.

44. KAY, SYLVIA C. *Reading Critically (in the Fields of Literature and History).* New York: Twayne Publishers, 1952.

45. KING, HAROLD V. "Foreign Language Reading as a Learning Activity." *Modern Language Journal,* Vol. XXXI (December, 1947), pp. 519–24.

46. LANE, FREDERIC C.; GOLDMAN, ERIC F.; and HUNT, ERLING M. *The World's History.* New York: Harcourt, Brace and Company, 1947 (Revised in 1954).

47. *Language Arts for Secondary Schools.* Resource Materials, Curriculum Bulletin Series. Dallas: Dallas Independent School District, 1953.

48. LAWRENCE, ARMON JAY. "A Vocabulary of Business and Economic Terms of Popular Usage." *Bulletin* of the Bureau of School Service, College of Education, University of Kentucky, Vol. XVII (March, 1945).

49. LAWRENCE, HARRIET. *Series on Famous Operas.* New York: Grosset and Dunlap, 1948–1953.

50. LEARY, BERNICE E. "Improving Reading Skills in Mathematics and Science." *High School Journal,* Vol. XXXVI (October, 1952), pp. 17–21.

51. LESLIE, LOUIS A. *Methods of Teaching Gregg Shorthand.* New York: Gregg Publishing Division, McGraw-Hill Book Company, 1953.

52. LESLIE, LOUIS A. *Tape Recording in Business Education.* St. Paul: Educational Services Division, Minnesota Mining and Manufacturing Company, 1953.

53. MALLINSON, GEORGE GREISEN. "How to Use the Textbook in Science Teaching." *School Science and Mathematics,* Vol. LIII (November, 1953), pp. 593–600.

54. MALLINSON, GEORGE GREISEN, and OTHERS. "Reading Difficulty of Textbooks for General Physical Science and Earth Science." *School Science and Mathematics,* Vol. LIV (November, 1954), pp. 612–16.

55. MALLINSON, GEORGE GREISEN, and OTHERS. "Reading Difficulty of Textbooks for General Science." *School Review,* Vol. LX (February, 1952), pp. 94–98.

56. MORTON, R. L. "Language and Meaning in Arithmetic." *Educational Research Bulletin* (College of Education, Ohio State University), Vol. XXXIV (November 9, 1955), pp. 197–204.

57. NATIONAL COUNCIL OF TEACHERS OF MATHEMATICS. *The Learning of Mathematics — Its Theory and Practice.* Twenty-First Yearbook. Washington, D.C.: National Council of Teachers of Mathematics, 1953.

58. NATIONAL SOCIETY FOR THE STUDY OF EDUCATION. *Reading in the High School and College.* Forty-Seventh Yearbook, Part II. Chicago: University of Chicago Press, 1948.

59. NYACK PUBLIC SCHOOLS. *Inside Our Schools,* Vol. II (March, 1954), Nyack, New York.

60. NYE, R. E. "If You Don't Use Syllables, What Do You Use?" *Music Educator's Journal,* Vol. XXXIX (April, 1953), pp. 41–42.

61. PARSTECK, BENNETT J. "The Newest Medium for Book Reports." *English Journal,* Vol. XLII (April, 1953), pp. 210–11.

62. PETERSON, ELEANOR. *Aspects of Readability in the Social Studies.* New York: Bureau of Publications, Teachers College, Columbia University, 1954.

63. PHELPS, MARGARET E. "The Evolution of a Reading Program in a Special English Class." Unpublished doctoral project. New York: Teachers College, Columbia University, 1955.

64. *Reading-Ease Calculator.* Chicago: Science Research Associates.
65. *The Reading Teacher,* "Literature for Children and Youth," Vol. IX (February, 1956), pp. 131–58.
66. RINKER, FLOYD. "Stimulating Creative Expression." *NEA Journal,* Vol. XLII (December, 1953), pp. 551–52.
67. RUTAN, E. J. "Word Study in Business Education." *Journal of Business Education,* Vol. XXI (March, 1946), pp. 29–30.
68. SCHERER, GEORGE A. C. "Importance of Auditory Comprehension." *German Quarterly,* Vol. XXV (November, 1952), pp. 223–29.
69. SHAEWITZ, LEONARD. "Semantics for Modern Languages." *Modern Language Journal,* Vol. XXXVII (April, 1953), pp. 177–80.
70. SHEPHERD, DAVID. "Effective Reading in the Social Studies." Unpublished doctoral project. New York: Teachers College, Columbia University, 1954.
71. SHORES, J. HARLAN, and SAUPE, J. L. "Reading for Problem-Solving in Science." *Journal of Educational Psychology,* Vol. XLIV (March, 1953), pp. 149–58.
72. *Social Studies, A Description of the Social Tests of the College Entrance Examination Board.* Princeton, New Jersey: Educational Testing Service, P.O. Box 592, 1953.
73. SPAULDING, SETH. "Three-Dimensional Word Repetition in Reading Material." *Modern Language Journal,* Vol. XXXVII (May, 1953), pp. 226–30.
74. SQUIRE, JAMES R. "Emotional Responses to a Short Story." *The Reading Teacher,* Vol. IX (October, 1955), pp. 30–35.
75. STRANG, RUTH, and OTHERS. *Study Type of Reading Exercises* (Revised). High School Level. New York: Bureau of Publications, Teachers College, Columbia University, 1956.
76. STRANG, RUTH, McCULLOUGH, CONSTANCE; and TRAXLER, ARTHUR E. *Problems in the Improvement of Reading* (Revised and Enlarged). New York: McGraw-Hill Book Company, 1955.
77. STRANG, RUTH, and ROBERTS, RALPH. *Teen-Age Tales.* Books I and II. STRANG, RUTH, and HEAVEY, REGINA, Book III. Boston: D. C. Heath and Company, 1953, 1955.
78. STRUCK, F. T. "102 Key Words." *Industrial Arts and Vocational Education,* Vol. XXXII (February, 1943), p. 57.
79. SUERKEN, E. H. "Basic Glossary and Vocabulary in Printing." *Industrial Arts and Vocational Education,* Vol. XLI (November, 1952), pp. 305–307.
80. "Teaching of Science in Grades VII, VIII and IX." *Review of Educational Research,* Vol. XV (October, 1945), pp. 289–97.
81. TRIGGS, FRANCES O. *We All Teach Reading.* Privately printed by the author, Frances O. Triggs, 419 West 119th Street, New York 27, New York, 1954.
82. WESLEY, EDGAR B., and ADAMS, MARY A. *Teaching Social Studies in Elementary Schools.* Boston: D. C. Heath and Company, 1946.
83. WHEELER, OPAL, and DEUCHER, SYBIL. *Series on Composers.* New York: E. P. Dutton and Company, 1936–1940.

84. WHIPPLE, G. W. "Vocabulary Development: Social Studies." *Education*, Vol. LXXI (May, 1951), pp. 564–66.

85. WILBORN, LEE J.; ALEXANDER, NELLE; and BRACKEN, DOROTHY KENDALL. *The Improvement of Reading in Secondary Schools.* Bulletin No. 540. Austin: Texas Education Agency, 1953.

86. WILLGING, HERBERT M. "A New Approach to the Reading Objective." *Modern Language Journal*, Vol. XXXII (February, 1948), pp. 108–11.

87. WILLIAMS, S. L., and ANDERSON, S. A. "Power of Words in Industrial Arts." *American Vocational Journal*, Vol. XXVII (December, 1953), p. 12.

88. WITHROW, DOROTHY. "The Philadelphia Secondary School Reading Program: Small Remedial Reading Classes and Individual Cases." Unpublished doctoral project. New York: Teachers College, Columbia University, 1955.

89. WITTY, PAUL. "Reading of Social Studies Materials." *Elementary English*, Vol. XXVII (January, 1950), pp. 1–8, 62.

90. WITTY, PAUL. *Reading Roundup, A New Basal Reading Literature Series.* Boston: D. C. Heath and Company, 1955.

91. WOOD, WILLIAM R. *Short, Short Stories.* New York: Harcourt, Brace and Company, 1951.

92. WOODRING, MAXIE N., and SANFORD, VERA. *Enriched Teaching of Mathematics in the Junior and Senior High School.* New York: Bureau of Publications, Teachers College, Columbia University, 1942.

SPECIAL READING GROUPS AND
READING CLINICS

MANY RETARDED READERS need individual help. Some of it can be given during the regular class period, as already described in the sections on individualization of instruction. Teachers may also devote some time to work with individual pupils during their free periods or after school. But there are still many students who need more expert and intensive help than teachers can give. These students may be referred to special small reading groups or to reading clinics.

Individual Help Given by Teachers

In addition to the classroom instruction in reading which every teacher gives to his class as a whole and to subgroups within his regular class, the skillful teacher often helps retarded readers individually (17). Here are some examples:

Bill, a senior in high school, was a slow reader and lacked confidence in his ability to read faster. However, his English teacher gave him extra time for examinations, which demonstrated to him that he had the power but not the speed; and this reassured him. His teacher also individualized his assignments, suggesting wide reading of easy material on his favorite topics instead of intensive reading of dull material. Independently he did exercises in a workbook, *How to Read Better and Faster* (Thomas Y. Crowell Company), which gave him practice in the skills in which he was weak. A comparable form of the reading test given at the end of the year showed an increase in speed of comprehension from the 21 to the 45 percentile and in level of comprehension from the 48 to the 57 percentile. This special consideration given to Bill by a friendly teacher was all that he needed to improve his reading.

Another English teacher helped Jean, whose reading test showed a low vocabulary score. The teacher taught her how to make notes of the unfamiliar and difficult words she found in her reading. Jean wrote each of these, with the meaning, on one side of a card and she wrote sentences using the word on the other side. By reviewing these words from time to time she increased the number of words she could recognize unerringly at sight. The teacher also took time to give Jean and several others special instruction in word meaning skills — using context clews, structural analysis, and the dictionary. They also browsed through and discussed Ernst's *In a Word* (8), which aroused their interest in word origins and meanings.

A social studies teacher found time to help Donald individually. Donald was having trouble organizing what he read and remembering it. The teacher showed that these two abilities go together; when facts are related, they are easier to remember. They started with selections that were very clearly structured; the author had made his organization obvious. Gradually they worked on finding the main ideas and their relations and supporting details in more difficult material. Donald was especially helped in writing well-organized paragraphs and compositions. First he selected a topic in which he was interested — "The Track Meet on Saturday." Then he thought of the main points of interest and the details related to each main point. Having organized the facts, he was able to write well-constructed paragraphs. He proved to himself that taking time to organize his history and other reading assignments paid off. His subjects became more interesting to him and he remembered what he had read. As a result, his attitude toward himself and his attitude toward school began to change for the better.

Although a teacher may find time to give intensive extra help to several seriously retarded readers in his classes, there is a limit to the individual work a teacher can do. If he spends a disproportionate amount of time with individual students, it may be at the expense of work with the whole class. Moreover, there are some reading problems that are baffling to the classroom teacher. He does not know the causes of these reading difficulties and the procedures he has used do not seem to be effective. These individuals he would like to refer to special reading classes or to a reading clinic.

The Special Reading Class

When the regular teachers are not able to meet the reading needs of certain individuals, small special classes may be formed. These have already been briefly described as special sections of English classes (see Chapter 5). The purpose of these classes is to give students with unrealized reading potentiality more intensive diagnosis and remedial work than is possible in the regular classes. The reading teacher tries to help the student discover the causes of his reading difficulty and to correct them.

To these special classes the teachers will refer students whose reading age is one or more years below their mental age and whom they have not been able to help much in their regular classes. They should not refer discipline problems, nor should they refer slow learners who are reading as well as they can and who need experiences other than reading through which they can learn the things necessary for a useful life.

The way in which students are referred to special reading classes or clinics is important; it largely determines the student's initial attitude toward the experience. Never should any stigma be attached to a special reading class or reading clinic. Teachers should try to build the attitude that these services offer a special opportunity to a limited number of students and that anyone who is accepted in the special reading class or clinic is indeed fortunate.

The special reading classes should be taught by a reading specialist or, at least, by a teacher who has studied problems in the improvement of reading of high-school-age students.

It is very important for the reading teacher to have an initial interview with the student referred to the special group. This enables the reading teacher to view the reading problem through the student's eyes; to understand the student's attitudes toward reading and toward himself; to discover earlier experiences, home conditions, present circumstances that may be interfering with reading improvement. In this initial interview the student may also describe previous attempts to improve, why they failed, and what he thinks will work best now. For example, in the first interview with a thirteen-year-old boy who spoke indistinctly and seemed apprehensive, the worker included the following questions in the course of the conversation:

The instructor fills in the interest inventory.

The right book for a particular pupil is a readable book.

Worker: Just tell me about yourself, Jim.

Jim: What?

Worker: Anything you want to.

Jim. Ask me.

Worker: Well, what about reading?

Jim: I don't like to read, unless it's interesting.

Worker: You like to read things you're interested in?

Jim: Yes, but I don't like to read aloud. . . .

Worker: When did reading get hard for you?

Jim: In the fourth grade.

Other questions that brought out valuable information were:

How does your family feel about your reading?

What do you do when you meet an unfamiliar word?

Tell me how you do your studying.

It became evident that the parents had unsuccessfully tried to help Jim with his reading. Their impatience and disappointment with his progress reinforced his negative self-concept and their anxiety about his reading was being transferred to the boy himself. Having sensed Jim's fear and anxiety about reading, the worker, in this first interview, selected very easy material for him to read and tried to maintain a relaxed and "easy-does-it" attitude.

If the student is highly motivated to work on improving his reading, the reading teacher will not go through a lengthy detailed diagnostic procedure. Such an approach might increase the student's sense of inadequacy, which so many reading cases feel acutely, as well as cause impatience over not making immediate progress in reading. Instead, the reading teacher will begin with several oral reading paragraphs that are likely to be suitable to the student. The following paragraphs are the two easiest ones from the *Diagnostic Reading Record*, published by the Teachers College Bureau of Publications:

Oral Reading Passage A

Fear, like anger, stops the flow of the digestive juices. In India a test was once used to tell whether or not a prisoner was guilty of a crime. The man was given a handful of dry rice to put in his mouth. He was told to keep the rice in his mouth a few minutes. If the prisoner had committed a crime and was very much frightened, his saliva would stop flowing and the rice would remain dry. If he was not guilty and had no fear of being punished, his saliva would flow as usual and the rice would be wet.

Oral Reading Passage B

The earth has written its own story. Like all the books in the world, it cannot tell everything. Like all very old books, this book of the earth has missing pages. In places the words are dim or in a language men have not yet learned to understand. But the book is there — a thrilling story of strange and mysterious things, of living creatures so small they have to be imagined, and of monsters the like of which we shall never see alive. The pages of the book are the layers of rock that lie one on top of another.

As the student reads, the teacher notes his attitude — whether he is anxious, embarrassed, apologetic, indifferent, hopeful, or overoptimistic. The teacher also notes poor phrasing, lack of expression, and errors in pronunciation and the omission, repetition, and substitution of words or letters. By asking the student to give the gist or the main idea of the paragraph, the important details, and the meaning of certain words and phrases, the teacher can ascertain the student's ability to comprehend. The same procedure may be used with paragraphs from a book which the student chooses to read from among several on the table. If the student is "test-shy," much diagnostic information may be obtained from this informal procedure of having him read aloud or silently material of known level of difficulty. Immediately following the oral reading, the teacher may give instruction on the specific kind of errors that he makes.

This initial informal diagnostic procedure may be followed by a variety of reading games, dramatized reading, the making of various kinds of word or story books, or other appropriate practice and instruction as indicated by the student's need.

Interwoven with instruction and practice will be various tests and other diagnostic procedures as they seem to be needed and as the student shows readiness for them. For example, if the student makes errors in perceiving words, he may be given a visual screening test (see page 324). If no eye difficulties are evident, tests of visual discrimination may be given. These consist of distinguishing from among four words the one that is different or noting the distinguishing detail in two words, one of which makes sense in a sentence, as for example:

$$\text{The boy} \left\{ \begin{array}{l} \text{was} \\ \text{saw} \end{array} \right. \text{the dog.}$$

$$\text{The gangster} \left\{ \begin{array}{l} \text{want} \\ \text{went} \end{array} \right. \text{to jail.}$$

Visual and auditory efficiency (see page 324) should always be checked early. If eye difficulties or lack of visual discrimination do not seem to account for the student's poor perception, further study is indicated. His method of attacking words should be closely observed and certain word recognition skills may need to be developed. Going more deeply into the problem, the reading teacher may find the difficulty is associated with the student's concept of himself or with fear of failure, or shame in not being able to read better.

In the special reading class the students should have a wealth of reading materials and practice exercises. There will be books and magazines on all levels of difficulty, from picture books with one or two simple words on a page and the first-grade level of *My Weekly Reader* to adult fiction and texts and reference books used in high school classes. There will be many different practice books from which students can select the kinds of exercises they need to correct specific difficulties (see Appendix, page 348). When students are working independently, the teacher will guide each in his selection and use of these materials.

Students in the special reading class should also work part of the time in pairs and in groups. This group work provides the stimulus they need — the knowledge of results and progress they are making, the fun of dramatized reading and playing reading games, the sharing of best methods of accomplishing certain kinds of reading tasks, and the building of self-esteem through the encouraging comments of other students — "You only made one mistake this time" or "We liked your story; you read it *very* well."

With older students who are gadget-oriented, some of the reading machines may be highly motivating. They have hopes that here is something new that will really help them to read better. And some students who have good basic vocabulary and comprehension skills are helped to read faster by these mechanical devices (see Appendix, page 358). If money is available some of these devices may be bought to use with some students for certain purposes indicated by the study of the individual.

The reading teacher should also be aware of emotional difficulties in reading. He should recognize emotional conflicts that are preventing the individual from concentrating. He may detect unconscious resistance to reading stemming from hostility toward parents or teachers, or from fear and anxiety. These feelings may make it impossible for him to put forth the effort that reading demands.

Twelve-year-old Fred's interest in a book on the weather could not break through his general disinterest in and fear of reading. The mother apparently had given the child a concept of himself as inadequate, and had conveyed to him her disappointment in his low reading level. During the interviews with the reading teacher, Fred expressed his anxiety in various ways: He would guess wildly at the meaning of the word rather than admit he did not know it. He would say, "Don't tell me," when he came to a difficult word. When he saw the worker making notes he became worried and said, "What did

I miss?" As part of the front he was putting up, he would often say, "This book is too easy," and he expressed contempt for the books he was given to read. When telling about a test in school, he said his score was "on the bad side of medium." The worker encouraged the boy to tell about things he did well, and often made such comments as, "You must be very proud of that report," "Good luck in the track meet." He was pleased by praise, pleased to hear something positive about himself. The worker's attitude of positive expectancy toward him helped him to change his feelings of inferiority about himself.

If the reading teacher has had preparation in counseling and psychotherapy, he may deal with problems such as these individually or in group therapy. Otherwise he will have to seek more expert aid in mental hygiene or guidance clinics.

Intensive Work with Individual Cases

More intensive work with individual cases is carried on in reading clinics. These are the students who need more individual attention than can be given them in the regular classroom or in special reading classes. Each case is unique and the work develops according to the intellectual and emotional needs of the individual. The person assigned to the case works within the area of his competency. If he is qualified primarily as a reading teacher, he uses his knowledge and skill in this field within the framework of a warm, constructive relationship. As the client makes progress in reading, he gains in self-esteem and self-confidence which often spreads to other areas of his life. Thus the reading specialist's work often has therapeutic effects, although he is not, strictly speaking, a therapist, unless he has obtained this additional training. If for emotional reasons the client seems inaccessible to reading instruction, as is true in perhaps about 3 per cent of the cases, the reading specialist may refer him for a psychological or psychiatric service.

Excerpts from a tape-recorded series of interviews will illustrate some of the principles and procedures in working with serious and often baffling reading problems.

A boy, Donald, thirteen and a half years old in the eighth grade, was referred to the High School and College Reading Center, Teachers College, Columbia University, by a tutor who had been working with him. His parents were foreign born, the father being a tradesman and the mother a housewife. He had a brother sixteen years old, who Donald said used to have a reading problem.

On the Stanford-Binet test administered when Donald was eight years old

Individual intelligence test.

Learning the short sounds of vowels for further individual progress in the initial stages of reading.

the IQ was 112. Another form administered five years later gave these results:

Chronological Age: 13 years, 3 months
Mental Age: 14 years, 2 months
IQ: 108
Rating: Average
Percentile: 58

On the Pintner General Ability, Intermediate Group Test he scored at the 78 percentile. According to the Gray Standardized Oral Reading Paragraphs, given when Donald was 13 years, 3 months, he was reading on the first-grade level. An excerpt from the letter written by the school counselor, at the time of referral, said: "Donald failed all major subjects during the first ten-week period; passed only music and ceramic shop. He showed need for personal adjustment in areas of courtesy, dependability, cooperation, self-control, and effort. He is restless, craves attention, and has a very short attention span. . . . Poor achievement was attributed to emotional factors."

Following are short excerpts from the first fifteen interviews:

First interview. Donald, accompanied by his father, arrived early. Worker introduced herself, shook hands with the father. The father left and Donald went to another room with the worker. He had not said a word since arriving except a mumbled "hello."

Worker: My, it's hot in here. Would you please open the window? (*Donald nodded and tried a window. It would not open. He shrugged and walked away.*)

Worker: Maybe the other window will open. (*Donald tried it, found it would open, so gave it a big shove and opened it as far as it would go. Worker thanked him. They sat down and Donald watched her as she laid out a pencil and paper and some other materials. He said nothing. Worker talked a bit about her watch which had a broken hand.*)

Worker: Donald, can you tell me something about your reading problem and why you are here?

Donald: What's to tell? (*Shrugs*) Don't know where to begin.

Worker: Just any place.

Donald: Just can't read.

Worker: Do you know why you can't read?

Donald: Just can't. Don't know the words.

Worker: Do big words give you trouble?

Donald: Just can't read. (*Shrugs*)

Worker: You just can't read. (*Donald shrugs, says nothing. Long silence.*)

(*The worker then asks about Donald's hobbies and pets. Donald says he builds model airplanes and has a mutt named Honey. There is a silence during which Donald looked up at the worker rather apprehensively.*)

Worker: Did you worry a bit about meeting me for the first time?

Donald: Ya.

Worker: You wondered what I would be like, didn't you?

Donald: Ya.

Worker: Did you want to come?

Donald: Sure, nuthin' can happen to me. Nuthin' to lose. Everything to gain.

Worker: Of course, you have everything to gain. (*Donald nodded but said nothing.*) Can you tell me more about your reading problems now?

Donald: Just can't read. Don't really know what gives trouble — just can't read. (*When asked about reading at home Donald says he has newspapers and magazines at home but it is his father mostly who reads them.*)

Donald: My father reads to me sometimes if I ask him. He's always after me to read, though. (*Donald does not want to talk about his brother who he said "used to have a reading problem."*)

Worker: How do you feel when you try to read in school and can't? (*Donald shrugs, says nothing.*)

Worker: Do you feel discouraged?

Donald: Ya.

Worker: What do you feel like doing?

Donald: Throwing the book down. (*He tells about a tutor he had and said, "I didn't learn nuthin'." Then he volunteers more information about another tutor.*)

Donald: We were working with a book, *Why Johnny Can't Read.*

Worker: You were working with a book called *Why Johnny Can't Read?*

Donald: Ya, with the vocabulary. You see, the teacher gives lessons out of the book. I didn't read it. She told me that was the way. The teacher gives the lesson (*pause*). But I didn't learn nuthin'. (*long silence*)

(*Worker asked Donald to select something from several books, magazines, and booklets on various levels of difficulty. He selected an article in a Reader's Digest Skill Builder, third-grade level, entitled "The Lincoln Penny." He read word by word, slowly and laboriously, with many mistakes. He tried to figure out words he didn't know by sounding the first letter and guessing at the rest. He didn't notice periods or question marks. He seemed not to see endings such as "ing," "ed," or "s." He said "even" for "ever," "it" for "in," "set" for "sit," "came" for "come," etc. After reading a paragraph, Donald put the booklet down and leaned back in his chair.*)

Worker: Would you like me to read the rest of the article to you?

Donald: Ya. (*Worker finished reading article.*)

Donald: I forgot to tell you. We have guidance at school.

Worker: Yes?

Donald: Ya, each class has a guidance teacher. Ours is a man. You can talk over your problems. If you want, you can see him privately in his office.

Worker: Have you ever talked over anything with him?

Donald: No.

Worker: Do you like to talk to people?

Donald: Some people.

Worker: Have you ever tried to figure out why you like to talk to some people more than to others?

Donald: It's if they're interested in what you are.

Worker: Do you talk with your brother?

Donald: Naw, my father mostly.

(*Worker asked Donald about the best time for him to come. He said he didn't know — worker would have to talk with his father.*)

Second interview. Worker handed Donald a slip of paper on which was typed: "The room is very warm. Please open the window that is not behind you." Donald looked a bit puzzled at first, then he grinned and opened the window.

After a short conversation about school and homework in which Donald volunteered the information that he had failed in science, English, and social studies and would be left back if he failed them at the end of this term, worker asked Donald to dictate to her the directions for making a model plane. This would be typed in dialogue form for reading next time by Donald and worker. He read "The Lincoln Penny" again and was tested on about a third of the Dolch basic vocabulary words. At the close of the interview, the worker handed him this direction: "Time is up. Please close the window."

Donald: Where did you get them? (*grinning as he closed the window*)

Worker: I typed them.

Donald: May I keep them?

Worker: Sure. (*Donald put the slips of paper in his shirt pocket.*)

Fourth interview. Worker explained to Donald that another worker was going to give him the Stanford-Binet test today.

In the fifth and sixth interviews, worker tested Donald on Dolch basic words and found that he knew 159 of the 220. She rewrote in simplified form a news item for him to read.

Donald: I don't like it. I can't get it. I don't remember the words even when I do know them here.

(*Donald then traced his route to the Reading Center on a subway map the worker had brought for him. He said: "This is nice. You can figure out a lot of things." Worker gave him the map to keep.*)
(*Donald enjoyed putting together some scrambled sentences. He said: "This is fun. It's like TV — Beat the Clock." Then, "It's easy when you know the words."*)

After the sixth interview Donald's father wanted to find out how Donald was doing. During the conversation he made remarks such as: "Oh, such a time as we have with him! He has so much trouble at school."
Worker: Trouble?
Father: Yes, he can't read, you know. They give a test and he gets a zero because he can't read it to know what to do. Then he gets on the defensive and he wants to fight. He has a red D in conduct. Oh, such a time! (*holding his head*) . . . He isn't stupid, is he?
Worker: Oh, no. Donald isn't stupid.
Father: He had an intelligence test, didn't he? Can you tell me how he did?
(*Worker started to explain about intelligence test — father interrupted.*)
Father: You don't want to tell me. It wasn't good.
Worker: Oh, yes, Donald ranks average plus.
Father: (*Face lighting up*) Why, that's good.
Worker: Of course.
Father: I try to help him one night a week, but I get so impatient.
Worker: Every parent wants his child to read and to do well. It is hard not to put pressure on them. Hard not to get impatient.
(*When they joined Donald he was pulling a new bright yellow scarf out of a package.*)
Worker: Oh, a lovely new scarf! (*Donald grinned.*)
Father: Oh, such a color! But on "doll face", anything looks good! (*Walks over and knots scarf around Donald's neck. Donald stands still, grinning rather sheepishly.*)

In the next interviews the worker spent some time in talking with Donald about anything that seemed to be of immediate concern to him. The specific reading procedures that seemed to be most effective were:
Various reading games, such as scrambled sentences.
Experience reading — accounts Donald had written or dictated and worker had typed.
Film strip — Donald operated machine.
Giving adjectives to describe various things — his dog, the subway, etc.
Worker: I don't know your brother. Could you describe him to me so that I would know him if I met him?

Donald: Don't want to. I don't like to talk about people. (*Pause*) It isn't really that I don't want to do it but I just don't like to talk.

Worker: Well, what would you like to describe?

Donald: The subway. I hate it. It stinks.

Worker: That's a word that tells me exactly how you feel about the subway (*laughing*).

Donald (*laughing*): I hate it. It's crowded, noisy, cold, dingy, dirty, inconvenient.

At the end of the eighth interview, Donald selected *King Arthur and His Knights,* a simplified version, to read, and worker spent part of the next period reading the second chapter to him.

Thirteenth interview. Donald arrived early as usual.

Donald: You know my friend that sent in an application — he hasn't had an answer yet — and I was wondering . . . could he come when I do?

Worker: Would you like that?

Donald: Ya.

Worker: All right, bring him along next time.

Donald: He's here now . . . out in the hall.

Worker (*trying not to show her surprise*): All right, bring him in. (*Donald hustled out and returned quickly with his friend.*)

Donald: This is my friend, John. He can't read any better'n me.

Fourteenth interview. Donald arrived alone. He said that John was ill; showed worker a slip of paper and said, "I came by myself today. My father wrote down the directions."

Worker: Good for you. (*Worker noticed a comic book on the desk.*)

Worker: Was this comic book here?

Donald: No, I brought it.

Worker: Can you read it?

Donald: No, but I wish I could. John reads these . . . he has a lot of them. A whole stack. . . . He reads them pretty good.

Worker: Let's see what you can do.

(*Worker gives necessary instruction. Later Donald expresses his feeling about school — "School's just no good. . . . They don't teach me anything."*)

In the fifteenth and sixteenth interviews, the two boys took turns reading from a booklet, *The Fireman.* Later they listened to themselves on the tape. Played a game called *Look* (like Bingo but uses words). Worker pronounced words — boys identified beginning, middle, and ending sounds and reviewed some of basic vocabulary.

The opportunities offered at the clinic are discussed
with the parent.

Fifteenth interview. Donald and John came together.

Donald: You know, I read my social studies book and you know the name of this school is Emerson?

Worker: Yes.

Donald: And you know, he's a famous man.

Worker: That's right.

Donald: He's the one that said, he said like this, he said that if we want to have peace, we gotta have schools.

Worker: That's right. We have to educate people.

Donald: Ya. . . . I read it good, too. My social studies book.

Worker: Good for you, Donald. . . .

Donald suddenly said: I wanta read.

Worker: You want to read now.

Donald: Ya. I like to read. I couldn't read enough in school. . . . They wouldn't let me. . . .

Worker: They wouldn't let you?

Donald: Naw. . . . The other kids wanted to read. . . . And I wanta read. I wanta read a book that I like to read. I don't want none of those books (*pointing to some paper-back booklets*). I wanta read some hard books, hard-cover books.

Teacher: Yes.

In subsequent interviews similar procedures were used, with John who had more motivation to learn to read but less ability than Donald, stimulating Donald to read better.

In a telephone conversation the father reported much satisfaction with Donald's progress. He said that Donald was willing now to read in school, that his marks had improved in conduct as well as in his subjects.

Although each case is unique, Donald was in some ways like many other boys with serious reading problems. His mental age was higher than his reading age; he was failing in his school subjects; his parents were anxious about his poor reading and impatient with him.

In the first interview the worker had to "play by ear." She treated him courteously, assumed he had initiative and ability to do the simple task she suggested — open the window. When he failed to open the one window, she did not do it herself. Instead she asked him to try the other window. This he opened successfully. Later it became clear that this kind of experience during the reading period was very important for him; he needed to take initiative, to move away from his overdependency and fear of growing up.

Since he knew he was coming to the Reading Center because of his reading difficulty, the worker met his expectation by asking about his reading. To this approach Donald was very unresponsive. But after the worker had reinforced his one positive insight by saying, "Of course, you have everything to gain," he spoke more freely and volunteered information about reading at home, his relation with his father, his feeling about reading in school, and the tutors he had had.

To obtain some direct understanding of his reading difficulty, the worker asked him to read a paragraph from a book he had chosen among several on the table. This informal oral reading test confirmed the previous appraisal of his reading and gave more detail about his difficulties.

Clews to the underlying problem were obtained even in the first interview. His resistance to reading was evident. In later interviews, too, he repeatedly made statements such as, "I didn't learn nuthin'," "I don't remember words even when I know them," "I'll forget this," "School's just no good. They don't teach me anything." At one point when the worker said, "If you want to remember it, you won't forget it," Donald replied, "You think I don't want to remember" — almost as though he had some insight into why he was not learning. Other clews as to the forces at work in preventing his progress in reading were his father's concern and pressure on him to read, his reference to the guidance teacher with whom he might like to talk, and his significant statement about liking to talk with people "if they're interested in what you are."

From the very first interview the worker presented herself as a warm, understanding person who enjoyed the boy and expected the best of him. She avoided putting pressure on him as his family did, and showed interest in him as a person. Acting on the tentative hypothesis that Donald was resisting reading because he did not want to give up the dependency of childhood or to lose the special attention his reading problem gave him, the worker helped him to discover that he could enjoy the satisfactions of a relationship with a motherly person and at the same time learn to read. Reading games, acting out printed directions, and putting together scrambled sentences aroused responses such as, "This is fun. It's like TV — Beat the Clock. . . . It's easy when you know the words." These pleasant experiences with reading gradually led to an intrinsic interest in reading and the spontaneous statement in the fifteenth interview, "I wanta read."

As one works with an initially baffling reading case, understanding unfolds. There is no substitute for sensitivity to the individual, skill in using reading methods and materials, and resourcefulness in meeting his needs as they gradually emerge during the contacts with him.

Procedures in a Summer Reading Center

At the High School and College Reading Center, Teachers College, Columbia University, a variety of activities are offered during a five weeks' summer session to persons from twelve to twenty-one years of age with a wide range of reading proficiency. These activities may be illustrated by briefly summarizing work with one of the Reading Center clients.

Jerry was thirteen and a half years old when he entered the Reading Center. His parents both had a high school education. His father had a white-collar job and his mother was a housewife. English had always been spoken in the home. At this time Jerry had just completed the seventh grade of a junior high school.

On the Wechsler-Bellevue test given a month before entering the Reading Center, he obtained a verbal IQ of 82 and a performance IQ of 97. On the Gates Basic Reading Tests, given during the summer — Reading to Understand Directions — he scored Grade 2.8; Reading to Appreciate General Significance, Grade 2.8; Reading to Predict Outcomes, Grade 2.9. On the Diagnostic Spelling Test he rated Grade 1.

He began school in a first grade which had fifty to sixty children. He failed the second grade twice, but went ahead with his age group when he transferred to another school at that time. His hearing difficulty and slow learning help to explain his early school trouble. His parents have a strong desire for him to learn to read and the vocational goal of carpenter is acceptable to them and to the boy.

Individual work. For one hour each day Jerry worked with his summer reading teacher, one of the graduate students taking the case study course in reading on the high school and college level. In the first interview with Jerry, the worker's purpose was to establish a friendly relation and to look for a starting point at which to help Jerry with his reading. They talked about his school program, his interests, his reading, and his hobbies. The following are excerpts from the interview during which they explored the subject of reading:

Worker: How about reading classes? Do you have special reading classes?

Jerry: Just a group for four of us poor readers.

Worker: Has it helped you to improve?

Jerry: Quite a bit.

Worker: Have you any idea what your trouble is in reading?

Jerry: Well, I sound the words but I can't put them together. . . .

Worker: What about reading for fun? Do you ever do that?

Jerry: Sometimes I read the comics like the other kids; sometimes I can't read them.

Worker: Do you ever read a book for fun?

Jerry: No. My dad helps me to read. He keeps me for half an hour extra and if I don't do good he keeps me for another half hour. He tells me words but I forget them. About four lines down I don't remember the word.

Worker: Do you have a good memory for other things?

Jerry: Yes. I can read signs like, "No right turn," and that.

(*Jerry gives quite a bit of detail about a lamp he made in shop and put in his father's room. He likes to make things with his hands. The worker asked him to tell more about the lamp and as Jerry talked he wrote some of the words he mentioned, such as* hammer, file, screwdriver, saw, nails, shellac, sandpaper. *In trying to read these words, Jerry got several right. They stopped at the word* sandpaper.)

Worker: What do you do when you come to a word like that?

Jerry: I sound part of it . . . *and*

Worker: What then?

Jerry: I try to say the word.

Worker: Well, what is it? What sound is this (*pointing to* s)?

Jerry: No sound.

Worker: It's *ssss.* If you tie that with *and,* you get *sand.*

(*They then discussed the need for being able to read directions for making things, such as puppets, which Jerry said he liked to make.*)

Worker: We might think about making puppets. You could read the directions and maybe write plays and read them. Well, our time is up now.

Jerry: Is time up? It just seems like a few minutes.

Worker: Well, time goes fast when you're busy. I'll see you on Monday and we can both think about plans for our summer work.

The next period Jerry talked about his interests. The worker again used the procedure of writing some of the words Jerry used as he talked. Then the worker asked him to listen to the words as he said them and tell which began with the same sound. Jerry had difficulty in doing this. Knowing this, the worker in subsequent interviews gave Jerry practice in distinguishing initial, middle, and final sounds of words. Before the end of the period, Jerry told about his week end at the lake and the worker wrote what Jerry dictated:

"The bungalow was close to the water. You can go swimming any time you want. There was no kitchen in the house. You had to go to the cafeteria next door to eat."

This was the first page in a booklet which Jerry decided to call "My Trips." They also planned to begin work on the puppets.

In the next interview the worker brought the following directions for making puppets: (*These directions were later published in* The Reading Center Gazette.)

How to Make Puppets

Materials:
cardboard about 3" by 4"
powder paste
newspaper
poster paint
brushes
string
pan and jar
shellac.

Directions:
Step 1:
Roll a piece of cardboard to fit
around your finger. Tie it with
string. This makes the neck of
the puppet.

Step 2:
Roll paper around this to shape
the head. Tie with string.

Step 3:
Put lumps of paper and paste on for
eyes, nose, etc.

Step 4:
Place strips on the head. Put paste
on each strip. Put on about three
layers and smooth them out.

Step 5:
Let it dry.

Step 1

Step 2

Step 3

Step 4

Along with the work on the puppets, the stories which Jerry dictated and read, selections from Grade 3 *Reader's Digest Skill Builders,* and several easy books such as a simplified version of *Davy Crockett,* Jerry did reading exercises which the teacher prepared especially for him. The following are typical examples:

| cardboard | string | paper | roll | paste | strips |
| paint | tear | tie | tightly | hair | puppet clothes |

1. Use these words to fill in the blanks:

    The box is made of heavy ——.
    It is tied with strong ——.
    Every night I read the ——.
    I watched a funny —— on TV.
    His —— were all dirty and torn.
    I will —— the devil puppet red.
    Hold the puppet —— in your hand.

2. Put the words in boxes:

Words starting with letter c	Words starting with letter p	Words starting with letter s	Words starting with letter t

3. How many syllables in

    bungalow ——
    swimming ——
    garage ——
    next ——
    cafeteria ——
    kitchen ——

Every day Jerry took some of his work home to show his mother and father the progress he was making. One day, in response to the worker's question, "How do your parents feel about your reading lately?" Jerry said, "They think I'm doing pretty good. My dad bought me a siren for my bike because I could read those things perfectly."

Writing the script for the puppet play and learning to read it effectively provided strong motivation. The puppet play was finally given in the large group and won enthusiastic applause.

In the last interview Jerry asked for the worker's address so that he could write to him about his reading in the future. They discussed the possibility of using his puppets at the public school which Jerry would attend in the fall.

Large group experiences. During the first fifty-minute period each day Jerry met with a group of about twenty students, some non-readers, others concerned with achieving greater efficiency in reading to meet the more exacting demands of college. In the first period the aim of getting acquainted was realized by having the students pair off, tell each other about themselves, and then report back to the group what they had learned about the other fellow. In the same period, the whole group enjoyed a story read to them by the teacher. Each wrote, or dictated, to one of the graduate students observing the group who served as his "secretary," a summary of the story. These summaries gave valuable information on the individual's listening comprehension. If that proved to be superior to their comprehension when reading the same kind of material, reading potentiality was indicated. In the next period they were divided into groups roughly according to reading level and given appropriate standardized reading tests. Subsequent periods in the large group were spent in giving a spelling test, working individually on spelling, beginning with their present grade level and progressing as fast as they were able; in group exercises and instruction in vocabulary and reading skills used by all members of the group; in reading games, presentations of puppet shows, plays, and other programs prepared in the small groups; and in work on the *Reading Center Gazette* to which all were encouraged to contribute accounts of experiences, book reviews, comments about the Reading Center, jokes, riddles, crossword puzzles, poems, and interviews with persons associated with the Reading Center.

The following brief excerpts from the *Reading Center Gazette* give an idea of the variety of contributions:

BAD OLE BEACH

Full of sand. There's water, crowded, noisy with kids digging holes in the sand — that's the beach. Disagreeable old sand getting into my food, flies biting me, burning ole sun streaming down.

JUNIOR HIGH GROUP LEARNS ABOUT AFRICA

. . . Mr. S__ is a lecturer on the staff of the University of Natal and is here at T.C. looking for new ideas which will aid him in helping boys and girls who have not kept up in their reading classes. . . . When the group learned that Mr. S__ was from Africa they immediately wanted to know about the cannibals, the lions and elephants, the tribal warriors and the tribal customs. He explained to the group that South Africa was really very civilized and their cities are much like our own. . . .

COMMUTING CAN BE FUN

I had never done any commuting until I had to commute on the trains and buses to get to the Reading Center. I might say, too, that I have never spent a summer going to school either. So this has been an interesting experience for me, particularly since I usually think of a summer vacation as being able to be lazy, sleeping late in the morning, and in general, taking life easy. . . .

CURIOUS GEORGE

(A Book I've Liked)

George lived in a zoo. One day he stole the zoo keeper's key and ran away. He catches a bus and goes to a hotel. . . . I like the book because it is fun, and it tells of all the tricks the monkey did, and how curious he was.

THE DOOR

The massive door loomed before him. Slowly, yet without hesitation, he approached it. As he came nearer he grew more uneasy. Clenching his fists, he forced himself to go on. Nearer he came, nearer and nearer to the door of fate. . . .

RAGS' TERRIBLE NIGHT

I was shut up in the house getting ready to watch "This is Your Life" . . . that is how it was when it happened. My brother, Jimmy, breaking rules again, had my dog Rags, off the leash. . . .

VIEWS OF THE HIGH SCHOOL AND COLLEGE READING CENTER BY THOSE WHO ATTEND IT

In the third hour the individual teacher goes over exactly what each student needs. I bring my chemistry book in and he gives me study hints, like showing me good ways to outline, etc.

I think what helps me the most here in the Reading Center is having an individual teacher helping me with my own reading problems. No two people are exactly the same in anything. So it is with reading. With an individual teacher we can be helped with our own problem and learn at our own rate.

Before I came to the Reading Center I read very little but now I like to read. I had never read the New York Times but now I do. Everybody here is so nice and friendly.

Some illustrations of words formed from the same root were also included:

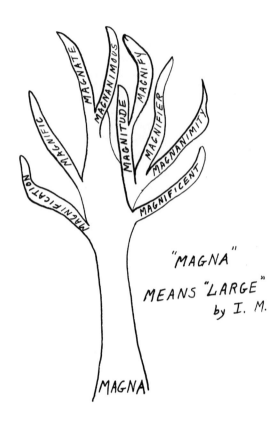

"MAGNA"
MEANS "LARGE"
by I. M.

Enough copies of the *Gazette* were mimeographed to give to members of the Reading Center and to sell to graduate students. The proceeds from the sale were used for an all-day outing at the end of the session.

Small group experiences. In addition to this group work for one period each day, Jerry had another fifty minutes with a group of five having similar reading difficulties. In this group they worked more intensively on specific problems, received much individual attention from the teacher, and enjoyed a number of interesting experiences. In the individual period, the worker prepared Jerry to participate in the small group, as, for example, in doing pantomimes in which the student acted out a story after reading it from a card. Another time members of the group were playing the roles of movie stars, lawyers, and people in other vocations. Jerry took the part of the interviewer and had to read the questions about their views on the importance of reading.

Evaluation. In oral reading Jerry had developed facility in sounding the initial consonants; he had gained considerable ability to divide words into syllables and had learned many new words at sight. He still has trouble with difficult combinations like *ph* and in blending sounds. He has built confidence and new interests and has changed his attitude toward reading through the experience. The worker, acting on the tentative hypothesis that part of Jerry's problem was having lost out on basic reading instruction in the primary grades and not having the necessary remedial work in the subsequent upper grades to which he was promoted by age rather than achievement, sought to:

1. provide experiences that required reading, used his manual skills, and stimulated his imagination;

2. build confidence through success in a new activity (puppets) in which he had not already failed and in the daily reading experiences;

3. build a sight vocabulary through experience reading;

4. begin study of word attack skills;

5. teach spelling systematically;

6. provide purposeful situations for oral reading, such as the script for the puppet play; and

7. establish a happy, secure atmosphere in which learning could take place.

Not being a therapist, the worker did not delve into possible deeper subconscious motives that might be involved in the reading problem. He worked within the area of his competence as an imaginative, creative, sensitive reading teacher.

During the winter session the work in the Teachers College High School and College Reading Center is mostly with individual cases. In some instances the worker may meet with one or two additional clients at the same time, if doing so seems to be of benefit to all. The general policy is to begin with the reading problem as presented by the client and to gain incidental diagnostic information continuously while working with him. More specialized information, such as scores and observations in individual testing situations, is obtained by a qualified worker as the need is indicated and the client shows readiness to accept the more formal testing procedure. The relationship between the client and worker is considered of central importance. Consequently, the worker will not probe for information, if such probing may cause hostility toward the worker and destroy the relationship. Within the framework of a friendly, understanding relationship, the worker will use appropriate reading techniques and suitable reading materials which reinforce the good relationship, as the client begins to see for himself that he can improve in reading.

In both winter and summer sessions, the focus is on the education of the graduate students who work with cases under supervision. They have also the opportunity of observing groups and hearing and analyzing current cases as they are presented in the class sessions. A number of the advanced students carry on research in the field of high school and college reading.

A follow-up of students who had attended this Reading Center showed individual differences in the experiences which seemed to them most valuable. One student marked practically every activity as "not at all helpful," while others marked all but two activities as having helped "very, very much." Most of those who replied reported as helpful the systematic practice on words in the Stanford speller. Outlining, doing exercises in a variety of workbooks, and reading stories of their own choice just for pleasure were generally rated, "helped me a good deal." Some liked vocabulary games, cards, making pages for the picture dictionary, and writing stories about a picture. Those who took part in a dramatized reading of a play, "The Ins and Outs," and in special demonstration lessons were enthusiastic about these experiences. All but one who wrote for the *Reading Center Gazette* marked this as having helped "very, very much."

The comments made by several students suggest goals for other special reading classes:

". . . The tests I took helped me to overcome my test phobia. They also, believe it or not, made me overcome my inferiority complex which had become serious in my mind."

"I had learned to concentrate . . . [and] to get work done with people talking."

"I learned to be critical of material I read, to skim and to analyze my work this year."

"This year at school I was able to pick out the important things from what I had to read; also I find I am able to look over a paragraph and understand most of what it says without reading every word. I have found it very helpful in later reading a book if I first examine it. . . . The knowledge that I gain about the book before really reading it makes the actual reading a lot easier. All these things I learned at the Reading Center."

Another student emphasized another aspect of communication:

"The Reading Center has helped me to express my thoughts in class. It has also helped me in my speech, spelling, grammar, and understanding new ideas."

Although not generally recognized by the students, a very important condition conducive to learning was the friendly, accepting attitude of teachers and students toward one another. One older boy expressed his feeling about the atmosphere in the group in these words: "Everyone here is so kind and helpful. It gives me confidence in myself and in my work."

A Public School Reading Clinic

Many school systems have established reading clinics that serve an individual school or a number of schools in a district or county. The St. Louis Public Schools Reading Clinics serve as a fine example of this kind of service. Their procedures are described in an issue of the *Saint Louis Public School Journal* (22). A brief account taken from that issue will acquaint teachers with the kind of service they may expect for the students whom they refer to a reading clinic.

The St. Louis reading clinics offer four kinds of services:

1. Diagnosis of reading disability.
2. Remedial teaching for severely retarded students.
3. Consultant service for classroom teachers.
4. In-service education for classroom teachers.

Diagnosis

When a teacher recognizes that a student needs special help, he consults with the principal. The principal confers with the student's father or mother. If the parent agrees to take him to the clinic, the principal makes an appointment for the first interview. Referrals are made only through the principal. The mother comes with her child to the reading clinic at the appropriate time and fills out a form which calls for information about the child useful in understanding his reading problem.

A physical examination is given. Reading problems, of course, cannot be attributed entirely to physical handicaps, though it is true that about half of the clinic reading cases show some physical handicap which may hinder learning. Therefore, it is well to check on possible physical conditions that may contribute to the reading problem. Prominent among the physical handicaps are visual defects. Almost half of the St. Louis clinic cases failed the visual screening test. These clients are referred for more thorough ophthalmological examination. Hearing defects handicap students in beginning reading where phonetic methods are used. Even a slight hearing defect may affect a child's language development. Although only 18 per cent of the St. Louis reading clinic cases showed a hearing loss of 10 per cent or higher, a hearing test should be given to all clinic cases.

It is important to know whether the retardation in reading is part of a general mental retardation or caused by other factors. For this purpose, non-language intelligence tests are given by a trained psychologist. The individual test is necessary because the poor readers will not be able to

The reading game with words.

Reading level may be discovered as the pupil reads aloud from a book of known difficulty.

The silent reading test includes a vocabulary test.

Associating the word with the picture.

Learning through the kinesthetic approach to reading.

Eye defects are detected by a visual screening test and referred to an ophthalmologist for correction.

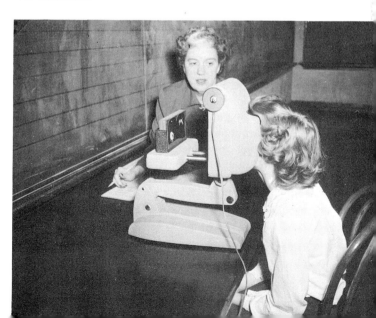

demonstrate their true mental ability on group intelligence tests that require reading.

Oral reading tests give valuable information about the client's reading level, his mechanical difficulties, and often his attitudes toward reading. If a disc recording is made of the first test, it can be compared with another recording made after his treatment at the clinic. This will give the client and the parent objective evidence of progress he has made.

The most common difficulty reported in the St. Louis reading clinics — 94 per cent, or 864 cases — was "helplessness in using word perception techniques. These children have never learned or have never been taught to associate sounds with symbols at all or have such distorted notions about independent word attack that their inadequate techniques are practically useless" (22, p. 11).

Silent reading tests are also used in the clinic. Some of these are the standardized reading tests selected especially for each student; others are informal tests having more specific diagnostic value. These tests show the individual's "disability pattern" and are used to plan the individual remedial program.

A photographic record of eye movements is always of interest to students and is of value in studying the eye movement pattern, especially of individuals who have few word recognition difficulties.

Although the relation of left-handedness to reading has not been clearly established, most reading clinics give some attention to this problem. Left-handedness is part of a pattern of cerebral dominance. Ordinarily the left hand and the left eye are controlled by the right side of the brain and the right hand and the right eye by the left side of the brain. In some children this is not the case and what is called *mixed dominance* results. Consequently, some children with mixed dominance may have a tendency to say *was* instead of *saw* and reverse other letters and sometimes whole words. Cases in the St. Louis clinics thus far have not shown mixed dominance alone to be a serious factor in reading retardation. Reversal tendencies, where they exist, can be corrected without involving the theory of cerebral dominance.

In the St. Louis clinics, emotional disturbance appeared to be a relatively minor factor; only 6 per cent of the cases were diagnosed as showing evidence of emotional difficulties severe enough to interfere seriously with their learning to read. Other clinics, using different diagnostic procedures and having cases referred not only from the schools but by parents, social agencies, and other sources find emotional difficulties associated with the large majority of reading problems. In these other clinics emotional difficulties loom large and personality tests are included for all cases that show serious emotional involvement. A group of tests, given by highly

trained psychologists, including the Rorschach, the Thematic Apperception Test, the Bender Gestalt, and the Macover Draw-a-Person Test, often
uncovers important information on personality structure and gives clews
for treatment.

The interpretation and synthesis of information from these various
sources is the most difficult part of the diagnostic procedure. It involves
a sequence analysis of the data and the forming of *tentative* hypotheses
which serve as guides to first steps in the treatment of the case. These
hypotheses are continuously modified as the worker gains new insights
from his day-by-day observations of the individual's behavior and performance on reading tasks.

Remedial teaching

The reading teachers in the clinic try to give each client the instruction
and practice he needs in accord with the diagnostic information obtained
for each individual. In the St. Louis clinics, in view of the general lack of
word perception techniques, a good deal of emphasis is put on associating
sound with symbol and on structural analysis of words. Other methods
and materials of instruction similar to many already described are used.
A few students who have failed to learn by the phonetic or "look-and-
say" method, learn by the tracing, or kinesthetic method. This method, as
described by Grace Fernald (10), brings successful word recognition to
certain individuals who think of themselves as unable to read. The
confidence they gain from mastering some words by this method enables
them to go ahead with more rapid methods of vocabulary building and
reading.

Training in alertness is needed by some "lazy" high school students.
They profit by having a mechanical stimulus to make a quick association
between their perception of a word or phrase and its meaning. This kind
of stimulus is provided by a mechanical device such as the *Flashmeter* or
Timex, which exposes words or phrases for a small fraction of a second.
If the specific basic reading skills have been acquired, a mechanical device
may bring them to high levels of efficiency. Some students enjoy using
the individual metronoscope, which uses a roll somewhat like that of a
player piano to expose phrases in their meaningful context. It is used to
increase their rate of reading and possibly to enlarge their recognition span.
Others may be made confused and anxious by any such pressure methods.

In the clinic as well as in the classroom, reading materials are of crucial
importance. The retarded readers of high school age have mature interests; they dislike being offered books about the activities of small children,
even though they are on their reading level. Fortunately, an increasingly
large number of books and magazines is being made available to meet

the combination of mature interest and easy reading levels required for adolescent retarded readers (see Appendix, pages 351–353).

Consultant service

A large part of the clinic work is wasted unless contact is made between the clinic and the schools. Teachers need to know how to make classroom adjustments for students who have been at the clinic. They also need suggestions of methods and materials for helping and preventing reading difficulties too numerous for the clinics to handle.

In the St. Louis schools a classroom consultant connected with each clinic is available for service in a school at the request of the principal. This consultant assists in the planning and administering of the testing program, in adjusting materials and instruction to individual needs, in grouping students and providing teaching and learning materials. He may also demonstrate techniques of teaching small groups.

In-service education

A feature of the reading clinic, far-reaching in its influence, is the in-service education of a limited number of teachers each year.

> If widespread improvement of reading programs is to be attained, it can be achieved only by our classroom teachers with the support and assistance of the principals.
>
> With this objective in mind, present practice is to maintain a small permanent clinic staff and to bring into the clinics six temporary teachers for one semester. The temporary teachers thus have an opportunity to become familiar with diagnostic and teaching techniques for severely retarded readers. After a semester of clinical experience, these teachers are reassigned to classroom work, where, it is anticipated, they will assist in building strong classroom programs (22, p. 20).

In this way the influence of the reading clinic is multiplied tremendously as each teacher who has had the clinic experience uses it with the hundreds of children whom she teaches.

A University Reading Clinic

Many school systems cannot afford reading clinics or do not think their system warrants the establishment of clinics since there are private clinics or clinics operated by colleges and universities in their neighborhoods. The Reading Clinic in Psychological Services at Southern Methodist University is an example of a reading clinic which serves a large area of one state. Like a number of other university clinics, the Reading Clinic at Southern Methodist offers many services, among which are:

1. A diagnostic service.
2. A remedial service for public school students.

A clinic has special reading materials and equipment.

3. Laboratory experiences for students and teachers enrolled in university courses.
4. Consultant service to school systems for in-service teacher training.
5. An adult service.
6. A diagnostic, remedial, and developmental college reading program.

Diagnosis

Referrals come to the Southern Methodist University Reading Clinic from numerous sources. They may come from teachers, principals, superintendents, nurses, pediatricians, psychologists, social agencies, child guidance clinics, optometrists, ophthalmologists, parents or friends. After the client decides on the service an appointment is made for the initial interview with one of the instructors.

At the initial interview certain routine information is secured from the parent, such as age of student, grade placement, etc. Then other inquiries are made: Did the student attend kindergarten? How old was he when he entered first grade? Has he failed? If so, what grade? Does he like school? What are his favorite subjects? Does he dislike reading? What is the reading problem as you see it? What illnesses, injuries, operations has he had? Who is his doctor? When was his last physical check-up? What are his special interests, hobbies, etc.? In addition, the teacher listens for bits of information which might indicate there were certain stresses and strains in the child's social and emotional life. Especially are ages and attainments of brothers and sisters noted; likewise, if relatives outside the immediate family circle reside in the home mention is made in the record. Any differences in the opinion of those handling the child concerning him, his ability, his talents, or his special problems are added to the record. Also, the parent asks what questions he wishes to ask and fills in the following rating on the student:

Parents' Rating of the Child's Qualities (31)

Rate the child with reference to other children of his age by drawing a circle around one of the three numbers before each trait. Use 1 to indicate a high amount of the trait, 2 an average amount of trait, 3 a lesser amount. For example, a circle around 1 before the trait "general health" indicates superior physical condition; around 2, average physical condition; around 3, poor physical condition. Encircle the question mark to convey uncertainty about the trait.

PHYSICAL TRAITS

1 2 3 ? General health
1 2 3 ? Immunity to colds and diseases
1 2 3 ? Sensory development (vision, hearing, etc.)
1 2 3 ? Muscular coordination and strength
1 2 3 ? Regular and undisturbed sleep habits

SOCIAL TRAITS AND ATTITUDES

1 2 3 ?   Socially active in school endeavor
1 2 3 ?   Popular in school
1 2 3 ?   Gregarious
1 2 3 ?   Diplomatic and considerate
1 2 3 ?   Accepts responsibility
1 2 3 ?   Interested in school work
1 2 3 ?   Appreciates beauty and has good taste
1 2 3 ?   Cooperative and shares with others
1 2 3 ?   Adjusts satisfactorily to failure
1 2 3 ?   Trustworthy
1 2 3 ?   Courteous and well-mannered
1 2 3 ?   Unselfish and fair
1 2 3 ?   Prejudiced toward races and social groups

MENTAL QUALITIES

1 2 3 ?   General intelligence
1 2 3 ?   Initiative and self-direction
1 2 3 ?   Artistic ability (music, art, etc.)
1 2 3 ?   Creative ability
1 2 3 ?   Mechanical ability
1 2 3 ?   Oral expression
1 2 3 ?   Success in school work

EMOTIONAL ADJUSTMENT

1 2 3 ?   Happy, wholesome nature
1 2 3 ?   Calm and poised
1 2 3 ?   Wholesome attitudes in sex problems
1 2 3 ?   Secure and confident generally
1 2 3 ?   Free from evasions and rationalizations
1 2 3 ?   Free from nervous habits (nail biting, etc.)
1 2 3 ?   Well-developed sense of humor

WORK HABITS

1 2 3 ?   Industrious
1 2 3 ?   Orderly and neat
1 2 3 ?   Efficient in study and individual work
1 2 3 ?   Efficient in group endeavor

Describe noticeable and frequent difficulties or irregularities in behavior.

To this information is added what the instructor can obtain from the school records of tests given, attendance, behavior involvements, etc. The student's present teacher and former teachers may furnish many insights as the result of informal observations. If others are involved — such as guidance clinic personnel, psychologists, pediatricians — information from these sources is added to the record.

An informal interview with the student is desirable, not only for what the instructor can find out but also to build rapport. Here the worker has an opportunity to discover what the student's evaluation of his own reading difficulty may be. The more skillful the interviewer, the more valuable the information.

Actual diagnosis of the student's reading ability covers several sessions, includes many different types of tests, and will probably involve the two other divisions of Psychological Services. Tests of mental ability and tests which screen for emotional disturbances are given by the Testing and Guidance Division. Formal hearing tests, if informal ones and observation indicate a need, are handled by the Speech Clinic, which also conducts speech screening tests. The Reading Clinic screens for visual difficulties, photographs eye movements, gives dominance tests, administers several written tests of silent reading, and gives a complete diagnostic battery of tests. Included also is an interest inventory.

Reading Clinic instructors are interested in knowing whether or not their students have visual difficulties. For this purpose the Keystone Telebinocular is used in the clinic. This test yields information in the following areas: simultaneous vision, vertical imbalance, lateral imbalance, fusion, right eye visual efficiency, left eye visual efficiency, stereopsis, and color perception at far point, lateral imbalance, fusion, visual acuity of right eye, and visual acuity of left eye at near point. Since the test is a screening device, the aim is to pick up those who should be referred to ophthalmologists. Aside from the actual visual information the tester may catch patterns of emotional response from the student which will aid him in future work with the student.

If the case seems very involved from a reading performance standpoint, the eye movements of the student may be photographed by the ophthalmograph. The eye movement record on film will give information as to how many fixations the eyes made per line of print, how the return sweep was made, number of regressive eye movements, and the number of words read per minute. The ophthalmograph is used often in research projects as well as routinely in the clinic.

Dominance tests of laterality (see Appendix, page 358) are given to determine which hand, foot, and eye are preferred. The information secured from these tests is mostly helpful in pointing out some difficulties which the student may have in reading from left to right and thus indicating whether or not education in this respect is needed. The findings on these tests may or may not indicate causes of the failure to progress satisfactorily.

Tests of silent reading ability are given to determine proficiencies and deficiencies in comprehension, vocabulary, and rate. These tests when

One part of an informal dominance test.

For research purposes tests of cerebral dominance may be used to throw light on a controversial problem.

Informal diagnosing is as important as formal testing.

combined yield a grade level score for silent reading. Other tests of silent reading — reading for general significance, reading to predict outcome, reading to gather details, and reading to follow directions — may also be given.

The Gates Diagnostic Reading Test gives the instructor still more insight into the student's reading problems. These tests include oral reading (which may be recorded on a disc or tape), oral vocabulary, reversals, phrase perception, word perception, spelling, visual perception techniques, and auditory techniques. High school students will be given special tests on reading in various fields, as social studies and science, and additional tests on oral and silent word attack. Added to this may be a test on study habits.

Since reading which a student does in a clinic is isolated from any continuous unit, project, or activity, the approach is usually from an interest point of view. Interest inventories, such as the one on page 327, and informal interviews are used to give the teacher hints as to what books would appeal to the student. Using the student's interests as a springboard, the teacher guides him to a specially selected library when the time comes for choosing reading material.

By the time the diagnosis is completed, the instructor has gathered together the following:

1. Information from parents, principals, present and former teachers, psychologists, pediatricians, speech therapist, and possibly social worker.
2. Results of mental tests and screening devices for emotional disturbances.
3. Results of hearing tests.
4. Results of visual screening devices.
5. Film showing eye movements.
6. Results of informal hand and eye preference tests.
7. Scores on silent reading tests, including comprehension, vocabulary, and rate.
8. Scores on all the subtests of a diagnostic battery of tests.
9. Indication of interests according to parent, student, interest tests, and inventories.

As a result of the accumulation of data, the instructor tries to determine some of the causes for this particular student's disability. In his study he will be asking himself some of these questions:

Since causes are multiple, what causes operate in this case?

What physical defects enter into the cause? Vision? Hearing? Speech? Glandular disturbances? Infections? Low metabolism? Circulatory disorders? Malnutrition? Severe illness? Injury? Major operations?

What mental factors enter this disability? What neurological factors? Are there emotional involvements? Might the social and economic background produce emotional causes? Is there a maladjusted home? Is there divorce? Is there a domineering member of the family? Or a perfectionist? Is there sibling rivalry? Or rivalry between friends? Or within a social group? Or in the school environment? Are there personality clashes in the home? In school?

What educational causes enter into this disability? Are there gaps in instruction? Were there absences at crucial times in the development of basic skills? Or school changes? Was there a sufficient readiness period? Was the first grade overly crowded? Were promotional policies favorable to this student? What methods of instruction were used? Was a variety of methods used? Were word attack skills taught? Was there an abundance of reading materials?

A second parent interview is held in order to report what the diagnosis has revealed and to describe the "picture" as the instructor sees it. This is also an excellent time to do some counseling and guidance with the parent as to his present role. This may be a chance for the instructor to counsel, for example, the parent who constantly compares the poor reader with a brother or sister or cousin who has made excellent progress in reading, or who does not show enough affection and respect for the child and his potential ability, or who puts too much pressure on the child to read better.

Kottmeyer Interest Inventory * (15)

1. What do you like to do best when you have some spare time? _____
   _____
2. What do you usually do after school? _____
   In the evening? _____ On Saturdays? _____
   On Sundays? _____
   How old are your brothers and sisters? _____
3. To which clubs do you belong? _____
   Do you go to Sunday school or church? _____
   Do you take any special lessons? _____
4. Which of your tools or toys do you like best? _____
   Do you let other children use your things? _____
   What tool or toy would you like to have? _____
5. How often do you go to the movies? _____
   With whom do you go? _____ Which is the best movie
   you ever saw? _____ What kind of movie

* Adapted from Paul Witty.

do you like best? _____ Who is your favorite movie
actor? _____ Actress? _____
6. Have you ever been to a farm? ____ Circus? ____ Zoo? ____ Art
Museum? ____ Amusement Park? ____ Concert? ____ Municipal
Opera? (local) ____ Picnic? ____ Ball game? ____ Summer camp?
____ Y.M.C.A.? ____ Swimming Pool? ____ Have you ever taken
a trip by boat? ____ Train? ____ Bus? ____ Car? ____ Airplane?
____ Where did you go? _____
7. What do you want to be when you grow up? _____
What do your parents want you to be? _____
8. Which radio and television programs do you like best? _____

How long do you listen to the radio and television every day? _____
To how many programs do you always listen? _____
9. What kind of pet do you have? _____ Hobby? _____
Collection? _____
10. Do you like school? ____ What subject do you like best? _____
Which subject do you dislike? _____
11. Do you like to read? ____ Do you like to have someone read to you? ____
How much time do you spend in reading story books? _____
Do your parents tell you to read? ____ Do your parents read much? ____
Which books have you read lately? _____

Do you have a library card? ____ How often do you get library books?
____ How many books do you own? ____ Are there any books you
would like to own? _____

About how many books are in your home? _____ What kinds of books
do you like best? _____
Which parts of the newspaper do you read? _____

Which part first? _____ Which part do you like the best?

Which magazines do you get at your home? _____
Do you read them? _____ Which magazines do you like best? _____

The diagnostic information deemed useful to the classroom teacher and
the principal is sent to the school. Results of vision and hearing tests are
useful to the classroom teacher as are the grade level scores on certain
reading tests. The complex causes of the reading difficulty are explained
simply and recommendations that are possible for the teacher to carry
out are suggested.

Remedial procedures

Remedial teaching of reading is determined by the results of the diagnosis. Since no two diagnoses yield exactly the same results, no two re-

medial programs are exactly alike. The course of action which the reading specialist will follow is not determined solely by the results of the tests but will be changed and modified as he works with the student, watches his responses, and sees him make progress as a result of certain activities but fail to progress as the result of others.

If we risk the danger of oversimplification, we might take a look at an example of what can be done in aiding students who have relatively simple and uncomplicated reading problems. The following remedial procedures might be used if the problem were chiefly one of *comprehension:*

1. Fit materials to individual's level of reading achievement.
2. Use material high in interest.
3. Explain various purposes in reading.
4. Teach student the reading problems characteristic of the various content fields.
5. Give practice in the basic reading skills in which the client is weak.
6. Increase speed as an aid to comprehension and develop a feeling for appropriate speed according to the purpose in reading and material read.
7. If possible, give enriching experiences with use of many visual aids.
8. Develop vocabulary through word files, student dictionaries, film strips, vocabulary games, and wide reading.
9. Develop the habit of looking for a writer's pattern of thought.
10. Teach the student to study paragraph patterns and study writing techniques as an aid to reading.
11. Teach the student to practice the use of the study-reading formula, SQ3R.
12. Call attention to clews in organizing, such as italicized words and paragraph headings.
13. Encourage outlining and summarizing as aids to comprehension.

When the diagnosis indicates among other things a problem of *rate of reading*, these methods are recommended:

1. Teach the psychology of the reading process.
2. Eliminate: vocalizing while reading silently, pointing along the line of print with the finger, moving the head.
3. Select reading materials high in interest level and low in vocabulary load.
4. Use materials which are at the student's reading level.
5. Teach student to change rate of reading when purpose and material change.
6. Give help in vocabulary building.
7. Teach appropriate use of skimming and skimming techniques.

Through a one-way-view mirror a student watches the instructor help children in a reading clinic.

Group tachistoscopic training.

Practice on the individual tachistoscope.

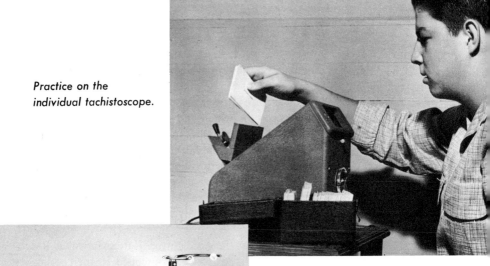

The ophthalmograph has been used to record eye movements on film.

An older pupil works on the accelerator to increase speed of comprehension.

8. Teach the student to practice key-word skimming.
9. Teach paragraph patterns for quick recognition of paragraph form.
10. Give much practice in reading from various content fields.
11. Use practice exercises in which the student reads for a specific purpose.
12. Keep records of rate and comprehension from day to day.
13. Encourage wide reading and introduce student to many types of books.
14. Stimulate interest in all types of reading materials.
15. Give tachistoscopic training either by use of homemade devices (15) or mechanical ones.
16. Use pacing devices such as the Accelerator, Rate Controller, Rateometer, Reading Pacer, Shadowscope, Controlled Reader.

When the diagnosis indicates a meager *vocabulary* among other things:
1. Stimulate wide reading on student's level.
2. Encourage study of unknown words in natural reading situations.
3. Have student make his own dictionary.
4. Teach context clews.
5. Show the student how to play reading games with new words.
6. Teach the student to systematically review new words.
7. Show the student how to use new words in creative situations.
8. Have the student tell the story of words and give origin of words.
9. Get the student to make a routine study of roots, prefixes, and suffixes.
10. Continually practice new words in many oral and written situations.
11. Have the student make a study of shades of meanings and implied meanings.
12. Introduce practice exercises which use new words.
13. Use film strips and movies.
14. Use Minnesota Efficient Reading Series on Tachistoscope (see Appendix, page 358).

When the diagnosis indicates among other things a lack of *word recognition and word attack skills:*
1. Discover level of this student's sight vocabulary and build from there.
2. Introduce methods of recognizing words other than "look-say."
3. Give practice in phonics, beginning with initial consonants, blends, speech consonants, long and short vowels, phonograms, prefixes and suffixes, roots, etc.
4. Teach other word attack or word recognition skills and the appropriate use of them.

5. Teach use of context clews.
6. Teach structural analysis.
7. Teach and give much practice on rules of syllabication.
8. Use film strips, such as films on phonics.
9. Use kinesthetic method.
10. Give practice in use of dictionary.
11. Use many reading games for practice.
12. Guide in the use of reading workbooks especially designed for improving word recognition skills.

From a reservoir of procedures and materials the reading teacher draws whatever may be of value in working with individual cases.   Mrs. Camilla Anthony, Reading Clinic Teacher, Dallas Independent School District, described her method in her report of two reading cases:

The first of these two cases is about Th— who was withdrawing further into his shell of daydreaming and refused to play with boys his own age. He would not touch books unless he was forced to. He had a feeling of inadequacy and felt ridiculed by his classmates because he had failed to read as he should.   He also felt keenly the disappointment of his father and mother, although they were very understanding.

Th— looked the Reading Clinic over; the teacher explained the purpose of the different pieces of equipment, and he immediately responded to the situation.   Looking at it from the point of view of a doctor, he diagnosed his own reading and went to work.   Progress was evident from the beginning. He continually evaluated his own progress and often made suggestions for changing material.   He seemed to enjoy working in the clinic because of the individual assignments and the lack of competition.   Material of high interest was necessary and the classics revised by Dr. Kottmeyer were a great help. Comprehension exercises were a challenge to him and regular practice on the tachistoscope improved his visual coordination and his attention span. He used the SRA Reading Accelerator to improve his speed of free reading, keeping a record of the increase of the number of words read per minute.

Th— is now in the eighth grade. He has made the honor roll once this year and only lacked a few points of making it another time.   He was recently voted cheer leader for next year by the student body and has had parts in several dramatic presentations.

After thirteen months in the clinic, Th— showed three years, six months' gain in vocabulary; five years, two months' gain in comprehension; and two years, eight months' gain in speed.

The second case showed much more resistance to reading and emphasizes the fact that all cases are different and each will have to be handled in its own way.

It was during the opening weeks of the Reading Clinic that I became aware of C—. Each day it seemed the mail brought another notice to the effect that C—, by all means, must get into the Reading Clinic this year. There was a report from the Research Department showing that he had scored very high on his intelligence test and the psychologist recommended the Reading Clinic. There was a carbon copy of a letter from the Superintendent in Charge of Instruction reminding the principal to get in touch with the Reading Clinic early in September to determine when C— might be admitted. There was a message from the Reading Clinic at Southern Methodist University where C— had had a short summer course, and along with this a call from both his parent and the principal of the school. C— I must see, and as soon as possible.

C— came to the clinic with his mother for his first appointment. At first glance, I could see he was a very frustrated boy and reluctant to enter another situation that involved reading. His eyes darted from place to place and refused to rest on anything that resembled a book. Games and puzzles which usually catch the eye of retarded readers did not appeal to C— because his mother had purchased most of them and used them with him at home. He was not interested in the mechanical devices of the clinic. He had seen them in his other clinic experience and since they were not new to him he did not show the interest most pupils evidence in them.

I talked with C— using an interest inventory which led him into discussing some things he liked, exposed him briefly to a primary reading test for word recognition, but seeing that he knew practically no words, I removed it quickly and changed to flashing numbers on the tachistoscope. This he could do successfully on the smaller digits, so I concluded his first visit while I felt that he was reasonably satisfied with himself and with me. I asked him to tell his mother to come back in to arrange a schedule for him and told him to go on to the car to wait for her.

She was aware of the severe difficulty C— was having and admitted that both she and her husband had tried to teach him to read using a great deal of force and pressure. I asked her to leave off all reading at home until I asked her to help. We arranged a schedule (semi-private) for C— and I undertook what looked to me at that time the impossible task of teaching C— to read.

The first few sessions I read stories of high interest, used numbers in the tachistoscope, and devised a few new puzzles to hold his interest. He could sit in his chair only a few minutes before he would lift his foot into the seat. A few seconds later he would rise to one knee and lift himself to the back of the seat, leaving one leg hanging over the seat. I ignored this and simply changed the activity as often as I could. The first reading I gave C— was in the form of jokes. I put them on the bulletin board near the tachistoscope and, as I hoped, he noticed them and asked about them. I read them to him and he was amused. The next day he attempted to read them himself and I helped him without making any comment on his reading. He wanted to memorize them so he could tell them to his friends. From this beginning I led him into the simple books by Walt Disney. I usually sit near my pupils for guided reading, but he informed me that he had had people sit over him and try to make him read until he could not stand it, so for a time I sat across a table from him and read upside down.

I refrained from any pressure, any criticism, or any type of discipline. I always smiled at C— regardless of his progress (or lack of it) or his behavior. This completely baffled him, but he soon responded and accepted me as a friend. Then he began to open up and tell me things. Some of these I discussed with his mother, because he revealed a strong jealousy toward his younger sister who was in the second grade and already reading better than he did.

I tried all of my old tricks and many new ones; none seemed to be just the right one for C—. Finally, he pointed the way for me. I enrolled a younger boy with an even lower reading ability, but with a much better attitude toward reading. He started reading low first-grade books as a part of his program, and to my surprise C— asked if he could watch the book as J— read. In this way C— soon developed a sight vocabulary big enough to read second- and third-grade material. I had a great deal of highly interesting material at this level. C— has begun to read! The formal report for this year shows very little *numerical* progress, but when I return from my lunch each day and find C— and J— with a chair between them for me, ready to read, I know my time has not been wasted.

Retesting

Since the clinic follows the University schedule, retesting is done after the student has had remedial work in the clinic for not less than four or five months and preferably at the end of eight or nine months, according to the severity of the disability. Tests are not given again in the areas of mental ability, emotional disturbances, vision, hearing, and preference. Retesting, administering a different form of the same test, will be done for silent reading, reading for various purposes, and all subtests of the diagnostic battery. Eye movements will be rephotographed and tape recording of oral reading will be made again.

As a result of comparing the retest scores with the initial test scores, progress can be determined in terms of grade levels. Confidence, assurance, and improvement in personality and behavior, important by-products of remedial reading, are usually reported by parents and teachers.

A high percentage of students who attend reading clinics gain one, two, and sometimes three grade levels in eight or nine months. This kind of success, however, is never guaranteed and is not attained by some students even after extensive diagnosis and intensive remedial teaching. Failure to improve in reading will be found just as in any other area of education because of the many factors preventing progress in reading, such as irremediable physical defects, deep-seated emotional problems, low mental ability, family and school conditions that cannot be changed at present, and the instructor's lack of control over these factors.

Final interviews

Final interviews involve the student, the parents, his teacher, the principal, and perhaps the counselor. To each is given the record of the student's progress. This may include a list of his outstanding gains, mention of the areas in which some progress was made, and the points at which more effort need be expended. Included, also, may be some recommendations for further work along certain lines. From the student, teacher, parent, and others the worker gathers opinions to add to his record.

Laboratory experiences for students and teachers enrolled in university courses

For students and teachers enrolled in courses in how to teach reading, how to diagnose and remediate in reading, and how to use children's literature with pupils, the university Reading Clinic offers valuable experiences. They may observe the instructors through a one-way view mirror, they may help check the pupil's practice exercises, they may play reading games with the pupils, they may make intensive study of reading interests and search out appropriate books in accordance with that interest and the pupil's reading level, or they may make an intensive study of a case history. The Reading Clinic also serves the needs of graduate students who are interested in doing research in reading, giving advanced psychological tests, or studying methods relative to teaching high school English.

Consultant service

The members of the Reading Clinic staff can help school systems with in-service teacher education programs. They give talks on all phases of the reading problem, conduct demonstrations, and appear as a panel for answering questions raised by teachers, consultants, principals, and superintendents. They sponsor local and national reading organizations, and often plan and present from two- to five-day reading conferences. Reading workshops are also coordinated with the work of the Reading Clinic. The following is a description of consultant work rendered by the

Southern Methodist University Reading Clinic to one private school. The school requested a reading consultant for an in-service teacher training program, testers for a comprehensive testing program, and clinical help for certain students whose test scores, when reinforced by teacher judgment, indicated need for such service. The request was made on the basis of a nine-month program. The Director of the Reading Clinic was to work with the teachers as a group, in small groups, and on an individual basis. A member of the Clinic staff administered and scored tests and later worked with individual cases.

Plans were formulated by the Director of the school and the Director of the Reading Clinic during the spring and summer months. At the beginning of the fall term capacity tests and survey reading tests were given to all students enrolled from the first through the twelfth grades. These scores were studied and, in consideration of the teacher's judgment, recommendations were made that some pupils be placed in the regular clinical program. Schedules were arranged and upon entrance into the Reading Clinic these students were given a complete diagnosis and continuing remediation. The Director of the Reading Clinic carried on regular monthly meetings with the entire staff of the elementary and secondary schools and arranged small group meetings for special purposes.

The in-service teacher training program provided various experiences for the total teaching staff. Lectures in general considered the nature of the reading process and the reading needs of pupils. Specifically, the following phases of the developmental reading program were studied: readiness; the sight vocabulary; word attack skills; developing comprehension, vocabulary, and speed; reading in the content fields; reading for various purposes including recreational, creative, critical, etc. Teachers were encouraged to study their pupils in detail and to suggest changes in classroom organization and procedures. Small group meetings were devoted to a discussion of specific reading problems at the various grade levels and of problems of particular pupils. Small groups also saw demonstrations by reading experts and exhibits of reading aids. They visited the Reading Clinic in order to become better acquainted with its services and to better understand the work which was being done by and for the pupils in their classes who were enrolled in the Clinic.

The service the Clinic rendered the school requesting the consultant service was threefold: In-service teacher training, a testing service, and a clinical service for students needing this service.

University and adult services

The university reading program is conducted in the Reading Clinic. The diagnosing may be done on the basis of freshman testing, or departmental testing, or testing for a school within the university. Individual diagnosing is also available. The course for reading improvement is open to any regularly enrolled student on the university campus.

The adult reading service is a community offering. Of late there has been widespread interest among adults, particularly businessmen, in the improvement of reading skills with emphasis on rate of comprehension. Courses for adults may be open to any adult in the community or they may be given "on demand" by certain businesses for their executive staffs or other groups within their organizations who would profit from such a course. Reading improvement for the executive is often included in business institutes such as the ones held for several summers in Glenwood Springs, Colorado, by the Institute of Management of Southern Methodist University and in Dallas, Texas, by the Southwestern Institute for Chamber of Commerce Executives.

Concluding Statement

With in-service education of teachers in the reading clinic the school reading program is complete. Beginning with "every teacher a teacher of reading of his subject," we bring in consultants to help teachers give more effective instruction in reading in their subject, help schools to organize special classes, establish reading clinics to deal with the most complex and seriously retarded cases, and offer in-service education in the reading clinic to those teachers who want to learn more fully how to meet the needs of all the students in their classes.

The university offers many services to schools which do not have a reading consultant and reading clinics within their own systems. These include a diagnostic and remedial service for severely retarded pupils, laboratory experiences for teachers enrolled in university courses, and consultant services from the staff of the reading clinic. In addition to these services, many universities offer adult and college reading improvement courses. Although small remedial reading groups and clinical work with individual cases serve only a fraction of the students who need help in reading, they may be justified on other counts. They serve as laboratories for developing methods and materials which can be used in modified form in regular classes; they offer opportunities for teachers to observe how skilled reading teachers work with individuals and small groups; they help teachers to understand the complex causes of retardation in reading and what to do about them. In these ways the reading specialists in schools and clinics contribute to the developmental reading program (3, 29).

Learning word perception techniques using word wheels.

The Bingo game of words.

REFERENCES

1. BARBE, W. B. "Study of Reading Clinics." *School and Society*, Vol. LXXXII (October 29, 1955), pp. 138–39.
2. CURTISS, A. B. "Reading Improvement at Western Reserve." *American School Board Journal*, Vol. CXXX (November, 1955), pp. 31–32.
3. DEVER, KATHRYN IMOGENE. *Positions in the Field of Reading.* New York: Bureau of Publications, Teachers College, Columbia University, 1956.
4. DOLCH, EDWARD WILLIAM. *A Manual for Remedial Reading.* Champaign, Illinois: The Garrard Press, 1939.
5. DUREN, M., and LEWIS, M. A. "One Way to Meet Individual Differences." *National Elementary Principal*, Vol. XXXV (September, 1955), pp. 74–75.
6. ELLIS, ALBERT. "Results of Mental Hygiene Approach to Reading Disability Problems." *Journal of Consulting Psychology*, Vol. XIII (February, 1949), pp. 56–61.
7. EPHRON, BEULAH. *Emotional Difficulties in Reading.* New York: Julian Press, 1953.
8. ERNST, MARGARET S. *In a Word.* New York: Alfred A. Knopf, 1939.
9. ERNST, MARGARET S. *More about Words.* New York: Alfred A. Knopf, 1951.
10. FERNALD, GRACE. *Remedial Techniques in Basic School Subjects.* New York: McGraw-Hill Book Company, 1943.
11. GATES, ARTHUR I. *The Improvement of Reading, A Program of Diagnostic and Remedial Methods* (Third Edition). New York: The Macmillan Company, 1947.
12. GRAY, WILLIAM S. *Standardized Oral Reading Paragraphs.* Bloomington, Illinois: Public School Publishing Company, 1915.
13. JOHNSON, WENDELL. "An Open Letter to the Mother of a Stuttering Child." *You and Your Child*, Vol. III, No. 1 (April, 1941), pp. 68–75.
14. KOPEL, DAVID, and GEERDES, HAROLD. "A Survey of Clinical Procedures in the Diagnosis and Treatment of Poor Reading." *Journal of Educational Psychology.* Vol. XXXV (January, 1944), pp. 1–16.
15. KOTTMEYER, WILLIAM. *Handbook for Remedial Reading.* St. Louis, Missouri: Webster Publishing Company, 1947.
16. McCALLISTER, JAMES M. *Remedial and Corrective Instruction in Reading: A Program for the Upper Grades and High School.* New York: D. Appleton-Century Company, 1936.
17. PRESTON, RALPH C. "How English Teachers Can Help Retarded Readers." *English Journal*, Vol. XXXVI (March, 1947), pp. 137–40.
18. ROBINSON, HELEN M. *Clinical Studies in Reading, II, with Emphasis on Visual Problems.* Supplementary Educational Monographs, No. 77. Chicago: University of Chicago, 1953.
19. ROBINSON, HELEN M. (Editor.) *Corrective Reading in Classroom and Clinic.* Supplementary Educational Monographs, No. 79. Chicago: University of Chicago Press, 1953.

20. ROBINSON, HELEN M. *Why Pupils Fail in Reading.* Chicago: University of Chicago Press, 1946.
21. RUSSELL, DAVID H. "Reading Disabilities and Mental Health: A Review of Research." *Understanding the Child,* Vol. XVI (January, 1947), pp. 24–32.
22. "St. Louis Public Schools Reading Clinic." *The Saint Louis Public School Journal,* Research and Survey Series, Vol. III (February, 1949), pp. 1–20.
23. SCHUBERT, D. G. "Emotional and Personality Problems of Retarded Readers." *Journal of Exceptional Children,* Vol. XX (February, 1954), pp. 226–28.
24. SIEGELBAUM, M. "Mental Health and Remedial Reading." *High Points,* Vol. XXXVI (February, 1954), pp. 66–70.
25. SOFFIETTI, J. P. "Why Children Fail to Read." *Harvard Educational Review,* Vol. XXV, No. 2 (1955), pp. 63–84.
26. STAFF OF THE READING CLINICS OF THE UNIVERSITY OF CHICAGO. *Clinical Studies in Reading, I.* Supplementary Educational Monographs, No. 68. Chicago: University of Chicago Press, 1949.
27. STRANG, RUTH. "Interrelations of Guidance and Reading Problems." *Education,* Vol. LXXV (March, 1955), pp. 456–61.
28. STRANG, RUTH. "Personality Development and Reading Problems." *Claremont College Reading Conference, Tenth Yearbook,* 1945. Claremont, California: Claremont College Library, 1945.
29. STRANG, RUTH. "Positions in the Field of Reading." *The Reading Teacher,* Vol. IX (April, 1956), pp. 231–39.
30. WILBORN, LEE J.; ALEXANDER, NELLE; and BRACKEN, DOROTHY KENDALL. *The Improvement of Reading in Secondary Schools.* Bulletin 540. Austin: Texas Education Agency, 1953.
31. WITTY, PAUL, and KOPEL, DAVID. *Reading and the Educative Process.* Boston: Ginn and Company, 1939.
32. ZOLKOS, H. H. "What Research Says about Emotional Factors in Retardation in Reading." *Elementary School Journal,* Vol. LI (May, 1951), pp. 512–18.

APPENDIX

APPENDIX

TESTS

Tests of Reading Ability

California Reading Test. California Test Bureau, Los Angeles, California. Intermediate Battery for grades 7 to 9. Advanced Battery for grades 9 to 14.

Cooperative English Test. Educational Testing Service, Princeton, New Jersey. Test C1, for grades 7–12. Test C2 for grades 11–12 and college. For superior junior high school pupils and senior high school students, measuring vocabulary, speed of comprehension, and level of comprehension, with more emphasis on literary appreciation than most tests.

Diagnostic Reading Tests. (Higher level, grades 7–14.) Committee on Diagnostic Reading Tests, Inc., Kingscote Apartments, 3G, 419 West 119th Street, New York. Survey section of forty minutes (this part of test is available through Science Research Associates, Chicago, Illinois) and separate diagnostic sections. Usual tests of vocabulary and comprehension. Special features: test of auditory comprehension, tests of reading social studies and science, and a silent and oral test of word attack.

Durrell Analysis of Reading Difficulty, New Edition. World Book Company, Yonkers-on-Hudson, New York. A diagnostic test including paragraph reading, tachistoscopic procedures, tests of auditory and visual techniques, etc.

Gates Reading Readiness Tests. Bureau of Publications, Teachers College, Columbia University, New York. Includes five subtests. Time allowed, 50 minutes in two sittings.

Gates Reading Survey Test for Grades 3 to 10. Bureau of Publications, Teachers College, Columbia University, New York. Designed to measure word knowledge or vocabulary, power or level of comprehension, speed of reading, and accuracy of interpretation.

Gray Standardized Oral Reading Paragraphs, Grades 1 to 8. Public School Publishing Company, Bloomington, Illinois. Testing time, 5–10 minutes. An individual oral reading test made up of twelve paragraphs of increasing difficulty.

Iowa Every-Pupil Test of Basic Skills, Test A. Houghton Mifflin Company, Boston, Mass. For junior high school pupils generally low in reading ability. Information on paragraph comprehension, reading of details, organization, vocabulary, and total meaning. Test B covers reading of maps,

345

references, use of index, use of dictionary, and reading of graphs, charts and tables.

Iowa Silent Reading Tests, New Edition, Advanced Test. World Book Company, Yonkers-on-Hudson, New York. Consists of nine subjects and yields a total score.

Lee-Clark Reading Readiness Test. California Test Bureau, Los Angeles, California, 1943. Time allowed, 40 minutes in two sittings.

Metropolitan Readiness Tests. World Book Company, Yonkers-on-Hudson, New York, 1939. Includes six subtests. Time allowed, 70 minutes in three sittings.

SRA Reading Record. Science Research Associates, Chicago, Illinois. Testing time, 40 minutes. Includes a number of different reading skills.

Traxler Silent Reading Test. Public School Publishing Company, Bloomington, Illinois. Measures reading rate, story comprehension, word meaning, and paragraph comprehension.

Tests of Mental Ability

American Council on Education, Psychological Examination (High School Level). Educational Testing Service, Princeton, New Jersey. Gives scores for language reasoning and quantitative reasoning. New editions annually. Time, 60 minutes.

California Test of Mental Maturity. California Test Bureau, Los Angeles, California. Yields both quantitative and verbal scores.

SRA Primary Mental Abilities. Science Research Associates, Chicago, Illinois. Testing time, 60 minutes. Measures five primary mental abilities: verbal-meaning, space, reasoning, number, and word-fluency.

Most valuable would be the individual *Stanford-Binet*, the *Wechsler-Bellevue*, and the *Grace Arthur Performance Test* given by a trained psychologist.

Other Tests (*Auditory, Visual, Preference, Eye-Movements, Study Skills*, etc.)

ADC Audiometers. Audiometer Sales Corporation, Minneapolis, Minnesota. Instrument used for auditory test.

A.O. School Vision Screening Test. American Optical Co., Southbridge, Mass. A revised version of the Massachusetts Vision Test for quick screening to find students who need more thorough examination.

Harris Tests of Lateral Dominance. Ages 6–Adult. Psychological Corporation, New York. Individual tests for measuring hand, eye, and foot dominance.

Keystone Visual Survey Tests. Keystone View Company, Meadville, Pennsylvania. A series of brief screening tests to be used in the Keystone Telebinocular to determine if more detailed testing is necessary.

Leavell Hand-Eye Coordinator Tests. Keystone View Company, Meadville, Pennsylvania. Subjective analysis of Motor-Visual preference.

Maico Audiometers. The Maico Company, Minneapolis, Minnesota. Instrument used for auditory test.

Ophthalmograph. American Optical Company, Southbridge, Massachusetts. Instrument used for recording eye-movements.

School Ortho-Rater, Bausch and Lomb Optical Co., Rochester, New York. Instrument for quickly and accurately identifying children who need visual attention.

TRAXLER, ARTHUR E. *Survey of Study Habits*, Experimental Edition, Grades 8–14, Educational Records Bureau, New York, 1944. A study habits test.

WRENN, C. GILBERT. *Study-Habits Inventory*, Stanford University Press, Stanford, California, 1941. A study habits test.

FILMS, SLIDES, AND RECORDS

Audio-Visual Materials for Teaching Reading. Robert Leestma. Slater's Book Store, 336 S. State St., Ann Arbor, Michigan, 1954.

Better Reading. 12 minutes, sound, black and white. Encyclopaedia Britannica Films, Wilmette, Illinois, 1952.

Coronet Instructional Films. Chicago, Illinois.

The English Language: Story of Its Development. 11 minutes, sound, black and white, or color. Coronet Instructional Films, Chicago, 1953.

Enrichment Filmstrips (to accompany Landmark Books). 246 Fifth Avenue, New York.

Enrichment Records (to accompany Landmark Books). 246 Fifth Avenue, New York.

Filmstrips for Practice in Phonetic Skills. Scott, Foresman and Company, Chicago, Illinois. Rhyme Time, Beginning Sounds, Letters and Sounds, and Fun with Words.

Goals in Spelling. Popular Science Publishing Company, Inc., Audio-Visual Division, New York. (Phonics filmstrip developed in cooperation with Webster Publishing Company.) Hearing Sounds in Words, Consonant Sounds, Tricky Consonant Sounds, Long Vowel Sounds, Letters Which Work Together, and Studying Long Words.

The Harvard Films for the Improvement of Reading. Harvard University Press, Harvard University, Cambridge, Mass. 16 films, silent, black and white.

High-School Reading Training Films. Extension Division, State University of Iowa, Iowa City, Iowa. 14 films, silent, black and white.

How to Build a Better Paragraph. Coronet Instructional Films, Chicago, Illinois.

How Effective Is Your Reading? Coronet Instructional Films, Chicago, Illinois.

How to Prepare a Class Report. 11 minutes, sound, black and white, or color. Coronet Instructional Films, Chicago, Illinois, 1953.

How to Read Novels. Coronet Instructional Films, Chicago, Illinois.

How to Read Plays. Coronet Instructional Films, Chicago, Illinois.

How to Read Poetry. Coronet Instructional Films, Chicago, Illinois.

Learning To Study. 7 filmstrips, junior and senior high school and college, Jam Handy Filmstrips:

Study Headquarters	33 frames
Getting Down to Work	34 frames
Using a Textbook	26 frames
Taking Notes in Class	29 frames
Giving a Book Report	29 frames
Writing a Research Paper	32 frames
Reviewing	27 frames

Literature Appreciation. 11 to 13 minutes, sound, black and white, or color. A series including *How to Read Novels, How to Read Essays, How to Read Poetry.* Coronet Instructional Films, Chicago, Illinois, 1952–1953.

Minnesota Efficient Reading Series. Keystone View Company, Meadville, Pennsylvania. A series of slides to be used on the Keystone Tachistoscope, includes prefixes, suffixes, and roots.

Recordings for Teaching Literature and Language in the High Schools. Arno Jewett, United States Office of Education, Washington, D. C.

Words: Their Origin, Use, and Spelling. The Society for Visual Education, Inc., 1345 Diversey Parkway, Chicago 14, Illinois.

TEXTS, WORKBOOKS, READERS, GAMES, AND DEVICES FOR RETARDED READERS

BAILEY, MATILDA, and LEAVELL, ULLIN W. *Mastery of Reading Series.* New York: American Book Company, 1951.

BREUD, F. S., and SEALE, E. C. *My Word Book.* Chicago: Lyons and Carnahan, 1950.

BRIGGS, ALLEN F. *Ad-It-On.* Alpine, Texas: Sul Ross State Teachers College. (A game available from the author.)

CENTER, STELLA S., and PERSONS, GLADYS L. *Reading and Thinking* Series. New York: The Macmillan Company, 1940.

DOLCH, EDWARD. *Dolch Reading Materials.* Champaign, Illinois: The Garrard Press. Picture Word Cards, Popper Words, Basic Sight Cards, Sight Phrase Cards, Group Word Teaching Game (like Bingo), Consonant Lotto, Vowel Lotto, Take, Group Sounding Game, Sight Syllable Solitaire, Know Your States, etc.

DURRELL, DONALD D., and SULLIVAN, HELEN. *Building Word Power*, Revised. Yonkers-on-Hudson, New York: World Book Company.

GATES, ARTHUR I., and PEARDON, CELESTE C. *Gates-Peardon Practice Exercises in Reading.* New York: Bureau of Publications, Teachers College, Columbia University.

GUILER, W. S., and COLEMAN, J. H. *Reading for Meaning.* Workbooks for grades 4–12. Philadelphia: J. B. Lippincott and Company.

HERZBERG, MAX J., and OTHERS. *For Better Reading Series.* Boston: Houghton Mifflin Company, 1940.

HOVIOUS, CAROL. *Wings for Reading.* Boston: D. C. Heath and Company, 1952.

JOHNSON, ELEANOR M., and OTHERS. *Diagnostic Reading Workbooks: Adventure Trails, Exploring Today, Looking Ahead.* Columbus, Ohio: Charles E. Merrill Company, 1936.

JOHNSON, ELEANOR M., and OTHERS. *Reading Skilltext Series.* Grade 1 — Senior High. Columbus, Ohio: Charles E. Merrill Company.

KELLEY, VICTOR H., and GREENE, HARRY A. *Better Reading and Study Habits.* Yonkers-on-Hudson, New York: World Book Company.

KOTTMEYER, WILLIAM, and LAMBADER, MAY B. *Spelling Magic,* Book 1 and Book 2. St. Louis: Webster Publishing Company.

LEE, J. M. *Spelling Today,* Books 1, 2, 3, 4. New York: Charles Scribner's Sons, 1950.

MC CALL, WILLIAM A., and CRABBS, LELA MAE. *Standard Test Lessons in Reading,* Books A, B, C, and D (grades 2–12). New York: Teachers College, Columbia University, 1950.

MONROE, MARION; HORSMAN, GWEN; and GRAY, WILLIAM S. *Basic Reading Skills for High School Use.* Chicago: Scott, Foresman and Company, 1948.

MURPHY, GEORGE; MILLER, HELEN RAND; and OTHERS. *Let's Read:* New Series, Books I and II. New York: Henry Holt and Company, 1953.

My Weekly Reader. 400 South Front Street, Columbus 15, Ohio: American Education Press.

NEIGHEN, M.; PRATT, M.; and HALVORSEN, M. *Phonics We Use,* Books A, B, C, and D. Chicago: Lyons and Carnahan, 1950.

100 Keystone Exercise Sheets. For Use with Leavell-Development Service. Pads A, B, and C. Meadville, Pennsylvania: Keystone View Company, 1955.

ORR, ETHEL M.; HOLSTON, EVELYN T.; and CENTER, STELLA S. *Reading Today Series.* New York: Charles Scribner's Sons, 1947.

PARKER, DON H. *The SRA Reading Laboratory.* Chicago: Science Research Associates. Materials and exercises from grades 3 to 12.

PERSING, CHESTER L.; LEARY, BERNICE E.; and OTHERS. *The Discovery Series.* New York: Harcourt, Brace and Company, 1940–41.

Rapid Reading Kit. Chicago, Ill.: Foundation for Better Reading, 20 West Jackson Blvd., 1955. Kit includes hand tachistoscope, cards for use in it, and a reading manual.

Reader's Digest Reading Skill Builder. 353 Fourth Avenue, New York 10, New York: Reader's Digest Educational Service.

Reader's Digest Reading Workbook. Grades 2–6. 353 Fourth Avenue, New York 10, New York: Reader's Digest Educational Service.

Reading Adventures, by editors of *My Weekly Reader.* 400 South Front Street, Columbus 15, Ohio: American Education Press.

ROBERTSON, M. S. *Veteran's Reader.* Austin, Texas: The Steck Company.

Scholastic Magazine. 351 Fourth Avenue, New York: Scholastic Corporation.

SIMPSON, ELIZABETH A. *SRA Better Reading Books,* Books 1, 2, and 3. Chicago: Science Research Associates, 1950.

SMITH, CARLEY A., and KING, IDA LEE. *How to Read Better.* Austin, Texas: The Steck Company.

SPENCER, PAUL R., and HORST, HELEN W. *Finding New Trails.* Chicago: Lyons and Carnahan, 1946.

SRA Life Adjustment Booklets and Better Living Booklet Series. Chicago: Science Research Associates.

STONE, CLARENCE R. *The Eye and Ear Fun Series,* Books 1–4. St. Louis: Webster Publishing Company.

STONE, CLARENCE R., and GROVER, CHARLES C. *Practice Readers,* Books 1–6. St. Louis: Webster Publishing Company.

STRANG, RUTH. *Study-Type of Reading Exercises.* High School and College Levels. New York: Bureau of Publications, Teachers College, Columbia University.

The Syllabascope. Washington 16, D. C. Wordcrafters Guild, St. Albans School. A device for teaching word analysis. Teacher and pupil syllabascopes available together with word sets and blank packs.

TRIGGS, FRANCES O. *Reading Exercises* (to accompany Diagnostic Reading Tests). Order from author, Frances O. Triggs, Kingscote Apt. 3G, 419 West 119th Street, New York 27, New York.

Webster Word Wheels. St. Louis: Webster Publishing Company.

WITTY, PAUL. *How to Become a Better Reader.* Chicago: Science Research Associates. Grade 9 through Adult.

WITTY, PAUL. *How to Improve Your Reading.* Chicago: Science Research Associates. Grades 7 through 9.

BOOK LISTS FOR RETARDED READERS AND SLOW LEARNERS

BERGLUND, ALBERT O., Compiler. *Easy Books Interesting to Children of Junior High School Age Who Have Reading Difficulties.* Winnetka, Illinois: Winnetka Educational Press, 1948.

BEUST, NORA E., Editor. *Books and Records to Help Build International Understanding.* Washington, D. C.: U. S. Department of Education.

BRODERICK, GERTRUDE, and BEUST, NORA E., Editors. *A List of Recommended Books with a Limited Listing of Recordings.* Washington, D. C.: U. S. Department of Education.

Books for Adult Beginners, Grades I–VII, Revised Edition. Chicago: American Library Association.

Books for Retarded Readers. Springfield, Illinois: Illinois State Library, 1951.

Books for the Slow Learner. Compiled by the California State Commission on Developmental Reading. National Association of Secondary-School Principals Bulletin, Vol. XXV, Section II (February, 1951), pp. 40–42.

CARPENTER, HELEN MC CRACKEN. *Gateways to American History: An Annotated Graded List of Books for Slow Learners in Junior High School.* New York: H. W. Wilson Company, 1942.

CARR, CONSTANCE, Compiler. *Substitutes for the Comic Books.* Reprint from *Elementary English*, April and May, 1951. Chicago: National Council of Teachers of English, 1951.

D'AMICO, LOUIS A.; FATTU, NICHOLAS A.; and STANDLEE, LLOYD S. *An Annotated Bibliography of Adult Literacy Training Materials.* Bloomington: Bulletin of the Institute of Education Research at Indiana University, Vol. I, No. 3, 1954.

EAKIN, MARY, Compiler. "Trade Books for Poor Readers." *Clinical Studies in Reading*, II; with Emphasis on Vision Problems. Edited by Helen M. Robinson. Supplementary Educational Monograph, No. 77. Chicago: University of Chicago Press, 1953, pp. 177–81.

Fare for the Reluctant Reader. Capital Area School Development Association. Albany, New York: New York State College for Teachers, 1952.

HILL, MARGARET KEYSER, Compiler. Bibliography of Reading Lists for Retarded Readers. College of Education Series, No. 37. Iowa City: State University of Iowa, 1953.

KUDER, FREDERIC G., and CRAWFORD, LURA. *Kuder Book List.* Chicago: Science Research Associates.

LA PLANTE, EFFIE. *Rapid Reading Books.* Chicago: Board of Education, Chicago Public Schools, 1952.

LUTZ, UNA DELL, Compiler. "Books for Severely Retarded Junior High School Readers." *English Journal*, Vol. XXXIX (October, 1950), pp. 439–41.

ROBINSON, HELEN M., Editor. "Remedial Reading Materials and Equipment." *Clinical Studies in Reading*, II: with Emphasis on Vision Problems. Supplementary Educational Monograph, No. 77. Chicago: University of Chicago Press, 1953, pp. 172–76.

SMITH, DORA V. *Junior High School Ladder, Spring, 1954.* University of Minnesota, Minneapolis, 1954.

SPACHE, GEORGE. *Good Books for Poor Readers.* Gainesville, Florida: Reading Laboratory and Clinic, University of Florida, 1954.

STRANG, RUTH M.; GILBERT, CHRISTINE; and SCOGGIN, MARGARET. *Gateways to Readable Books: An Annotated Graded List of Books in Many Fields for Adolescents Who Find Reading Difficult,* Revised. New York: H. W. Wilson Company, 1952.

SULLIVAN, HELEN BLAIR, Compiler. *Selected List of Books for Remedial Reading.* Boston: Educational Clinic, Boston University, 1950.

WARNER, DOROTHY, Compiler. *Bibliography of Reading Materials for the Mentally Retarded on the Secondary Level.* Topeka, Kansas: State Department of Public Instruction, Division of Special Education.

SERIES OF BOOKS FOR RETARDED AND RELUCTANT READERS OF HIGH SCHOOL AGE

(Higher in interest than in difficulty)

All About Books. By various authors. New York: Random House. *All About Dinosaurs, All About Radio and Television, All About the Sea, All About Volcanoes and Earthquakes,* etc.

American Adventure Series. Chicago: Wheeler Publishing Company. *Daniel Boone, Buffalo Bill, The Rush for Gold, Fur Trappers of Old West, Wild Bill Hickok, Cowboys and Cattle Trails,* etc.

American Heritage Series. By various authors. New York: Aladdin Books, American Book Company. *Cowman's Kingdom, Back of Beyond, The Country of the Hawk, Printer's Devil, Wheat Won't Wait, Jed Smith, Trail Blazer,* etc.

Aviation Readers. Henry J. Lent, and Others. New York: The Macmillan Company. *Straight Up* (Grade 1), *Straight Down, Planes for Bob and Andy, Airplanes at Work, Men Who Gave Us Wings, Aviation Science for Boys and Girls,* etc.

Basic Vocabulary Series. Edward W. and Marguerite P. Dolch. Champaign, Illinois: The Garrard Press. *Folk Stories, Animal Stories, "Why" Stories, Dog Stories, Pueblo Stories, Tepee Stories, Wigwam Stories.*

Childhood of Famous Americans Series. By various authors. Indianapolis: Bobbs-Merrill Company. Approximately seventy-five biographies such as *Tom Edison, Luther Burbank, Audubon, Lou Gehrig, Amelia Earhart,* etc.

An Easy to Read Book. Nashville, Tennessee: Abingdon Press. *Country Boy, Tools for Andy, Speckles Goes to School, A House for Leander,* etc.

Easy to Read Books. Cowboy Series. Chicago: Beckley-Cardy Company. *Cowboy Sam, Cowboy Sam and Freddy, Cowboy Sam and the Rodeo, Cowboy Sam and the Rustlers, Cowboy Sam and Porky.*

Everyreader Series. By various authors. Adapted by William Kottmeyer. St. Louis: Webster Publishing Company. *Ben Hur, Cases of Sherlock*

Holmes, Count of Monte Cristo, Flamingo Feather, Ivanhoe, Juarez, Simon Bolivar, etc.

Famous Story Series. By various authors. Adapted by Frank L. Beals. Philadelphia: Benjamin H. Sanborn Company. *Robinson Crusoe, Moby Dick, The Deerslayer, Two Years Before the Mast, Treasure Island, Three Musketeers.*

The First Book Series. By various authors. New York: Franklin Watts, Inc. *The First Book of Electricity, The First Book of Science Experiments, The First Book of Snakes, The First Book of Stones, The First Book of Baseball, The First Book of Space Travel, The First Book of Words, The First Book of Horses*, etc.

Globe Modernized Classics. 175 Fifth Avenue, New York: Globe Book Company. *A Connecticut Yankee, Last of the Mohicans, David Copperfield, Tale of Two Cities, Ivanhoe, Treasure Island*, etc.

Landmark Series. By various authors. New York: Random House. *The Pony Express, Paul Revere, The Vikings, Mr. Bell Invents the Telephone, Clipper Ship Days, The Story of the U. S. Marines, The Wright Brothers*, etc.

Modern Adventure Stories. Evanston, Illinois: Row, Peterson and Company. *The Strange Paper Clue, The Man with the Pointed Beard, Find Formula X–48.*

Pleasure Reading Series. Edward W. Dolch, Marguerite P. Dolch, and Beulah F. Jackson. Champaign, Illinois: The Garrard Press. *Fairy Stories, Famous Stories, Aesop's Stories, Bible Stories, Gospel Stories, Old World Stories, Far East Stories, Greek Stories.*

Reading-Motivated Series. By various authors. San Francisco: Harr Wagner Publishing Company. *Desert Treasure, The Adventures of Canolles, The Secret of Lonesome Valley.*

Real Book Series. By various authors. Garden City, New York: Garden City Books. *The Real Book About Space Travel, The Real Book About Daniel Boone, The Real Book About Pirates, The Real Book of American Tall Tales*, etc.

Series for Servicemen. Madison 3, Wisconsin: U. S. Armed Forces Institute. *Stories for Today, Stories Worth Knowing.*

Simplified Classics. By various authors. Chicago: Scott, Foresman and Company. *Around the World in Eighty Days, David Copperfield, Huckleberry Finn, Lorna Doone, Silas Marner, Treasure Island, 1001 Nights*, etc.

Teen-Age Tales. Books I to VI. Ruth Strang, Ralph Roberts, and Regina Heavey. Boston: D. C. Heath and Company. (Simplified modern stories for teen-agers.)

Treasure Book Series. R. A. Pulliam and O. N. Darby. Austin, Texas: The Steck Company. *Gulliver's Travels, Rip Van Winkle and the Legend of Sleepy Hollow, Kidnapped.*

Unitext Series. By various authors. Evanston, Illinois: Row, Peterson and Company. Paper-covered booklets, usually 36 pages. This series is in five main divisions, three of which are at the elementary school level: (a) THE BASIC SCIENCE EDUCATION SERIES: Animals and Their Young, How the Sun Helps Us, Electricity, Machines, etc. (over fifty titles); (b) THE BASIC SOCIAL EDUCATION SERIES: *Down the Santa Fe Trail, Prairie Children, On the Airways,* etc. (fifteen titles); and (c) REAL PEOPLE: four sets of six titles each, such as *Christopher Columbus, Benjamin Franklin, Daniel Boone, Jane Addams.*

Walt Disney Story Books. Boston: D. C. Heath and Co. *Here They Are, Donald Duck and His Nephews, Water Babies, Circus and Other Stories, Donald Duck and His Friends, Pinocchio, Mickey Never Fails, School Days in Disneyville, Mickey Sees the U. S. A.,* etc.

Winston Adventure Books. By various authors. Philadelphia: John C. Winston Company. *A Pirate Flag for Monterey, Drummer for Vincennes, Mosquitoes in the Big Ditch, River of the West, War of the Mayan King, Island Fortress,* etc.

World Geography Readers. By various authors. Columbus, Ohio: Charles E. Merrill Company. Twenty paper-covered booklets. *Norway and Sweden, British Isles, Australia and New Zealand,* etc.

World Landmark Books. By various authors. New York: Random House. *The Adventures and Discoveries of Marco Polo, Mary, Queen of Scots, Napoleon and the Battle of Waterloo, King Arthur and His Knights, Royal Canadian Mounted Police,* etc.

BOOK LISTS FOR THE AVERAGE AND SUPERIOR READER

ARBUTHNOT, MAY HILL, and OTHERS. *Children's Books Too Good to Miss.* Cleveland, Ohio: Press of Western Reserve University, 1953.

ASSOCIATION FOR CHILDHOOD EDUCATION INTERNATIONAL. *Bibliography of Books for Children* (current edition), Washington, D. C.: Association of Childhood Education International, 1200 15th Street, N. W.

Back Talk. About Books for the Teen-Ager. New York: New York Public Library.

Books for You. A List for Leisure Reading for Use by Students in Senior High School. Compiled by the Committee on Senior High Book List. Chicago: National Council of Teachers of English, 1951.

Children's Catalogue. New York: H. W. Wilson Co.

COLBY, JEAN, Editor. *The Junior Reviewer,* Catalogue of the Best Books for Children. 1954–56 edition. 241 Greenwood St., Newton Center 59, Massachusetts.

Current Books. Junior and Senior Booklist of Secondary Education Board. Milton, Massachusetts: Secondary Education Board, April, 1953.

HAEBICH, KATHRYN A. *Vocations in Fact and Fiction.* Chicago: American Library Association, 1953. (Some titles are suggested for retarded readers, also.)

The Horn Book, 248 Boylston St., Boston 6, Massachusetts (only magazine devoted entirely to children's books).

JEWETT, ARNO. *Aids for Knowing Books for Teen-Agers*. Washington 25, D. C.: U. S. Department of Health and Welfare, Office of Education.

Junior Libraries. 62 West 45th Street, New York 36.

MISSISSIPPI DEPARTMENT OF EDUCATION. *A Suggested List of Books for Mississippi School Libraries*. Jackson, Mississippi: School Library Supervisor, Division of Instruction, Department of Education, 1955.

NEW YORK PUBLIC LIBRARY. *Books for the Teenage*. New York: New York Public Library.

Reading Ladders for Human Relations (Rev. Ed.). Washington 6, D. C.: The American Council on Education.

STEFFERUD, ALFRED, Editor. *The Wonderful World of Books*. New York: The New American Library of World Literature and Houghton Mifflin Company, 1952.

Spring and fall book lists from all leading publishers.

STORIES, PLAYS, AND BOOKS FOR STUDY OF PERSONALITY AND SOCIAL RELATIONS

"The Buffalo Dance" by Cornelia Meigs
"The Catalogue Girl" by Jesse Stuart
"The Interlopers" by Saki
"Learning to Speak" by Helen Keller
Letters to Jane, by J. Schultz
"Little Britches" by Ralph Moody
"The Night of the Storm" by Zona Gale
"Spark Neglected" by Leo Tolstoy
"Spring of Hope" by Alden Hatch
Teen Theatre, by Edwin and Nathalie Gross
"The Thousand Dollar Bill" by Manuel Komroff
"The Valiant," a play, by Holworthy Hall and Robert Middlemass
"A Voice in a Hundred Years" by Constance B. Burnett
Death Be Not Proud by John Gunther
Father Flanagan of Boys' Town by Fulton Oursler
The Lone Cowboy by Will James
The Promised Land by Mary Antin
The Thread That Runs So True by Jesse Stuart

DIAGNOSTIC SPELLING TEST *

* Developed by Helen Carey and Dorothy Withrow.

(To determine instructional spelling level)

Dictate the following list of seventy words. They are listed by grade level, ten words to each level. The first level on which a student misspells two or more words is probably his instructional spelling level. For a more accurate diagnosis a larger sampling of words may be dictated. It is not likely that a student's instructional level will be above that determined by this test, but it may well be below it.

Grade 2	Grade 3	Grade 4	Grade 5
1. about	11. ache	21. coast	31. arithmetic
2. brother	12. chapter	22. cocoa	32. author
3. chair	13. feast	23. doctor	33. dentist
4. lion	14. lose	24. everywhere	34. English
5. name	15. meal	25. fought	35. fourteen
6. next	16. monkey	26. greedy	36. loose
7. room	17. picture	27. guide	37. procession
8. were	18. piece	28. medicine	38. pronounce
9. where	19. stairs	29. watch	39. volunteer
10. your	20. woman	30. women	40. wrap

Grade 6	Grade 7	Grade 8
41. accident	51. accommodation	61. abundant
42. although	52. acquaintance	62. appropriate
43. conceal	53. beginning	63. cafeteria
44. correspondent	54. brought	64. complexion
45. difference	55. character	65. congratulate
46. excellent	56. commercial	66. curiosity
47. freight	57. disappointment	67. prejudice
48. laboratory	58. government	68. privilege
49. pamphlet	59. principal	69. quarrel
50. relief	60. villain	70. restaurant

DIRECTIONS FOR SPELLING FILE

1. On one side of a small slip of paper, or on a 3 by 5 inch card, write, correctly, the word you have misspelled.

2. Under the word write it again in syllables.

3. Then write the part of speech which the word is, or the parts of speech which it may be.

4. On the other side of the paper write a sentence of your own, using the word.

5. If the word may be more than one part of speech, underline the part of speech which applies to your use of the word in your sentence.

6. Use a classroom dictionary for syllables and parts of speech.

7. Keep your words in alphabetical order in an envelope. Your slips of paper should be uniform in size. Your writing should be legible and fairly large.

SPELLING RULES

Final *e*:

1. Words ending in silent *e* usually drop the final *e* before the addition of suffixes beginning with a vowel.

   EXAMPLES: *write, writing; use, usable; approve, approval*

   ONE EXCEPTION: After *c* or *g* if the suffix begins with *a* or *o* the *e* is retained.

   EXAMPLES: *change, changeable; courage, courageous*

2. Words ending in silent *e* keep the final *e* before the addition of suffixes beginning with a consonant.

   EXAMPLES: *care, careful; safe, safety; nine, nineteen*

ie and ei:

> Put *i* before *e*
> Except after *c*
> Or when sounded like *a*
> As in *neighbor* and *weigh*.

   EXAMPLES: *receive, receipt, ceiling, veil, sleigh, believe, niece, piece*
   EXCEPTIONS: *ancient, seize, either, neither, leisure, financier, weird*

Final *y*:

1. When final *y* follows a vowel (a, e, i, o, u) it is necessary to add only *s*.

   EXAMPLES: *play, plays; day, days; monkey, monkeys*

2. When final *y* follows a consonant (any letter other than a vowel) change the *y* to *i* and add *es*.

   EXAMPLES: *try, tries; carry, carries; apply, applies*

Doubling final consonant:

Words of one syllable ending in a single consonant preceded by a single vowel, double the final consonant when a suffix is added. This rule also applies to words of more than one syllable if the accent is on the *last* syllable.

EXAMPLES: *drop, dropped; beg, begged; occur, occurred; begin, beginning*

MECHANICAL AIDS

AVR RATEOMETER. Audio-Visual Research, Chicago, Illinois. A device for improving speed of reading.

CONTROLLED READER. Educational Developmental Laboratories, Inc., New York, N. Y. A machine which uses filmstrips for improvement of reading (readiness period through fault level).

KEYSTONE TACHISTOSCOPE. Keystone View Company, Meadville, Pennsylvania. Device for presenting digits, phrases, sentences, affixes, etc. (timed or untimed) by use of slides.

LEAVELL HAND-EYE COORDINATOR. Keystone View Company, Meadville, Pennsylvania. Offers training in hand-eye coordination.

PERCEPTASCOPE. Perceptual Development Laboratories, St. Louis 5, Missouri. Combines training with films and training in tachistoscopic techniques.

READING PACER. Keystone View Company, Meadville, Pennsylvania. Device for improving speed of reading.

READING RATE CONTROLLER. Stereo Optical Company, Chicago, Illinois. Device for improving speed of reading.

RENSHAW TACHISTOSCOPIC TRAINER. Stereo Optical Company, Chicago, Illinois. An individual tachistoscope.

SHADOWSCOPE READING PACER. Lafayette Instrument Company, Lafayette, Indiana. Device for improving speed of reading.

SRA READING ACCELERATOR, MODEL II. Science Research Associates, Chicago, Illinois. Device for improving speed of reading.

TIMEX. Educational Developmental Laboratories, Inc., New York, N. Y. A tachistoscopic device.

INDEX

INDEX